7-16-16

Happy Birthday

Lucille

Love Paula

More God's Abundance

Joyful Devotions for Every Season

EDITED BY

Kathy Collard Miller

STARBURST PUBLISHERS

P.O. Box 4123, Lancaster, Pennsylvania 17604

To schedule author appearances, write: Author Appearances, Starburst Promotions, P.O. Box 4123, Lancaster, Pennsylvania 17604 or call (717) 293-0939. Website: www.starburstpublishers.com.

CREDITS:
Cover design by Richmond & Williams
Text design and composition by John Reinhardt Book Design

All scripture was taken from the New International Version unless otherwise indicated.

MORE GOD'S ABUNDANCE

First Printing, August, 1999

ISBN 1-892016-15-X
Library of Congress Catalog Number: 99-63788
Printed in the United States of America

To Florence and Marita Littauer

May you experience even more of God's abundance
for being a source of inspiration, encouragement,
and a godly example to me.

Contents

Introduction

Have you ever read to the end of a book and been sad that you were finished? I've heard from so many of you that that was your response to reading the original *God's Abundance*. Well, I didn't want you to suffer for too long without something more to enjoy—even though some of you report you're on your second time through *God's Abundance*. So here is another dose of encouragement, inspiration, and enlightenment to motivate you to look at life with a view toward enjoying all of life that God gives you.

There are some changes in the format that I think you'll enjoy. Instead of being arranged by month, you'll find four main sections based on the four seasons of the year. But don't worry, all the wonderful touches are back. You'll find a thought-provoking quote to begin with, and then some great information or inspiration through someone's experience or exhortation. Capping it off will be a pertinent Scripture and then a motivational tip to put everything together like a beautiful present with a big bow on top! You're going to love it.

I want you to see fulfilled in your life Jesus' promise of complete living as He said in John 10:10: *The thief comes only to steal and kill and destroy; I have come that they may have life, and have it to the full* (NIV). The thieves of apathy, discouragement, and selfishness can so easily bombard us and keep our eyes on ourselves. But with the selections you read here, you'll be enlivened to see the spiritual message in the ordinary, to choose joy in the midst of the daily, and to seek God in the midst of the common events of life.

God is everywhere, and through soaking in these selections, you'll have your eyes opened to His fingerprint of love in everything in your life. Enjoy!

Kathy Collard Miller

Spring

Spring shouts, "More!" It's the season when earth comes alive again and we see God's handiwork of abundance surrounding us. Just as He designed for this season to testify of His goodness, He wants us to enjoy His abundant goodness in our lives. We can do that through these selections which speak of God's love and generosity. As you and I enjoy Spring, let's allow our soul to spring alive through focusing on God each and every day.

Every Problem
Holds Positive Possibilities

ROBERT H. SCHULLER

*The greatest thing is to be found at one's post as a child of God,
living each day as though it were our last, but planning as though
our world might last a hundred years.*

C. S. Lewis

Every problem contains secret ingredients of some creative potential either for yourself or for someone else.

There are two sides to every coin. What may be a problem to someone can be a profitable business for others. For instance, rats and mice are plagues to the human world. However, the presence of rats and mice in America alone results in tens of millions of dollars in our economy. Rats and mice are responsible for thousands of jobs! Factories make mousetraps. Families are supported from the income of exterminators of such pests.

Similarly, every human problem holds possibilities for someone willing to look for them.

Bankruptcy was such a horrible experience for one man that he decided to help others who were going through it. Today he is a counselor to those who are having to declare bankruptcy.

One man's problem is another man's opportunity. Consequently, hospitals exist because people are sick. Lawyers are in business because people violate laws in a moment of weakness or ignorance. Mortuaries, cemeteries, colleges, churches, and universities all exist for the purpose of helping people through their problem times.

You can turn your pain into profanity—or into poetry.

It is the glory of God to conceal a thing.
Proverbs 25:2

> If you delegate a chore to a child, change your
> thinking from expecting perfection to rejoicing
> in whatever they can accomplish.

Easter Story Cookies
KATHY COLLARD MILLER

Taking all the evidence together, it is not too much to say that there is no single historic incident better or more variously supported than the resurrection of Christ.

Brooke Foss Westcott

Would you like a way to make the true meaning of Easter clear to the children in your life? Here's a project that I recently learned of, although I haven't been able to track down its original source. It's to be made the evening before Easter.

You will need:

1 c. whole pecans   zipper baggie
1 tsp. vinegar   wooden spoon
3 egg whites   tape
pinch salt   Bible
1c. sugar

Preheat the oven to 300 degrees. That's important; don't wait until you're half done with the recipe. Place the pecans in a zipper baggie and let the children beat them with the wooden spoon to break into small pieces. Explain that after Jesus was arrested, he was beaten by the Roman soldiers. Read John 19:1–3.

Let each child smell the vinegar. Put one teaspoon of vinegar into a mixing bowl. Explain that when Jesus was thirsty on the cross he was given vinegar to drink. Read John 19:28–30.

Add egg whites to the vinegar. Eggs represent life. Explain that Jesus gave His life to give us life. Read John 10:10, 11.

Sprinkle a little salt into each child's hand. Let them taste it and brush the rest into the bowl. Explain that this represents the salty tears shed by Jesus' followers and the sourness of our own sin. Read Luke 23:27.

So far the ingredients are not very appetizing, but now add one cup of sugar. Explain that the sweetest part of the story is that Jesus died because He loves us. He wants us to know and belong to Him. Read Psalm 34:8 and John 3:16.

Beat with a mixer on high speed for 12 to 15 minutes until stiff peaks are formed. Explain that the color white represents the purity in God's eyes of those whose sins have been cleansed by Jesus. Read Isaiah 1:18 and John 3:1–3.

Fold in broken nuts. Drop by teaspoonfuls onto a wax paper covered cookie sheet. Explain that each mound represents the rocky tomb where Jesus' body was laid. Read Matthew 27:57–60.

Put the cookie sheet in the oven, close the door, and turn the oven *off*. Yes, off! Give each child a piece of tape and seal the oven door. Explain that Jesus' tomb was sealed. Read Matthew 27:65–66.

Go to bed! Explain that they may feel sad to leave the cookies in the oven overnight just like Jesus' followers were in despair when the tomb was sealed. Read John 16:20, 22.

On Easter morning, open the oven and give everyone a cookie. Notice the cracked surface and take a bite. The cookies are hollow! On the first Easter, Jesus' followers were amazed to find the tomb open and empty. Read Matthew 28:1–9.

Jesus said to her, "I am the resurrection and the life. He who believes in Me will live, even though he dies."
John 11:25

For Easter, read *The Parable of the Lily* (Liz Curtis Higgs, Thomas Nelson) to your children.

Slow Down That Conversation

GARY SMALLEY

Loving your wife is not to love her as a saint, but as a sinner. If we love her for her saintliness, we do not love her at all.

Mike Mason

Not long ago, Norma and I were asked to give a person a gift of money. When we first talked about this opportunity, I threw out the dollar amount I felt we should provide, and Norma reacted negatively. When she said what she wanted to give, I reacted negatively.

Without intending to, we began to argue about this issue. But neither of us had a full understanding of what the other person thought and felt. That's when we slowed down, counted to ten, and started over. This time, we used quick listening to really hear the other person and understand the whys of what each of us had said.

Soon we saw that both of us had valid reasons behind our thoughts, and we quickly came to a solution that honored our feelings and our friend.

For more than twenty years, we've been working at slowing down our conversation whenever friction begins to mount, concentrating on asking honoring questions to find out all the facts and feelings of the other person. And it still amazes me how much that commitment to honor each other in our conversations has enabled us to understand and value each other better.

If you love those who love you, what reward will you get?
Matthew 5:46

Write down the ten things you love most about your spouse.
Thank God for him or her and focus on the positives.

Thinking With The Heart

JODI KARNICK

Do more than listen; understand.

John H. Rhoades

When Ryan first came to live as my foster son, it was his last hope. He was facing a long stay in Juvenile Detention Center if it didn't work out. A small fourteen-year-old with dreams bigger than the narrow-minded community he had come from, Ryan seemed lost.

Away from home, in the halls of the school where his name rang over the loudspeaker more regularly than the bell, he had been labeled a trouble-maker, and he lived up to that reputation by ditching classes, getting into fights, and sometimes, cutting school altogether.

As I left the school counselor's office one day, his words echoed in my head, "Ryan is incapable of exhibiting human kindness. If this doesn't change, I'll have no reason not to recommend that he be placed in the Juvenile Detention Center at the end of this year."

"Ryan," I questioned as we left the school, "what's going on?"

"No one understands me, that's all."

"You have to start thinking with your heart before you act," I instructed. "Got it?"

We drove into Minneapolis together that afternoon. It was a long and quiet trip with Ryan keeping to himself and me preoccupied with my own thoughts.

We decided to stop for lunch and as we walked through the crowded streets, Ryan eyed everything, unsure of his big city surroundings.

"I have ten dollars," he stated. "Can I buy something?"

"Not today."

"I never get anything," he pouted. "I never have as much as anyone else. Never!"

Rounding the block, we happened on a beautiful, outdoor restaurant.

"This looks nice," I offered. "Want to eat here?"

"What is she doing?" Ryan asked, ignoring me and eyeing an older woman sitting on a park bench, clinging to a weathered shopping bag.

I explained that the woman was homeless and was perhaps lonely or scared, and then advised him to stop staring.

"I'm going to make reservations," I said. "Are you coming?"

"In a minute. I'm going to look at CD's. I won't buy one," he assured me, stepping off the curb and disappearing on the other side of the street.

I stood in the long line in front of the restaurant, checking for Ryan's faded denim jacket through the crowd. I had seen him stop briefly at a flower vendor on the corner but now, he was nowhere in sight. Afraid we would miss our reservation, I went in search of him. He wasn't in the music store or at any of the other vendors' stands and with a huff of disappointment, I hurried back toward the restaurant.

"Here," I heard a familiar voice saying.

I turned around to find Ryan handing the woman on the corner a bouquet of flowers. "These are for you."

Ryan looked embarrassed as he turned and moved in my direction.

"What?" he said. "Sometimes you have to think with your heart."

I realized again that day that there is always hope for every one of us.

Have you given up on someone whom you love? Don't stop praying for them. God will answer.

If you have any encouragement from being united with Christ, if any comfort from His love, if any fellowship with the Spirit, if any tenderness and compassion . . .

Philippians 2:1

Today, do something nice for someone you don't know.

Lessons From An Airplane Ride

JOANN MATTHEWS

It's not about us! It's all about Him, Jesus!
Bishop Nate Holcomb

Have you ever thought about the significance of an airplane ride? Probably not. One day, I did. I was not feeling particularly spiritual that day but in the midst of the chaos of boarding the plane, I focused on the change in dimensions and perspectives. Looking out the window of a plane gives a different view of the world. I saw God's handiwork, the magnificent sunsets and horizons, breathtaking clouds, and the ordered landscapes of the country.

I've also noticed that sometimes the weather conditions are different. I have taken off in Texas in 100-degree weather and arrived in Washington, D.C., during a rainstorm and vice versa. I have had bad experiences (you know the kind where people believe you made it up) and excellent ones (a red-eye from Boston to Dallas). I have been on the verge of a panic attack and have slept from the time the pilot said we could take off our seatbelts. I have had to endure drunks, crying babies, rude people, loud and disruptive conversations, and plain old indifference from the person sitting next to me. I have had a lot of space and at times have been a little too close for comfort. I have had looks of bigotry and looks of genuine care. I have had good food (or at least I was so hungry anything would have tasted good) and no food (sometimes I thought I would starve!).

What did I learn? The lessons of life. We are dealt circumstances that are out of our control like landing in a thunderstorm without an umbrella, but we still have a choice as to how we respond. At times, I thought God just didn't have the resources to take care of me and my family. Then when I looked out the plane window at a countryside full of trees, He reminded me that He has a never-ending supply of whatever I needed.

The longer I live, the more I am convinced that there is a lesson in every-thing. I have experienced deep pain, discouragement, and humiliation but after it was over or the situation healed, I realized that I had learned some-thing. I was a victor even though at the time, victory seemed too far away, just like the airport I'm flying to.

I've learned that if we don't learn the lesson the first time, God has to allow us to experience something similar. But when we allow Him to change us and our perspective, we are more grateful, loving, and kind.

There is a purpose in everything, even flying in a plane. The next time you fly, look out the window and see what you can learn.

"For in Him we live and move and have our being." As some of your own poets have said, "We are His offspring."

Acts 17:28

The next time you fly (on the airplane, of course), ask for the window seat. Keep your journal with you and write down your reflections.

For Our Own Good

JAMES DOBSON

Having given us the package, do you think God will deny us the ribbon?

Oswald. C.J. Hoffman

Ryan had a terrible ear infection when he was three years old that kept him (and us) awake most of the night. Shirley bundled up the toddler the next morning and took him to see the pediatrician. This doctor was an older man with very little patience for squirming kids. He wasn't overly fond of parents, either.

After examining Ryan, the doctor told Shirley that the infection had adhered itself to the eardrum and could only be treated by pulling the scab loose with a wicked little instrument. He warned that the procedure would hurt, and instructed Shirley to hold her son tightly on the table. Not only did this news alarm her, but enough of it was understood by Ryan to send him into orbit.

Shirley did the best she could. She put Ryan on the examining table and attempted to hold him down. When the doctor inserted the pick-like instrument in his ear, the child broke loose and screamed to high heaven. The pediatrician then became angry at Shirley and told her if she couldn't follow instructions she'd have to go get her husband. I was in the neighborhood and quickly came to the examining room. After hearing what was needed, I swallowed hard and wrapped my 200-pound, 6-foot-2inch frame around the toddler. It was one of the toughest moments in my career as a parent.

What made it so emotional was the horizontal mirror that Ryan was facing on the back side of the examining table. This made it possible for him to look directly at me as he screamed for mercy. I really believe I was in greater agony than my terrified little boy. It was too much. I turned him loose—and got a beefed-up version of the same bawling-out that Shirley had received a few minutes earlier. Finally, however, the grouchy pediatrician and I finished the task.

I reflected later on what I was feeling. Though Ryan was screaming and couldn't speak, he was "talking" to me with those big blue eyes. He was saying, "Daddy! Why are you doing this to me? I thought you loved me. I never thought you would do anything like this! Please! Stop hurting me!"

It was impossible to explain to Ryan that his suffering was necessary for his own good. How could I tell him of my compassion in that moment? I would gladly have taken his place on the table, if possible. But in his immature mind, I was a traitor who had callously abandoned him.

Then I realized that there must be times when God also feels our intense pain and suffers along with us. Wouldn't that be characteristic of a Father whose love was infinite? How He must hurt when we say in confusion, "How could You do this terrible thing, Lord? Why me? I thought I could trust You! I thought You were my friend!" How can He explain within our human limitations that our agony is necessary, that it *does* have a purpose, that there are answers to the tragedies of life? I wonder if He anticipates the day when He can make us understand what was occurring in our time of trial.

Blessed is the man who makes the LORD his trust, who does not look to the proud, to those who turn aside to false gods.
Psalm 40:4

Write down any decisions, relationships, or challenges you find difficult to trust God for and then burn the paper in a ceremony of dedication to God.

Love Is Difficult

SUSAN McELMURRY

To love is good, for love is difficult.
Rainer Maria Rilke

She sat on a desk swinging her legs back and forth and telling me all sorts of interesting but trivial details about her life. I sat at my desk, correcting papers, half-listening and half-wishing she would go away so I could finish and go home. It was Friday afternoon. I'd known "Jan," a new Christian, for a year and a half. She came in often to talk, but today I merely responded "Hmm" and "Oh, really?" for I was anxious to start my weekend. This went on for twenty minutes, when the idea hit me that she really needed to talk and have someone listen. I put down my pen and inquired, "Do you have something you need talk about?" Out it came. She had a confession to make. After many months of being off drugs, she had fallen that day and felt horrible about it. She did need to talk. So I listened and then we prayed.

On the way home, I thought about the passage in Galatians where Paul tells us to carry each other's burdens in order to fulfill the law of Christ. The words "carry" and "burdens" represent difficulty and work to me. I don't want that. My life is already too hard and too busy before adding someone else's burdens. But because God's Spirit within me gives freely and joyfully of time and energy, I can have enough to share.

My afternoon with "Jan" reminded me of how I must depend on His Spirit to be an encouragement to those around me. It would have been easier to continue only half-listening and finish those papers (I know for I have done that many times). But God provided the opportunity, the wisdom, and the energy to help this young believer carry her burden.

It can be difficult and tiring loving others. I need to be reminded frequently of God's desire for me to love others so that I don't become weary of helping my students. To do that, I need to rely on His Spirit and the hope He has given us.

If you're feeling weary of helping others, fill yourself up with God's love and let it spill out to others. He can replenish the supply as often as you need it.

Let us not become weary in doing good, for at the proper time we will reap a harvest if we do not give up.

Galatians 6:9

Take time each day to reflect on how God's Spirit has strengthened you to do things you didn't think you could do or normally would not do. It will help you remember that He is alive in you.

Come As You Are

Lucy Whitsett McGuire

We must not only give what we have; we must also give what we are.

Désiré Joseph Cardinal Mercier

"Mama, where did you get that ring?"

My friend Judy looked at her eight-year-old daughter, Laney, and explained, "Your father gave it to me, because today is our anniversary."

The family sat in the living room together. Laney looked back and forth at her parents, then solemnly walked over to her mother and patted her cheek. She hugged and kissed her and said, "Happy Anniversary, Mama." Then she walked over to her father and put her arms around his neck. She looked up at him without smiling and said, "I don't have anything to give you but myself. That's all I have to offer. Just me. I love you."

Both her parents were moved by this touching gesture. And the gift of her love meant even more because her parents understood that's how God wants us to come to Him. Just as we are.

Paul's prayer in Ephesians 3:18 asks God to give the reader "the power to comprehend . . . and know the love of Christ . . . that you may be filled with all the fullness of God."

In reading and meditating on that chapter years ago, I prayed, "How will we experience this love?" He told me several ways, but the last is the most important. It's a standing invitation—"Come."

When we come into His presence, He fills our hearts with a firm foundation of His marvelous love. As we reverently look into the face of our Father, we will know that we don't have anything to give but ourselves.

Are you trying to bring something to God, besides yourself, that you think will make you more acceptable or more worthy to be loved? Some people give money or time or energy, but God really only wants us to give ourselves.

The giving of money, time, and energy will be the result of coming to Him and knowing we are unconditionally loved and accepted.

Why not be like Laney and give yourself to your loving heavenly Father?

"Come, all you who are thirsty, come to the waters; and you who have no money, come, buy and eat! Come buy wine and milk without money and without cost."

Isaiah 55:1

Give love and you will always be able to afford a gift.

The Bedspread

ROSALIE J.G. MILLS

Down in the human heart, crush'd by the tempter, Feelings lie buried that grace can restore; Touched by a loving heart, wakened by kindness, Chords that were broken will vibrate once more.

Fanny J. Crosby

The crocheted squares stretched across the living room floor. It had taken months to complete, but what I call my "divorce bedspread" was finally coming together, figuratively as well as literally. It was large and wide enough to fit on top of a queen-sized bed, or cover top as well as sides of a twin. For me, it was the latter.

When my son and I moved into our apartment, his extra bunk bed and former dresser became my bedroom furniture. I had brought linens with me, but had forgotten they were all queen-sized. Nothing fit anymore.

I had been using his old bedspread, too. But as the months passed, I wanted something more feminine to decorate my room. Since purchasing something new was beyond my budget, I decided to crochet my own. After finding just the right colors of yarn on sale, I began what has become one of my most prized possessions.

Needlework has always been a stress reliever for me, and I definitely needed something calm in my life right then. Everything around me was filled with chaos—the divorce became final, I was raising a teenager alone, my best friend and confidant moved away, and I left my former church. I experienced raw emotions at every turn.

As I worked each square, I began to realize how much I needed something in my life to be coming together, to balance all that was falling apart. Somehow I knew I could survive as long as that one stable, creative process continued. With each square's completion, a piece of calm resulted. Anger, resentment, bitterness, unforgiveness, and rage seemed to be my constant companions, yet each time I began to crochet, a peace settled over my heart in anticipation of the new addition to my bedroom. Everything in my room had been given to me by friends or brought from my former home. This would be the first "new" addition that was mine alone.

Finally the big day came. The joining stitches completed, I removed the old spread and stored it away. As I unfolded my new creation and placed it across the bed, it became a tangible reminder that healing takes time, patience, and determination to make it through trials. When I arrive on the other side of the difficulty, there is always something beautiful created along the way. Like my "divorce bedspread," a symbol of victory in the midst of defeat.

If you're feeling like you'll never reach the other side of your trial, hang on. You will make it. And without you even knowing it, God is weaving a beautiful design into the fabric of your life.

Consider it pure joy, my brothers, whenever you face trials of many kinds,
because you know that the testing of your faith develops perseverance.
Perseverance must finish its work so that you may be mature and complete,
not lacking anything.

James 1:2–4

> When everything seems to be falling apart, find something
> creative you can do that brings things together again.

Overcoming Shyness

J. Oswald Sanders

*How can I lift a struggling soul and guide him if I never take his
arm?*

Viola Jacobson Berg

On one occasion when my wife and I had gone to the mountains for a time of retreat, she was brought to face anew the believer's responsibility for personal witness. Being of a shy and retiring disposition, she found witnessing to others a rather daunting experience. However, after meeting with the Lord at this time, she promised Him that henceforth she would be willing to witness for Him to anyone, anytime, anywhere. For her this was a costly commitment.

Only a day or two after our return to the city, as she was walking past an open-air evangelistic service, she noticed a young woman standing alone, listening to the message. As she passed her she felt the prompting of the Holy Spirit to go back and witness to her. Her recent resolve came to mind, so she retraced her steps.

After approaching the young woman, she discovered that she had only that day come to the city from the country, looking for employment. She knew no one and was desperately lonely. After further conversation she committed her life to the Lord, and later became a sincere Christian worker.

We who are enjoying the companionship of Christ should be sensitively alert to such opportunities, for we are surrounded by similarly lonely people who might be led to the Lord through a friendly touch, and find in Him the solution to their problem.

Lonely people often assume a protective mask to conceal their distress. We should be alert to pierce the mask and endeavor to overleap the barrier it creates.

Perfume and incense bring joy to the heart, and the pleasantness of one's friend springs from his earnest counsel.
Proverbs 27:9

When you begin to feel angry, stop and ask yourself, "What am I really angry about?" You may find it's something different than the immediate situation.

Last Name, Please?
D. J. NOTE

God did not save you to be a sensation.
He saved you to be a servant.
John E. Hunter

All kids fuss at having to carry out daily chores. When my children ask, "Why do I have to?" I just smile and ask, "What is your last name?"

After they respond, I tell them, "That makes us family, and families help one another."

I also remind them that Jesus came to serve, not just to be served. They can't deny their last name and they know they belong to a greater family, the family of God.

This simple reality check usually ends any potential mutiny, and the chores get accomplished.

Remind your children of the two families to which they belong: yours and the family of God. For each, they have a high standard to live up to.

. . . just as the Son of Man did not come to be served, but to serve, and to give His life as a ransom for many.

Matthew 20:28

Surprise your children with popcorn and their favorite video when chores are completed without a fuss.

Look Up!

CATHY S. CLARK

Keep your face to the sunshine and you cannot see the shadows.

Helen Keller

The drive home, though only ten miles, felt like an eternity. I turned my van onto the freeway and sighed at the view of the desolate desert valley. Cracked, dry earth spread like a dull, brown carpet, spotted with low, fat tumbleweeds and grass burned up by the sun. The barren surroundings only mirrored what I felt inside. "Can anything thrive in this desert?" I wondered. "Can I?" Discouragement, like a dust storm, had blown in and settled over me.

Just as I was about to make the usual turn to go home, my seven-year-old son pointed out the front window and exclaimed, "Mom, look! Up on the hill, there's a cross!"

On a hill overlooking the valley, stood a tall, white cross. For months I had driven this route daily, yet never lifted my eyes to see past the usual exit. If I had only looked up—beyond my normal scope of vision—I would have seen it. The cross, a fresh reminder of the only One who can shine hope into barrenness: Jesus.

So often I allow circumstances, disappointments, or cares of the world to obscure my eternal perspective. I can become so consumed with my view of the wilderness that I don't think to look beyond to the cross and to the hope of what lies ahead in eternity because of what my Savior accomplished on that cross. That's when I need someone to nudge me and say, "Look up! There's the cross! There is hope!"

Why are you downcast, O my soul? Why so disturbed within me? Put your hope in God, for I will yet praise him, my Savior and my God.
Psalm 42:5–6a

Photos make fun, personal postcards! Draw a center vertical line down the back. Address the right side and write your note on the left side. Stamp and mail!

Basket Of Blessings
AMBERLY NEESE

Necessity is the mother of invention.
Unknown

Early in our married life, my husband and I had limited financial resources. As Easter approached, we realized that although love was abundant and the desire to celebrate Christ was insatiable, money was tight. We were in desperate need of some creative (and cheap) ideas for filling Easter baskets, and fabricated a way to do so inexpensively.

We excitedly traveled to the nearby drugstore, purchased two dozen plastic eggs (that break in half for filling purposes), and returned home with our mission in focus. On small pieces of paper, my husband and I scribbled encouraging words, affirming Scriptures, and loving thoughts with the other in mind. We filled the plastic eggs with these tidbits of edification and placed them in the meager baskets. While Americans everywhere were getting filled up on chocolate bunnies and jellybeans, Scott and I enjoyed our "basket of blessings" filled with tenderness and care for each other.

We have continued our newlywed tradition throughout our marriage, despite an improved financial status and an occasional chocolate bunny. We eagerly anticipate sharing this inexpensive, yet invaluable, tradition with our children someday.

Pleasant words are a honeycomb, sweet to the soul and healing to the bones.
Proverbs 16:24

Write down scheduled "appointments" with family members
(i.e., dinner, bedtime story readings, sporting events)
on your calendar. This exercise helps a busy person say "no"
to unwanted time demands and protects true priorities.

Replanting The Family Tree
JEANNE ZORNES

People will not look forward to posterity, who never look backward to their ancestors.
Edmund Burke

When a nephew became engaged, his fiancee expressed to me the same bewilderment I'd experienced years earlier as a bride absorbed into a large and complicated family. For years, especially at family gatherings, I struggled with knowing who was related to who, and how.

That changed when I enlisted my mother-in-law's help in compiling a family history back about three generations. The extended family was delighted to have that information collected and typed, and I finally figured out who-belonged-where.

So when my nephew's fiancee came to me with questions of kinship lines and dates of family birthdays and anniversaries, I gave her what I wish I'd had in the beginning: a copy of the family history.

She was so grateful to get the story of her husband-to-be's heritage that I made the family history part of my wedding gift to other close relatives. When my own children marry, I plan to do the same for them.

In our computer-age focus on the future, we sometimes forget there's value in communicating the past. The Bible holds its share of family histories; I identify best with the genealogy in Nehemiah 7. Lost for seventy years after Jerusalem was destroyed, its discovery helped those rebuilding the city connect with their historical purpose. Similarly, I "connected" better with my earthly family when I learned its heritage. I also understood, from observing the "broken limbs" of broken lives, that God's eternal plan for bringing people to Himself included placing me just where I am.

Both the one who makes men holy and those who are made holy are of the same family.

Hebrews 2:11a

How far back can you trace your family history? How far back does your spiritual history go? Gather the testimonies of the family's living Christians and be sure to write your own.

Of Servants And Kings

DAWN RICHERSON

In the sight of God no man can look at himself
except when he is down on his knees.

Francois Mauriac

"Okay, Ma'am," Luke said as he took the Burger King crown off his head, "I shall now be your servant. What can I do for you? Anything! Really!"

The moment of child's play reminded me of our natural inclination to dismiss the possibility that a king could come to serve. Kings should wear crowns and bask in their glory, after all. Right?

The King of kings resisted the temptation to do so. Rather, He took up the towel of servanthood and washed clean the feet of those who called Him Lord. He humbled Himself, putting the needs of others before His own. He extended kindness in the face of mockery and false accusations. He loved even those who did not love Him.

Jesus set aside his kingly crown in favor of a crown of thorns. He showed us how to live at peace with all. He gave His very life in service and sacrifice. His choice of servanthood left no room for pride.

What crown do you wear with pride? What would it take for you or me to follow in the footsteps of our Lord, lay aside that shiny crown, and pick up the servant's towel?

Your attitude should be the same as that of Christ Jesus: Who, being in the very nature God, did not consider equality with God something to be grasped, but made himself nothing, taking the very nature of a servant, being made in human likeness. And being found in appearance as a man, he humbled himself and became obedient to death—even death on a cross!

Philippians 2:5–8

Keep your most treasured items together so that in case
of a disaster, you can gather them together at once.

Growing Room

LUCY WHITSET MCGUIRE

The great law of culture is: Let each become all that he is capable
of being; expand, if possible to his full growth; resisting all impedi-
ments, casting off all foreign, especially all noxious adhesions; and
show himself at length in his own shape and stature, be these what
they may.

Thomas Carlyle

A few years ago, my family planted thousands of pine seedlings on our tree
farm in Mississippi. We spaced them between six and ten feet apart, close
enough so they would stretch tall for the sun, but far enough apart to stand
alone. Forestry textbooks used to advise putting them next to each other,
then thinning them out later, but it was discovered that if they were too
close, they became diseased.

That's like me, I think. I need space around me wherever I go because I
am an introvert. That means I get my energy from being still and quiet.
Friends want me to do more with them, but I have to space how many meetings and social events I attend.

After I was first married, I tried to keep up with the customary social
obligations, but it became harder over the years. The busier I became, the
more stressed I felt. So, I learned to prioritize my time and simplify my activities.

I don't get to do everything I would like: attend Bible Studies, classes,
games, parties; but in the process of those losses, God taught me that He is

my portion. My happiness does not depend on how close I am to what's happening or how busy I am. I have to grow where I am planted, accept myself the way I am and ignore well-intentioned advice to do more.

Like plants, people need space to reach their potential. Sometimes that includes privacy—freedom from interrogation and expectations. Life is simpler when people respect each other's space, without nosy questions, frequent demands, and gossip.

Like people, plants need some time to themselves to grow uncrowded. My husband and I moved 1,000 miles away from our tree farm, and we were concerned about its maintenance without our frequent supervision. After being away for years, my husband came back to check on the farm. The farmer next to our acreage was sitting on his front porch talking to a friend, when my husband walked up to speak to them. They were surprised and pleased to see him and said, "We were just talking about your stand of trees! We have never seen any grow so fast and tall in all our lives! They're just blessed, that's what!"

We were relieved that the trees were growing to their potential. They were planted with the right amount of space, and God did the rest. It's the same with you and me.

He is like a tree planted by streams of water, which yields its fruit in due season and whose leaf does not wither. Whatever he does prospers.

Psalm 1:3

Make a list of everything you're doing and ask yourself whether it's what God wants you to do and for which you're suited.

Exercising Happiness

SANDY CATHCART

All misery is God unknown.

George MacDonald

If you met my friend Nelson, you would think he was one of the most joyful people in the world. His face shines with a perpetual smile and he finds humor in the most difficult situations. His laughter has become his trademark. I love to be around him because his good humor makes me forget my own troubles. To look at Nelson's smiling face you would think he never had a bad day. But I know better. Nelson's life has been full of the deepest of heartaches: a difficult childhood; a beloved wife who rejected God and him; his inability to father a child. He's known pain on a first-name basis. So what's his secret?

I recently asked him that very question. As usual, his famous laugh preceded his answer.

"It's easy," he smiled. "I exercise being happy. Life's too short to hang around in the doldrums. I get up in the morning and tell myself, 'This is going to be a good day.' It doesn't matter if the dog chews up my best pair of shoes and wets on the carpet before I get out the door. There are a lot of things in life that are going to try to change my mind, but I'm determined to have a good day."

"That's some determination," I answer.

"Not if you think about it," Nelson explains. "We exercise everything in life. If you want to get in shape, you exercise. If you want to be a godly woman, you exercise your faith. Why not exercise being happy?"

I had to admit he had a point. The more you exercise something, the stronger and better it gets, and happiness really is a matter of choice. If we're not exercising happiness, we're exercising sadness. "I think I'll try this," I said.

Nelson laughed. "It gets easier the more you exercise. Pretty soon, it becomes the natural thing to do."

I laughed.

"See. You're doing it already."

"Thanks," I said. "This is going to be a great day."

Since my conversation with Nelson, I've discovered that exercising happiness is a wonderful way to realize the full benefits of abundant life. What are you exercising?

This is the day the LORD has made; let us rejoice and be glad in it.
Psalm 118:24

> Make a goal of sending a greeting card to one friend each week, taking a moment to thank God and pray for their needs before sealing the envelope.

Once I Had A Favorite Pew

Doris C. Crandall

Repentance, to be of any avail, must work a change of heart and conduct.

Theodore Ledyard Cuyler

At the break between Sunday School and the beginning of the church service, I hurried into the sanctuary and placed my Bible and Sunday School literature in my favorite pew to save it for myself. Then I went about speaking to friends. "I've done that for years. There's no harm in it," I told myself, "and I'll be sure to get the seat I want."

When I invited Vivian and her family to visit our church, I was confident of the welcome they'd receive. "We have a great way of greeting visitors at our church. You'll see," I said.

Vivian seemed enthusiastic. "We'll visit next Sunday."

But on Sunday morning my husband was called out of town, and Billy, our youngest, was running a fever. I quickly ran down the street and explained that we couldn't be present.

"Vivian, do go on without us," I urged, and told her how to get to the church.

Anxiously, I awaited the Collins' return. At four o'clock I dialed her number.

"Hi," I said, "this is Ann. Did you go to our church this morning?"

"Yes," she replied. Nothing more.

Finally she continued. "The members greeted us where we sat, but—uh—well, we didn't get to sit together."

"Vivian, what happened?" I asked anxiously, "there's plenty of room in that church."

"Ann, many members were holding seats for themselves and their friends. There was no room for a family of six to sit together. We stopped at a pew where a lady sat alone, but she spread out her arms and said, 'I'm saving these seats.'"

"A lot of families don't sit together in church," Vivian continued, "but our children are young and, since we were in a new place, Jay and I wanted people to know we're all one family."

I tried to speak but my tongue seemed glued to my palate. Besides myself, I knew others who were addicted to seat-saving. I had failed to think how seat-saving might look to a visitor. How many guests had felt unwelcome upon finding places in our church reserved like those at some sports event? It must have made for a chilly atmosphere.

Of course, there are times when seat-saving is justifiable. Naturally a person with a hearing loss must sit in a certain location in order to hear God's message from the pastor. And a person in a wheelchair can't easily slip into a pew next to a pillar; however, these cases are in the minority.

I realized I had let others down, including my Master and visitors like the Collinses. So I confessed my sin, asked for forgiveness, and made a vow. Phooey to pew-saving in church! Now, it doesn't matter where I sit as long as I'm present to worship God.

Are you addicted to seat-saving? The next time you start to save your seat, look around and consider how it could make others feel.

. . . equip you with everything good for doing his will,
and may he work in us what is pleasing to him. . . .
Hebrews 13:21

After the children leave for school, take any items that haven't been put away and put them in "Toy Jail." They will have to pay a small amount per item to remove them.

A Planning Getaway
Pam Farrel

The heart of marriage is its communication system. It can be said that the success and happiness of any married pair is measurable in terms of the deepening dialogue which characterizes their union.

Dwight Small

Once a year, Bill and I set aside a special time away to talk over the business side of our lives. We set goals, talk finances, plan for the children's needs, and match calendars and do scheduling for the year. This valuable time away is when we discuss and evaluate our expectations. We talk over career plans, business items, pace of life—anything that either of us sees as a challenge to be overcome. By taking these regular planning getaways, we keep our anniversary and birthday getaways free from distractions—and then we can really enjoy each other rather than have the mood ruined by discussions about work or finances.

To get the most relaxation and direction out of your planning getaway, try these helpful hints:

Set a Date, Then Delegate: Share the responsibility for making reservations, child-care, or housesitting arrangements, and any other details. Decide who will do what. Get your trip off to a smooth start.

Play First: Plan a fun activity, a nap, and a good meal all before you begin setting goals or making decisions. You'll feel relaxed, refreshed, and ready to accomplish a lot.

Put First Things First: Remind yourself of your life priorities. If you've never written a mission statement for your relationship, start there. Write down the values and priorities that are important to both of you. Write down your goals and dreams. Having a plan for your relationship will build trust and confidence!

> *As charcoal to embers and as wood to fire,*
> *so is a quarrelsome man for kindling strife.*
>
> Proverbs 26:21

Use TV commercial time to get one chore done
or one step toward completion.

The Welcome Of Background Music
Patsy Clairmont

What oxygen is to the lungs, such is hope for the meaning of life.
Emil Brunner

I have found background music to be a pleasing greeting as guests arrive, though music can also be distracting if your friends feel they have to compete with it to converse. Sometimes the most accommodating background sound is silence, while other times music is a festive and hospitable addition.

Chimes on the porch can be a gentle touch; however, some are more like clanging cymbals that rankle the nervous system. But just as people see differently, we also hear differently. I stayed in a hotel recently where the housekeeper evidently thought I'd enjoy waking up at three in the morning to a hard-rock concert blaring from my radio. What may be a rip-snortin' clang to one may be an angelic choir to another. I have found that to be moderate in volume and style on the music dial is generally a good rule of thumb for guests. After everyone leaves, if you want to crank up your woofers and tweeters, have at it!

Speaking of tweeters, don't you just love the serenading songs of birds? In Michigan we are enchanted with the sound and sight of robins, our harbingers of spring. And with summer come troops of talented tweeters to our yards, and gardens, adding visual joy and distinctive songs. From the cooing mourning doves to the evening insistent whippoorwills and all the songsters in between (cardinals, bluebirds, finches), the outdoor concert drifts melodically into our home. Even the squawky blue jays' colorful rendition of "I did it my way" is appreciated in the mix. In the fall Michigan's sky fills with noisy, migrating Canadian geese. They honk as if to alert us to get out of town before the bitter winds blanket us in snow.

Much of the noise in our homes we create by the sounds from our own mouths. We are instructed to *make a joyful noise . . .* (Psalm 100:1a, KJV), which Les and I believe our mothers generally did. (Nah, they weren't perfect.) My mom filled our home with song as she worked around the house. That joyous offering convinced me she loved caring for us. And that thought added to my feelings of worth.

Can you list five sounds that have affected your life? What sounds comfort and encourage the people surrounding you? What is the quality of your words? How will you be remembered by those you love most? Is your home filled with celebration or contention? What will you do today to help arrange for your family and friends to experience a sweet serenade?

Listen, a noise on the mountains, like that of a great multitude! Listen, an uproar among the kingdoms, like nations massing together! The LORD Almighty is mustering an army for war.
Isaiah 13:4

Write a letter to someone who experienced those same five sounds and express how hearing those sounds now makes you feel.

Display Your Heritage In A Family Museum

Karen O'Connor

I desire no future that will break the ties of the past.
George Eliot

"Where did you get that beautiful old quilt? It looks hand-made," said the silver-haired woman, as she paused in front of the glass doors of the old cherry-wood bookcase that stands in the entry hall of our home. "And look at those lovely serving spoons and the Fostoria serving set. My grandmother had one just like it. And that old Bible. And the Shirley Temple drinking cup," she added. "What treasures!"

The guest in our home was referring to the heirlooms my husband Charles and I had on display in what has come to be known as "The Family Museum." Some years ago as we were packing and unpacking boxes during a move, we paused to look at all the items that had come down through the generations of our families: real china play dishes that were nearly a century old, my husband's first metronome from his childhood piano-playing days, his father's railroad pocket watch, a dictionary my grandfather had given me on my eighth birthday—and many more items of great personal value.

Charles suggested we select as many as our bookcase could artfully hold, clean them up, and put them on display. The books could go on a shelf in the den. But our heirlooms, many of them priceless to us, should be set out for friends and family to enjoy.

Today our collection of treasures is also a living museum as we periodically add small, special things that represent our ongoing lives: a yarn doll we bought in Mexico, a creche set made in Germany, our children's first shoes. Most important, however, our museum serves as an anchor to the past, as it reminds us of people and events that cannot be replaced or duplicated, especially in the lives of our sons and daughters and grandchildren.

If such a custom interests you, it is easy to get started.

• Ask your parents or other relatives for photos, shoes, trinkets, coins, spoons, cups, old books, a glass water pitcher, or other items that have special meaning to your family. Such things may already be in your possession or in an attic, basement, or closet of a family member.

Chances are your relatives would be proud and pleased to share them with you. My mother was so flattered when I asked her to save me one of my grandmother's hand-painted ice cream dishes, that she gave me the entire set on the spot! I kept one for myself and passed on the others to each of my grown daughters, my sister, and my niece.

• Place items on a shelf where they will be easily seen, or like us, buy or make a cabinet with glass doors for a permanent and safe display.

• Make your collection as personal as you wish. It can be a tribute to the past, a living memory of current times, or a blend of the two—a testimony to your individual and family connections.

• Put a sticker on the bottom of each treasure or heirloom in your family museum, noting the name of the persons (your children, for example, or other loved ones) you wish to leave them for after you're gone. Make a master list and keep it with your important papers, such as your will.

> *But seek first His kingdom and His righteousness, and all these things will be given to you as well.*
> Matthew 6:33

On the master list of your heirlooms, also note any information you know about the item: date of creation and whom it was first given to.

God's Silence
OSWALD CHAMBERS

Patience and diligence, like faith, remove mountains.
William Penn

Has God trusted you with a silence—a silence that is big with meaning? God's silences are His answers. Think of those days of absolute silence in the home at Bethany! Is there anything analogous to those days in your life? Can God trust you like that, or are you still asking for a visible answer? God will give you the blessings you ask if you will not go any further without them; but His silence is the sign that He is bringing you into a marvelous understanding of Himself. Are you mourning before God because you have not had an audible response? You will find that God has trusted you in the most intimate way possible, with an absolute silence, not of despair, but of pleasure, because He saw that you could stand a bigger revelation. If God has given you a silence, praise Him, He is bringing you into the great run of His purposes. The manifestation of the answer in time is a matter of God's sovereignty. Time is nothing to God. For a while you said, "I asked God to give me bread, and He gave me a stone." He did not, and today you find He gave you the bread of life.

A wonderful thing about God's silence is that the contagion of His stillness gets into you and you become perfectly confident—"I know God has heard me." His silence is the proof that He has. As long as you have the idea that God will bless you in answer to prayer, He will do it, but He will never give you the grace of silence. If Jesus Christ is bringing you into the understanding that prayer is for the glorifying of His Father, He will give you the first sign of His intimacy—silence.

Be still, and know that I am God . . .
Psalm 46:10

The next time you have your devotions, try to quiet your mind for one minute and just listen for God's voice.

My Special Friend

RUTH E. McDANIEL

The only way to have a friend is to be one.

Ralph Waldo Emerson

Friends! What a blessing they are, and how sad for those who have none. It's so easy to get friends; just follow Emerson's advice. God has blessed me with numerous friends of all ages. One of the newest is just eight years old. His name is Alex, and I call him my special friend.

This relationship evolved in a very natural way. Alex's parents own the house behind me and I introduced myself shortly after they moved in. Over the years, I've watched Alex grow and he became accustomed to seeing me stand at the back fence, chatting with his mother. Then, one day, early in the summer of 1998, Alex telephoned to ask me to meet him at the fence; he wanted to show me his newly acquired sea shell collection. That was the beginning of our daily talks. Throughout that summer and right up to the first cold day of autumn, he would stand at the fence and watch for me. As soon as I saw him, I would wave and hurry out to hear the latest.

People are curious about what we discuss. After all, there's quite a difference in our ages—nearly five decades, to be exact. The truth is, we talk about everything from Jesus and the Bible, to nature, animals, insects, friends, hobbies, and more. There's no end to the subjects that interest us. Alex allows me to view the world through his eyes, thus enabling me to write for his age group with some success. I give him my undivided attention, almost like a convenient, doting grandmother. It seems mutually beneficial.

At some point, it occurred to me that my relationship with the Lord is very similar to my friendship with Alex. I come to the Lord as a little child and He meets me where I am. He's available whenever I want to talk, and He gives me His undivided attention.

There is no end to the subjects we talk about. He is my very special Friend, and He loves me without reservation.

As time passes, I know that my relationship with Alex will change. He will seek my company less and less as his world expands. However, I will always treasure the times we now share and fondly remember our special friendship.

On the other hand, the Lord will never leave me. He will continue to draw close to me and love me, as long as I let Him, and our friendship will grow and grow, even after my life on earth has ended. This is truly one friendship that never dies.

You can have the same kind of friendship with Jesus. Just talk to Him like any friend. He promises to listen and respond. A person can never have too many friends—especially One who will love you forever.

A friend loves at all times. . . .
Proverbs 17:17a

Bake cookies and take them to a new neighbor;
begin your own back-fence friendship.

Let The Experts Do It

Gloria H. Dvorak

Whether it is a plumber, painter or just an extra
pair of hands, get help.

Nancy Miller

I was brought up to do things for myself because my parents could not afford to pay others to help us. My mother sewed her own curtains and draperies, cut the hedges, and painted all the walls in our home. My dad worked three jobs to pay all our bills so we could live in a nice neighborhood. Both parents were always weary and we kids helped as best as we could.

When I got married, I carried over this "do it yourself" attitude. But my husband believed in hiring qualified people to do the jobs we were not trained to do. I was not used to letting others help me nor was I willing to pay for their services.

I remember when we bought our first home and the children had made sticky finger marks all over the walls and banisters. I decided to paint the walls. I told my husband and he suggested I hire a painter. I didn't listen and thought that since my mother had done it, so could I. I concluded I could save a lot of money.

I eagerly embraced the challenge of painting but the smell soon overpowered me. When I tried to paint the inside of our closet that didn't have ventilation, I became dizzy and couldn't breathe. Then I opened the windows too wide and eventually got a terrible cold. When the kids came home from school, they walked on some paint droppings and spread it on the floors with their shoes. When my husband came home, supper was not cooked and I was too exhausted and sick to think about food. When my husband came in to inspect my painting, he pointed out all the spots I had missed, especially around the window frames. I didn't want to hear it! Instead of a thank-you, I was criticized for my hard work. From that time on, I never tackled a painting job in our home.

We have had many painters in over the years and I appreciate their professionalism and experience. I am now glad to pay them, knowing what a mess I had made.

Having experienced people work for us saves us time and stress. The money it costs is well spent, believe me!

Listen to advice and accept instruction, and in the end you will be wise.
Proverbs 19:20

If you've been putting off a project or chore, consider getting professional help to eliminate your procrastination.

When Our Wants Are Expensive

TERRY FITZGERALD SIECK

My needs are simple. My wants are expensive.

Miss Piggy

My three-year-old granddaughter, Olivia, and I went to "browse" in a toy store. She immediately spotted a bright pink tricycle and hopped on. As she pretended to peddle, I eyed the price tag. "Oh, Olivia," I bemoaned, "this is expensive."

"But I like 'expensive'!" she asserted.

I was both amused and amazed. It didn't take a child long to learn to like expensive.

Later, I thought about times when I had liked expensive. Several years ago I had wanted to live in an older, more stately, house. Although my parents had always preferred modern, my heart's desire was antique—a house with character, crown molding, plastered ceilings, hardwood floors, and solid brick fireplaces. My husband and I found such a house and put our modern one on the market. Just as the sale and purchase were coming together, everything fell apart. I cried. I crabbed. I prayed that God would work some miracle so that I could have "my" house. I liked expensive.

Then I thought about the house where my grandparents lived when I was a child. It wasn't expensive; indeed, it was hardly standing. Grandma and Grandpa were Midwestern farmers who eked out a living and managed to raise seven children. The house had no running water, but an outside well with a hand pump. They chopped the ice before we could use it in the winter. The privy was outdoors, too. Grandma burned corn cobs in her oven to make the heat for cooking. There was a pot-bellied stove in the living room, broken linoleum on the floors, and two small bedrooms for the kids: one for the five boys and one for the two girls. Instead of a TV, Grandpa played the harmonica and banjo. He also taught me to play rummy and let me win.

It wasn't much of a house, but it certainly was a home. I never heard Grandma pray, like I did, for a nicer house; in fact, I never heard her complain. Her needs were met—she had a home and a loving family. Her wants weren't expensive.

Too often we ask God to provide our wants and forget that he has met our needs. We don't focus on having a roof over our heads, running water, and food on the table. We take them for granted. Instead, we get preoccupied with our wants, and our wants are expensive: a bigger house, newer car, genuine jewelry, designer jeans, even pink tricycles.

Before I ask God for something, I now take time to ask myself, "Is this something I need, or is this something I want?" If it's something I want, then I ask, "Just how expensive is it?" Not only in terms of money, but of time, energy and things I may have to give up.

You and I can ask ourselves some other important questions. Is a new house worth working long hours at a stressful job? Are those hours at work more important than time with our families? Are we busier looking good on the outside than becoming good on the inside?

Our needs are simple. God meets them. Our wants are expensive and not necessarily needed. Consider carefully which you're asking for.

. . . do not worry about your life, what you will eat or drink;
or about your body, what you will wear. Is not life more important than food,
and the body more important than clothes?
Matthew 6:25

> Before you make a request of God, ask yourself,
> "Is this something I really need, or is it something I want?"

A Glimpse

DR. LARRY CRABB

*Mature people are made not out of good times
but out of bad times.*

Hyman Judah Schachtel

In six weeks I would be twenty-two years old. In three weeks I would be a husband. The first I was prepared for; the second, well, that's what I was here for.

I was sitting on an old worn-velvet loveseat in the preacher's living room. Nestled close beside me was Rachael, my beautiful bride-to-be. It would have been difficult to slide even a thin book between us.

Across from us, in separate chairs perhaps ten feet apart, sat the preacher and his wife, both in their late seventies. She nodded her gray head and smiled and listened and rocked as her hands worked a rapid rhythm with yarn and knitting needles. He was relaxed into an old stuffed recliner, busily jotting notes in a small, well-used black notebook.

As we discussed the details of our wedding ceremony, I found myself watching the old couple, not as preacher and preacher's wife, but as husband and wife. Suddenly something struck me. Those two, sitting in separate chairs with more than three yards between them, conveyed more love with a single meeting of their eyes than my fiancee and I were exchanging with all our snuggling, grinning, and whispered endearments.

I still remember thinking, "How do we get from here to there, from where we are in our eager young love to where they are in their loving maturity?"

Marriage is a stage on which real love—the kind the apostle Paul described as the greatest virtue—can be enacted for the world to see: the kind of love that enables us to endure wrong with patience, to resist evil with conviction, to enjoy the good things with gusto, to give richly of ourselves with humility, and to nourish another's soul with long-suffering.

When all these virtues are present, not only is each marriage partner in-comparably blessed, but sometimes a couple of young apprentices about to take their place on this same stage can catch a glimpse of what the marriage relationship *could* be—a glimpse that won't let them settle for anything less.

If any of you lacks wisdom, he should ask God, who gives generously to all without finding fault, and it will be given to him.

James 1:5

If you anticipate that you'll be put on hold when making a telephone call, have something to do while you wait.

Delight
JANET E. PRATT

He loves each one of us as if there were only one of us.

St. Augustine

I was browsing through the book of Psalms recently when I encountered a phrase that gave me a whole new perspective on God. It leaped out at me: "The Lord takes delight in His people." It was something I had never consid-ered before.

I know God loves me because He sent His Son to die for me. I know that because He loves me, He teaches and corrects me. But I've never thought about God taking *delight* in me. Curled up in my favorite chair, soaking in the view outside my window, I contemplated what it means to take delight in someone.

I take delight in my children. My daughter is bright, bubbly, and sensitive. Sometimes I watch her when she's not looking. I gaze at the delicate curve of her jaw line, her firm little chin, and I am awed by how beautiful she is. When her presence brightens a room, when I see her heart break over something she has done wrong, when she makes the effort to include a child others would rather ignore, my heart swells and I want to say, "She's mine. Isn't she just exquisite?"

My son is thirteen and he makes me laugh. He has a quick sense of humor and an enormous vocabulary, which includes words like *tenebrous*. The things that come out of his mouth often amaze and enchant me. I look at him and think, "What a marvelous human being."

Obviously, neither of them is perfect. There are times when I feel like locking them in their rooms until they are twenty-one. Still, I take pleasure in them.

Suddenly I realized that when I humbled myself and admitted I need a Savior, God beautified me with salvation. He no longer looks at me and sees my sin. He looks at me and sees the righteousness of His Son, Jesus Christ.

Satan may be pointing at me, saying, "Did you hear her yell at her kids? Did you see her doing eighty on the freeway? She forgot to read her Bible this morning," but I can just see God nudging the angel Gabriel and saying, "Look at her. Isn't she just exquisite? She's mine, you know. Did you hear how she made her friend laugh? Did you see her teach those children about Me?"

Gabriel must be looking at me, shaking his head, saying, "I just don't get it."

What a wonderful thought! I realized God's love is more than redemption and correction. It is also a love that comes from the heart of our Abba Father. And He delights in you, too!

For the LORD takes delight in His people; He crowns
the humble with salvation.

Psalm 149:4

Put aside the adult stuff today and play with your kids.
Find out what it means to delight in someone.

His Banqueting Table

JOAN CLAYTON

The Word of God nourishes the hungry soul.

Joan Clayton

Our new bird feeder was made of redwood cedar and I breathed deeply, relishing the smell. We filled it with all kinds of enticing seeds. My husband eagerly hung it on a strong branch of a nearby apricot tree.

We hurried and retreated to the safe distance of our swing and nestled down for a relaxing time of bird watching. We waited and watched. We did the same thing the next day and the next!

"What is wrong with those birds?" I impatiently exclaimed to my husband.

"Here is this beautiful banquet of food and they are ignoring it. All they have to do is receive it!"

Instantly in my heart, I felt the Lord was saying the same thing to me. God has provided a "banquet of food" for me in His Word. He satisfies the deepest longings of my soul. He has "spiritual food" for every need in my life. All I have to do is open His Word and receive it.

When I experience a "famine" in my life, I stumble around, faint with hunger, until I remember that my Heavenly Father, who feeds the birds of the air and the beasts of the field, will surely feed me and meet my every need.

"Look," I whispered to my husband one day. "The birds have found their food and they have told their friends."

I know where to find my "spiritual" food. I will tell my friends, too!

*Now He who supplies seed to the sower and bread for food will also supply
and increase your store of seed and will enlarge the harvest
of your righteousness.*

II Corinthians 9:10

Put a bird house or bird feeder out for the neighborhood birds.
You'll enjoy the reward of their singing.

The Present

DEBORAH SILLAS NELL

I expect to pass through life but once. If therefore, there be any kindness I can show, or any good thing I can do to any fellow being, let me do it now, and not defer or neglect it, as I shall not pass this way again.

William Penn

The last few weeks have been full of wonder. Rays of eternity like morning sunlight filter into each new day. In two weeks we will be moving to Pennsylvania. As we prepare to leave, stronger bonds of love and friendship are being cemented between us and the loved ones we are leaving.

Our days in California are numbered, so each day, each encounter is a gift. Our eyes and hearts have been opened to the treasure of the present moment. Our final hugs and words to a friend are priceless. We hold them close to our hearts. Each day is an open window of time illuminated with the knowledge that there is a departure date in the future. So we savor each day.

You and I should live in the same way, as if all our days are the last days here on earth. We each have a departure date for heaven. How thrilling if we could live each day knowing that any day could be our last. If we could just see each day as a gift, we could live life abundantly, just as Christ intended us to live.

I have fought the good fight, I have finished the race, I have kept the faith.
Now there is in store for me the crown of righteousness, which the Lord, the
righteous Judge, will award to me on that day—and not only to me, but also
to all who have longed for his appearing.

II Timothy 4:7–8

Keep a prayer journal. Record your prayer requests
and God's answers. In a year's time you will be amazed
at how faithful He is.

Celebrating Small Losses

SYLVIA DUNCAN

I celebrate myself and sing myself.
Walt Whitman

"Eat the foods you love and celebrate your losses," says Vicki Ellebrecht as she lectures at Weight Watcher's meetings. Nothing stops Vicki from encouraging her members On one occasion after being rescued from a flash flood, she lectured soaking wet. She is a woman who leads the way to permanent weight loss and better eating habits for life. It is a responsible job and Vicki does not shirk when she talks to people who want to take and keep off pounds. She has been encouraging Weight Watcher's groups for twenty-one years. She shines with enthusiasm and is a model of kindness with a strong energy level.

Each Saturday, Vicki talks to as many as one hundred twenty members and explains the program to all the newcomers. Five hours later as she ushers the last person out the door, she is still smiling and fresh. She has maintained her own weight over the years and offers key pieces of advice about eating habits.

"Don't deny yourself. Be good to yourself. Eat what you want but less of it." What if a gourmet gets carried away and eats too much of a much loved food?

Vicki has the answer to that, too.

"Plan ahead. Know exactly what you are going to eat for the day and stick to it but be sure to make it food you really like to eat."

Vicki knows that unusual eating patterns and festive foods can create havoc with an eating plan. It can be difficult to keep food intake under control when the clans gather. This dynamic leader always reminds herself and her members that nothing tastes as good as the feeling of being fit and healthy. She often goes back to the importance of eating food you love. "If you don't enjoy what you are eating, you won't change your lifestyle permanently. Then you'll be back where you started."

Vicki reminds everyone that you wouldn't say to a good friend, "You're a bad person because you gained weight." Her years of experience have shown it is better to encourage yourself with positive self-talk by remembering what you have done right—rather than what you've done wrong. Build on that. Vicki also believes in celebrating the smallest of weight losses. "Never say, 'Oh, only a half a pound lost.' Celebrate that half a pound gone."

For over two decades through several different programs, Vicki has maintained her own weight by planning ahead, treating herself well, and sharing her stories. She has been quick with compliments, quiet with sad members, and has reminded thousands of people to eat enjoyable food and celebrate small losses.

But the fruit of the Spirit is love, joy, peace, patience, kindness, goodness, faithfulness, gentleness and self control.
Galatians 5:22–23a

Make individual snack bags of your favorite foods.
Allow one a day.

Garden Blessings

BETTY CHAPMAN PLUDE

All through the long winter I dream of my garden. On the first warm day of spring I dig my fingers deep into the soft earth. I can feel its energy, and my spirits soar.

Helen Hays

As winter draws to an end, living in a state with four seasons, my soul yearns for the delights of spring and summer. My favorite focus is our flower garden, created to enjoy the large abundance of color from every location in our cottage-style home. My goal is to have a beautiful garden and have fun receiving many delightful blessings along the way.

Spring has finally arrived. As I stroll my way through the garden watering my color quilt of blossoms, stepping from one foot-shaped stepping stone to the next, I feel relaxed and I'm enjoying the outdoors. The birds singing their playful songs and energetic bumblebees flitting from one blossom to the next on the graceful, purple butterfly bush give me great pleasure.

Tucked sporadically throughout my garden, I have metal flower identification stakes with the names of my grandchildren, nieces, and nephews. I pray for or talk to whatever child's marker stands tall beside a colorful beauty. Sometimes I think about what that child is doing at the moment, in school, preschool, or napping. Even the grand baby who is yet in the womb has a marker standing by a beautiful, vibrant red rose bush.

When the children come to visit, following a hug, they run to the garden. Their happy voices exclaim, "There's my name! My flower has really growed."

"Yes," I respond, "Just as you have grown, taller and more beautiful."

Friends come to visit and observe the identification markers as we walk and enjoy the flowers. This creates great conversation and an idea is planted in their minds. Some return home and phone me excitedly to say they have tucked metal markers by their flowers to remember loved ones while enjoying and caring for their garden. One friend commented as she entered my front door.

"Betty, your nephew needs watering!"

My garden has turned into many unexpected blessings. It has blossomed into times of relaxation, a reminder to pray, an opportunity to share ideas with friends, and teaching the children to become more aware of the beauty of a garden. But most important, it tells them how important they are—and how loved.

The LORD will guide you always; He will satisfy your needs in a sun-scorched land and will strengthen your frame. You will be like a well-watered garden, like a spring whose waters never fail.

Isaiah 58:11

Instead of giving up food for Lent, choose to change an unattractive attitude or perspective.

From The Heart
STEPHANIE E. NICKEL

Live from your heart.
Richard Carlson, Ph. D.

Life is a treasure. The Creator of the universe has invested in our lives in countless ways. He has given each of His children gifts and abilities. To say it isn't so is to call Him a liar. Endeavoring to gain interest on this investment is not self-centered and prideful; it is biblical. I believe the parable of the talents refers to more than our financial resources.

Recently, my husband and I were invited to join the tenants of a nearby seniors building for supper. A lady seated beside Dave mentioned that they had missed my Christmas message this past holiday season. It turns out that they had previously used my writing, "A Walk through Bethlehem," during a time of corporate devotions. I was amazed and encouraged. That night, I came home and did something I hadn't done for a long time. I wrote from my heart. The result was a thirteen-stanza Easter poem. I dedicated "Reflections" to those seniors and hope that it will be an encouragement to them as they have been an encouragement to me.

You may not write. In fact, you may not consider your gifts and abilities all that noteworthy. That is often the way with the Lord's investment in our lives. Often it seems like second nature and we don't understand why others take notice. However, when we exercise the gifts God has given us, it will feel as if we're living from the heart, fulfilling something important.

There are things you do that make the world a brighter place. Perhaps you love children dearly. Even kind words and a smile may make all the difference in a child's day. Maybe you are given to hospitality. What a biblical calling! Maybe you work quietly in the background, willingly fulfilling the tasks that others find mundane. Believe me, there are plenty of us who are thankful that you serve the Lord in this way.

All of God's children have something special to offer. We must never minimize our importance to Him and to those around us. Until we get to heaven, we won't know how far-reaching our influence has been. God is looking for a return on His investment, and, because of His strength, motivation, and guidance, He will get one—through us!

We have different gifts, according to the grace given us.

Romans 12:6a

Try writing a poem, even if it's only a few lines.

Staying Power

PATTY STUMP

We must trust God. We must trust not only that He does what is best, but that He knows what is ahead.

Max Lucado

I enjoy uncertainty and thrive on adventure! I'm a natural at living life with a sense of reckless abandonment to the Lord, confident that curves encountered along the journey are merely bridges between where I've been and mountaintop experiences about to unfold.

Sounds great doesn't it? Yet in reality I don't thrive on adventure. In fact, I barely survive everyday routine and often struggle to juggle those things I see coming my way!

I'm more a creature of habit than I would like to admit, and stepping out of my "comfort zone" isn't always easy. Moving across the United States involved such a step. I'm not even sure how it happened, yet one day I found myself loading our Carolina furnishings onto a forty-foot moving truck headed to Arizona. What was I thinking? Arizona? Sure it was sunny, but what about the seasons? Certainly a pool would be nice, but nothing could replace the puddles left by summer showers. And was it true that Arizonans vacuumed their rock "lawns"? I'd grown up riding a mower!

The day before we began our cross-country journey, I heard Psalm 37:3 on the radio: "Dwell in the land and cultivate faithfulness." At the time I couldn't grasp what the verse would come to mean to me, yet through the years it has reminded me to have "staying power" in my faithfulness and yieldedness to the Lord regardless of my circumstances. "Staying power" comes from time spent with the Lord, coupled with a personal commitment to seek and follow Him every day in every way. When I fail to prioritize my relationship with Him, I lose perspective regarding the journey and forfeit the fullness of intimacy with Him. Plus, I lose a sense of expectancy regarding what He has in store.

Unexpected curves in life will continue to bring me face to face with breathtaking peaks and pinnacles, as well as heartbreaking valleys and deserts. I'm prayerful that as the Lord's plans for me unfold, I will respond to life's events with faith-filled momentum and a staying power that stems from knowing He loves me and gives to me from the abundance of His love!

If your faithfulness in trusting and serving the Lord is waning, reconsider how you can change your perspective to one of seeing life as an adventure. He knows the path ahead. Trust Him.

The LORD will guide you always.
Isaiah 58:11a

Send a note of encouragement to someone you know of
who is going through a time of transition. Through your
words, they too may experience "staying power"
to remain focused and faithful to the Lord.

Preparing For Spring
KAREN POLAND

Old promises must pledge themselves each day
Or, unrenewed, pass quietly away.
Calvin Miller

March is here, which means that the seasons are changing, and spring is very close. Just today I was thinking of all that we have to do around our house to prepare for spring. Things like removing all of the dead plants from the pots and replacing them with fresh potting soil and colorful flowers. We have to put fertilizer on the lawn in hopes that the brown of winter will turn to luscious green. And if I desire any fresh home-grown tomatoes this summer, I need to plow up the ground and plant them today.

Like life, our marriages go through seasons. I recall the summer after the birth of my second daughter. I was so emotionally and physically exhausted. Too often my poor husband would open the door after a long day of work to find all three of "his girls" crying. I felt at the time that being a mother took every ounce of my energy and left me nothing to offer our marriage. I wondered then if spring newness would ever replace the dryness that I felt. Our marriage was going through a time of winter coldness. It felt like there were no visible signs of growth. But just like the seasons, thank God that our marriage transitioned into springtime as well. There were times of hope, renewal, and excitement.

As we anticipate and prepare our front yards, what are we doing right now to welcome springtime into our marriages? Are there "weeds" of bitterness or unforgiveness growing that need to be pulled out by the roots to make room for new growth? Is there a particular fruit of the Spirit like love, patience, gentleness, or kindness that we desire to harvest that should be carefully planted right now? What about "pruning" our lives of those things that are hindering real growth in our relationship? Perhaps the potential for growth is hindered only by a need for nourishment or careful attention. Is there something we can be doing right now that will help bring on this new season?

Let us not become weary in doing good, for at the proper time we will reap a harvest if we do not give up.
Galatians 6:9

What one thing will you do today to communicate love to your spouse?

A Contented Silence

RUSTY FISCHER

True contentment is a real, even an active virtue—not only affirmative but creative. It is the power of getting out of any situation all there is in it.

G. K. Chesterton

After a recent job transfer took me far from home, I naturally turned to the TV for solace. During a storm the first month, I was in my new apartment and I unhooked my cable so lightning wouldn't damage my precious "friend." Too late. When I hooked the cable up the next day, I got nothing but a frosty screen and much hissing. Reluctantly I washed out a coffee can to begin my "New TV!" fund.

But then a strange thing happened. I found contentment! Without huge hours glued to the tube, I discovered the beauty of sunsets and the joy of peace and quiet. My daily stress headaches disappeared and I stopped taking those over-the-counter sleeping pills at night. I read all of those comforting bulletins and spiritual literature I picked up at church and had never gotten around to before. I lingered on the porch over long cups of tea, watching children and nature at play. I even found a reggae station on the radio and had never enjoyed dusting so much!

Yet above all, I finally found time amid my daily struggle . . . to pray. Where before I had always spent huge blocks of my time glued to a flickering box, now I sat quietly and talked with God. Thanked Him. Praised Him. And with each new, TV-less day I grew stronger. How disappointed I was when a friend came to visit and found that I had simply hooked the cable into the wrong outlet after the storm! The harsh, blaring sounds of canned laughter and screaming game show contestants now felt like an intrusion into my peaceful days. Shortly after she returned home, I turned the TV off for good and returned to my quiet routine of peace, quiet, and contentment. How

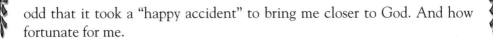

odd that it took a "happy accident" to bring me closer to God. And how fortunate for me.

But godliness with contentment is great gain.
I Timothy 6:6

Try turning off the TV for a specific period of time.
Write down all the benefits you experience.

College Boxes
KAYLEEN J. REUSSER

Children and adults of all ages seek constant satisfaction of their emotional needs, including the desire for love, social acceptance and self-respect.

Dr. James Dobson

The college years can be the best time of a person's life or the worst. Your church can help make the transition to high learning easier by giving each student a college box. A college box consists of stationery and personal items, such as folders, notebooks, envelopes, stamps, hi-liters, tape, scissors, thumb tacks, glue, pens, papers, pencils, aspirin, room deodorizer, gum, facial tissue, cups, hangers, Christian posters, snack items, toothpaste, and soap. All items are donated by the church and given to the students at no cost.

In the spring, coordinators offer sign-up sheets for persons who will be attending college in the fall and would like to receive a college box. Students are asked to print the name of the college they will be attending, if they are a freshman, and if they plan to commute or live on campus. This information helps coordinators determine quantities of items needed. For instance, a freshman living on campus could use a laundry basket, while a junior or commuter may not. Church members are encouraged to pray for each person on the list.

Coordinators prepare a chart of items and post it at the church with a mid-July due date. Church members sign their names by the items they wish to donate and bring them by the first of August so that the boxes can be prepared by the time students leave a few weeks later. Cash can be given to purchase items not received.

My purpose is that they may be encouraged in heart and united in love, so that they may have the full riches of complete understanding, in order that they may know the mystery of God, namely, Christ.

Colossians 2:2

Pray for students who you know are away from home
and facing new challenges daily.

Rainy Day Box
LAURA SABIN RILEY

Reflect upon your present blessings, of which every man has many;
not on your past misfortunes, of which all men have some.

Charles Dickens

I awoke to a screaming baby with a fever, a sink full of dirty dishes, a broken dishwasher, and a pile of laundry. By noon, I was feeling frazzled and defeated. The baby's crying had shattered my nerves, his fever increased, and I couldn't get him in to the doctor until late afternoon. The part for the dishwasher would be a week getting here and the pile in the sink was growing taller, not to mention the pile of laundry.

When I have a day that begins and progresses like the one above, I imagine that having a job outside the home would be more appealing, and easier! When my kids have a bad day, so do I. When they don't feel well, neither do I. The only abundance I experience on that kind of day is in the form of an abundant headache!

One simple way I've found to live in the abundant way I'd prefer, no matter what my circumstances, is to change my mind-set. I try to focus on more pleasant things. In the midst of such trials, I need to look to God. To help me do this, I have set up a rainy day box. This simple box is abundant with encouragement, as it contains affirming cards from friends and family, favorite Scripture verses written on index cards or slips of brightly colored paper, uplifting notes from my husband, even lyrics to a cheery song or poem clipped from a magazine. When I'm feeling discouraged or down in the dumps, I pull out my rainy day box and focus on the "things above," as well as the positive words of others. When I gird myself with strength this way, the challenges of the day don't seem so abundant.

Having a tough day, week, or month? Write down a few of your favorite Scriptures and start a rainy day box. Every time you receive an uplifting card or read an inspirational thought, add it to your collection. It will bring abundant sunshine to your next rainy day!

Set your minds on things above, not on earthly things.
Colossians 3:2

Keep the encouraging cards you receive from others
and read them often!

Pretzel Banners

Sarah Healton

Ere you left your room this morning, did you think to pray?
M. A. Kidder

Children and others love making banners for special occasions. The pretzel banner has always been one of my favorite crafts to use with children in church-related activities. Before we start making this craft, I tell the story about the origin of the pretzel.

A long time ago in Germany during the time of Lent, the forty days before Easter, eating eggs, milk, and fat were forbidden. In one village, the old baker began to experiment with how to make a special bread for his customers to eat during Lent. He took only flour, salt, and water mixed it together. Next he rolled it out into long, thin strips and twisted the loops to look like two arms crossed. Then he baked them. While they were still hot he sprinkled lots of salt on them. They became very popular with the people who thought they were a symbol for arms crossed in prayer. You can fold your arms and bow your head to illustrate. And so pretzels became a symbol of praying.

Each of you can make a banner of pretzels. What will you think of when you look at this banner?

Materials needed for this craft

- 1 piece of plain fabric 6"x 9" such as muslin or broadcloth
- 3 small pretzels (Have plenty of miniature pretzels on hand for the temptation to eat them will be great.)
- 9 tiny pieces of colored yarn or ribbon
- 1 plastic straw
- 12" of string
- Printed Bible verse to paste at the bottom of the banner.

Adult pre-preparation

- Make a 3/4" fold at the top of the cloth
- Stitch on sewing machine about 1/3". Be sure a straw will slide into the seam.

Making the banner

1. Push straw through the top seam of the banner.
2. Run a string through plastic straw to make a hanger.
3. Create a design on the banner by gluing on the pretzels, and colored yarn or ribbons.
4. Let dry before picking it up, about five minutes.
5. Encourage the children to talk about praying. If the children are old enough, encourage them to find Luke 11:1–2 verses in their Bibles. Watch the expressions on their faces as they read the very familiar lines in verse two which is the beginning of the Lord's Prayer.

> "... Lord, teach us to pray ..."
> Luke 11:1c

Make a banner for yourself and hang it on your bedroom door.

A Paneful Tap

LESLIE WHITWORTH

It comes the very moment you wake up each morning. All your wishes and hopes for the day rush at you like wild animals. And the first job each morning consists simply in shoving them all back; in listening to that other voice, taking that other point of view, letting that other, larger, stronger, quieter life come flowing in.

C. S. Lewis

Sometimes I am surprised at God's persistent desire to be with me. So often I focus on the doing and giving side of our relationship and miss out on the joy of just being in God's presence. Years ago, I was reminded of this in a unique way.

Each year an eastern phoebe builds her nest in the awning outside my children's bedroom window. One spring, as we watched, three oily, black birds emerged from their eggs. Through the pane, we monitored the rhythm of their every need. We knew when they threw back their double-jointed beaks and wailed for food. We watched their heads flop over in sleep. We worried as the funnel-shaped nest grew crowded.

One day as I vacuumed and watched mother bird fly to and fro with morsels of food, a bird vanished. It had been there a moment before, so I figured it had fallen out of the nest. I called my children and we went outside to check. We didn't find it, but our dog did. Gently, she laid the tiny bird down at my son's feet, unharmed. We brought it inside and fed it unceasingly. Two weeks later, we released Peeper, as we called him.

That fall, I went back to work as a teacher. I found it hard to get up early and spend time in prayer and devotion. As winter wore on, it was even more difficult to crawl out of my cozy bed. I tried propping myself up in bed to read and pray. Spring came and I got up, but I wandered outside to water the garden and feed the pets and soon all my time had slipped away. I offered quick prayers in the car or at my desk. In April, we "sprang forward" in time and my eyes stay glued shut when the alarm went off. Not bothering to sit, I sent up garbled prayers wrapped in unfinished dreams and drifted back to sleep.

One morning there was a knock at my window right at dawn. Tap, tap, tap, tap. I sat up in bed and looked. A black crested bird clung to the window frame and beat its beak against the windowpane.

"Go away!" I shouted and lay back down. Tap, tap, tap, tap, it persisted. I threw the pillow at the window. Tap, tap, tap, tap, it had gone around to the other window. I sat up and looked at the clock. I didn't have to be up for another half hour. Again it tapped. Unbelievable. "What do you want?" I shouted at the bird.

I told my children about it at breakfast. "It's Peeper! He wants to come inside," they said. The next morning at the same time "Peeper" returned. Again, I pitched pillows, ruffled shades, yelled. Peeper just kept on tapping. On the third day, I decided that God was trying to tell me something. I opened my eyes and said, "I'm up." I went into the kitchen, put coffee on, and sat down with my Bible. Peeper came back for about ten days. Each time I rose and prayed.

Peeper hasn't been back—there's no need. I'm now in the habit of spending time with God when I wake up. And if I'm ever tempted not to, I imagine God having to send Peeper back to remind me.

The Creator of the universe makes time for us every day. Do we do the same?

My soul waits for the Lord, more than watchmen wait for the morning, more than watchmen wait for the morning.

Psalm 130:6

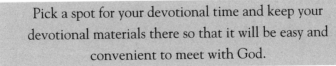

Pick a spot for your devotional time and keep your devotional materials there so that it will be easy and convenient to meet with God.

How To Make A Sweet Friend Feel Like $100,000 For Less Than 50 Cents

Susan Kimmel Wright

Little deeds of kindness,
Little words of love,
Help to make earth happy
Like the heaven above.

Julia Carney

At the end of each school year, my children and I struggled to come up with the perfect teacher recognition gift. Nothing in our price range ever seemed special enough to show appreciation for the extra effort our teachers had put into teaching a tough subject, their patience with immature behavior and attitudes, and the love and encouragement they'd shown.

Gift certificates were appreciated, but unimaginative. Special mementos tended to be expensive—and how many could a teacher display over the course of a long career? After years of this predictable struggle, my friend Ingrid gave me a solution that's never failed to delight the recipient.

Using a sheet of poster board, a marker, and some double-stick tape, we make a one-of-a-kind tribute with wrapped sweets. First, my children and I visit the candy store. We enjoy searching the shelves and bins for gums, candies, and small treats with names that can be used to create a message, the quirkier the better. Our basket, for example, might include: a "Jolly Rancher," a "Milky Way," a "$100 Grand" bar, a "Fifth Avenue," and Hershey "kisses" and "hugs."

We take the goodies home and get to work composing a message. Writing out our poster, we stop whenever we get to a candy name, and stick the piece of candy in that spot. A typical effort, using the selections listed above, might say:

"If you were a *Jolly Rancher*, instead of the best teacher in the *Milky Way*, your life might be more peaceful, but we're glad we have you! We wish we could give you *$100 Grand* and a ticker tape parade down 5th *Avenue*, but all we have are hugs and kisses. Thanks for a great year!"

Occasionally, we've varied our routine and attached items other than candy: "When your students drove you *nuts*, you must have needed to take some *pain reliever*, but you never complained." And sometimes other special people, like grandmas and bus drivers, deserve some recognition, too. Our favorite bus driver received a poster that referred to her driving in winter conditions that must have seemed like the high *Andes*.

When we give candy posters, we know our favorite people are getting a gift as special as they are. These are easy, inexpensive, and great fun to make. If you take some pictures—perhaps of your kids and the recipient with the poster—your "artistic efforts" won't be lost when the items are removed and used. That way, there's no waste or excessive accumulation, but the memory stays fresh to treasure.

Let my teaching fall like rain and my words descend like dew, like showers on new grass, like abundant rain on tender plants.

Deuteronomy 32:2

Try expressing your love and gratitude "sweetly" with a candy poster.

Easter Every Day

Susan Waterman Voss

It is the will and pleasure of the Father that he who sees the Son and believes in Him have eternal life.

Martin Luther

As I drove through silent streets that Easter morning, I thought of the women going to Christ's tomb. Did they, too, feel that they were the only people awake in the world? I was headed for the church and some last-minute organ practice before the sanctuary began to fill with worshipers.

The day progressed in the traditional manner for us. After the "Sonrise" service, my husband and I joined the congregation for Easter breakfast and attended the later morning service. Then it was off to the farm for dinner and Easter egg hunting with my husband's family.

Rosie, of course, was there. She had been with us in the morning as well. My husband was Rosie's grandson. While that alone would have made her precious in my eyes, there was much more to our relationship. A dear friend of our family, she had been a part of our lives for as long as I could remember.

Rosie was an important part of our church and community. Always willing to help out, never seeking thanks or recognition, she endeared herself to everyone. Her kindness resulted from Christian love—love that was evident in everything from the pies she made to the quilts she helped stitch for world relief efforts.

Rosie enjoyed her Easter day. After dinner, she sat holding her newest great-grandchild, and I marveled over her abundant faith and great strength and gentleness.

Later that afternoon, Rosie, sitting in a chair amidst family and friends, died. Soundlessly, her life slipped from her body and escaped to heaven.

Two days later, I stood in my classroom explaining to my students that I would be attending the funeral. Curious as always, one student asked, "When did she die?"

"On Sunday afternoon," I replied.

A child in the front row blurted out with great excitement, "On Easter? How neat!" Then he quickly apologized for fear of having offended me. I quickly assured him that I was in no way offended. He was absolutely right.

Christ's resurrection on Easter gives us the hope of eternal life. Because of that resurrection, Rosie now enjoys eternal life in heaven. What better way to celebrate Easter than to rejoice in the salvation Christ has given us? Had Rosie been given the opportunity to choose a day to be taken to her heavenly home, it might very well have been Easter day.

It occurred to me that perhaps God was weaving a heavenly message into our earthly sadness. Isn't every Christian's death an Easter celebration? Christ died on Good Friday to pay the ransom for our sins. His resurrection on Easter proved His success and great love for us.

When Christians die, they enjoy the greatest measure of Easter joy imaginable. Because of Christ's love, it's Easter every day. Our joy can be complete, even in death.

For to me, to live is Christ and to die is gain.
Philippians 1:21

When decorating Easter eggs, draw Christian symbols (crosses, butterflies, etc.) on eggs with a wax crayon before dipping in dye.

Pickle Tree Seeds

Marjorie K. Evans

Discretion of speech is more than eloquence.

Francis Bacon

It was spring and time to plant a garden. So early one Saturday morning, my husband, Ed, went out to the backyard to spade the garden plot. He had finished the digging and was raking the ground when our son and his family stopped to visit.

Five-year-old Cody dashed into the living room, gave me a bear hug and a kiss, then asked, "Where's Grandpa?"

"He's out in the back planting his garden," I replied. So Cody ran outside to see him.

Later Cody burst into the room, grabbed my hand, and exclaimed, "Grandma! Grandma! Come quick. Come and see how I helped Grandpa."

We hurried out to the backyard and over to the garden area. Beaming proudly, Cody announced, "See, Grandma, here's where I helped Grandpa plant carrots, and over here are radishes." Then he looked up at me for approval.

"That's wonderful, Cody. You really helped Grandpa, didn't you?"

"And then, Grandma," he excitedly proclaimed, "here's where I planted pickle tree seeds."

Of course I knew what he meant. But Cody's pronouncement that he had planted "pickle tree seeds" gave me a mental picture of a huge tree with juicy dill pickles hanging from each branch. And I chuckled inwardly.

"Honey, I think you mean cucumber seeds, don't you?"

"No, Grandma!" he insisted. "They're pickle tree seeds!"

No amount of explaining could change Cody's adamant declaration that pickle tree seeds were in that spot.

Then I thought of the times in my experience, when I, like Cody, have been positive that I'm right and others are mistaken. But, much to my chagrin and embarrassment, I discovered that, indeed, I was the one in the wrong.

Now I pray that the Lord will give me the wisdom to know when I've planted "pickle tree seeds" and the willingness to admit it. Will you commit with me to have such a teachable spirit?

Teach me, and I will be quiet; show me where I have been wrong.
Job 6:24

> When you listen to children, listen with your heart to what they are really saying—not just what you hear with your ears.

Pink And White Delight

ELLEN BERGH

A pot of strawberries gathered in the wood to mingle with your cream.
Ben Johnson

Spring brings the return of glorious strawberries and a perfect excuse to make a dessert just right for any night. For this "Pink and White Delight," you will need:

1 angel food cake—either bar shaped or round
1 container of strawberries (or frozen if fresh not available), sugar to taste
1 large container extra-creamy Cool Whip (or whipped cream if you are living dangerously)

Wash, hull, and slice berries; add sugar as desired. Reserve a few berries for garnish. Slice the top off the angel food cake; use toothpicks to mark around cake to get even cut if necessary.

Inside ½ inch from edge, cut all around the cake. Repeat around inner circle if using round cake. Gently tear angel food from cake, place in bowl, leave about 1-inch base to cake. You now have a hollow cake.

Combine berries, a dash of orange juice, and cake pieces. Toss and blend in ½ of Cool Whip. Pile this mixture back into your cake. Replace the top. With remainder of Cool Whip, frost outside of cake, garnish with reserved fruit, and chill two hours.

Stand back and enjoy the oohs and ahhs when you slice into your Pink and White Strawberry Delight.

Her children arise and call her blessed; her husband also, and he praises her.
Proverbs 31:28

Adding salt to strawberries as you rinse them will whisk away any sand on berries.

Awake To God

AUDREY ALLEN

God redecorates with each new season.
Catherine Duerr

The patio thermometer hasn't budged from its mark of 54 degrees even though I've downed two cups of steaming coffee and a banana muffin—but the day is still young. I put on a faded green sweatshirt, stuffed my feet into old tennis shoes, and headed out the door. I've been looking forward to this particular day for weeks and I'm prepared for almost anything—except rain, that is.

Once again, God's early morning sun casts its rays downward between gleaming, sunlit clouds. "You've done it again, God," I murmur thankfully, as I pull on my stiff, dirty, pink gloves.

Armed with all of the necessary tools, plants, and energy, I head for the flowerbeds, leaving my footprints in the glistening, dew-covered grass. The day is already filled with freshness and beauty, and with these tiny new plants at my side, I can envision bright colors and fullness yet to come.

Petunias, mums, and carnations are but a few of the plants my husband and I plan to add this year. We're thankful for the growth already present, like the baby pansies and impatiens now emerging from seeds and roots of last year's flowers.

Most of our perennial plants, as well as the palms and ferns, have survived the abnormally cold winter for this region of California. Flowering ornamental plum trees are loaded with pink blossoms, and signs of life are beginning to appear on the sticks and stems that will become bushes once again. Ah, yes, it's that time of year once again. It's spring.

This day is the beginning of even more beauty and color for these selected spots, not so much because of the work of my own hands, but the Hand of our Master. His awesome rays of warmth, His rich soil, and His powerful ability to create and make things grow are far more necessary than my presence in the garden.

This is my kind of day, the kind that lets me feel easily close to God. As I dig into the soil and work with these reminders of Him, I am again blessed with the confidence that He truly exists. His life and His breath are everywhere around me. I'm filled with His warmth and love.

Because of Him, the plants I stick into the earth today can grow and become beautiful summer flowers. And though I may not be ankle deep in fresh dirt tomorrow, these reminders will be here, growing, blooming, reseeding. Without Him, there would be nothing of this day.

God's abundance is present in our every day. Enjoy it.

This is the day the LORD has made; let us rejoice and be glad in it.
Psalm 118:24

Applying a pre-emergent to the soil will usually help reduce weed germination in your flowerbeds. But use this type of product only if you are *not* planning to sow seeds.

Summer

Summertime and the living is easy—or at least that's the way the song goes. Yet, if we're not careful, we can be distracted from an abundance in Christ through making plans for vacation or wanting to take it easy. Through your readings in this section, you'll have your attention continually brought back to God and "more" abundance. Enjoy your summer by drawing closer to a God who loves you mightily!

A Word Fitly Spoken

GLENNA M. CLARK

A powerful agent is the right word. Whenever we come upon one of those intensely right words in a book or a newspaper the resulting effect is physical as well as spiritual, and electrically prompt.

Samuel L. Clemens

"Gam-ma, you ugy."

Little Darcy enjoyed her daily telephone chat with her beloved grandmother. But one morning her horrified mother overheard this unexpected remark.

Stammering an embarrassed apology, Mother hung up the receiver. Turning to Darcy, she talked with her for some time. Then she explained how to make a proper apology.

Satisfied that Darcy understood, her mother called Gam-ma back. "Mother," she began, "Darcy has something she wants to say to you."

Taking the phone with confidence, Darcy apologized, "Gam-ma, I sorry you ugy."

We can all readily relate to the young mother's dismay. For all her lecturing she hadn't made herself clear. Yet Darcy thought she was obeying with her "apology."

Every day, Bible translators work at making themselves understood. Of course, "out there" the situation is much more serious. The possibility of a misunderstood translation demands careful checking of the work with the national speakers.

One day Dick Hohulin, a translator in the Philippines, was checking his rough draft of Mark 8:7 with his co-translator, Anuden. This story about Jesus feeding the multitude tells of Him blessing (or giving thanks for) the fish.

When Anuden read Dick's first attempt, he threw back his head with a long hearty laugh. Dick's innocent failure to insert the small article, "ni" before the word "fish" meant the readers would see it as, "Jesus thanked the fish."

I often think of these stories of misunderstood words. They are reminders of how easy it is to not make ourselves clear, especially when we try to express our Christian faith to others.

Are you and I making ourselves clearly understood? If we don't make the effort to convey ideas clearly, we can't expect our hearers to make the effort to interpret them. Let's be sure to avoid "Christianeze" when speaking of Jesus to others. They won't know the meaning of words like justification, sanctification, or redemption. By conveying the wonderful message of God's unconditional love in clear, basic language, we'll show our own love and interest in those for whom Christ died.

> . . . if the trumpet does not sound a clear call, who will get ready for battle? So
> it is with you. Unless you speak intelligible words with your tongue, how will
> anyone know what you are saying?
>
> I Corinthians 14:8–9

If you have a difficult choice to make, write out the pros
and cons to help you decide.

Communicate In Love

DAVID AND CLAUDIA ARP

Conversation: A fair for the display of the minor mental commodities, each exhibitor being too intent upon the arrangement of his own wares to observe those of his neighbor.

Ambrose Bierce

If you want to really communicate with your mate, you need to learn how to speak the truth in love. That rules out yelling and angry looks along with negative, attacking words.

Communicating the truth in love includes being willing to listen with love. And you must listen for the total message. "Why don't you listen to me?" is more than a trite question. Spouses in every stage and walk of life desperately desire to have their spouses listen to them. So why is listening so hard? And when we do listen, why do we so often misunderstand what the other person says?

One reason is that we are only listening to the words. And as important as the words are, they are only 7 percent of the total message! What you say is only a tiny part of the message. No wonder so many conversations are unheard dialogues. That's scary! If you don't understand the message, you'll have difficulty responding.

So what is the other 93 percent of the message? The tone of voice is 38 percent; how you say something is five times more powerful than what you say. So start listening for your tone of voice. That still leaves 55 percent of the message. And that's what you don't say in words—the shrugs, glares, and all other nonverbal messages. We all know "the look."

Think about this: What message do you really give if you say the right words, but your tone and look contradict them? Nothing devastates loving communication as much as a mixed message of loving words spoken in a bitter tone of voice! So as you listen to your spouse, also listen to your own message and make sure your words, nonverbal communication, and tone of your voice convey the same loving message.

> *. . . speaking the truth in love*
> Ephesians 4:15

Have a family meeting and determine the ten rules of your household. Then decide on a logical consequence for each one if broken.

The Short Version

KATHERINE LUNDGREN

There is no power like that of oratory.
H. Clay

When it comes to details, I have a million of them. My mind thinks of all the reasons, purposes, causes and effects, even the speculations. My feelings and emotions add intensity or confusion to the facts. When I want to discuss these things with my husband, I drive him crazy. What he wants to hear is the bottom line, the short story, just the point. He doesn't want a long speech.

This difference was the cause of difficulties in our first few years of marriage. I had so much to say. He didn't want all that information. Gradually I improved by being more concise when I speak and now he listens better by considering more carefully what I say. It's been a beneficial process even though it was hard. (I still have so much to say.)

Even if my husband can't handle all my detailed descriptions all the time, I know God handles them just fine because of His unlimited knowledge. Since Jesus knows best, I can trust Him for all the possible scenarios of my life. I don't have to worry when the pieces don't add up because He knows all the hidden details. God's wonderful love and attention invite me to pour out my heart and mind to Him—especially when others can't handle hearing all the trivialities.

You and I can stop trying to understand everything and learn to obey God's voice. That way we'll lean on His understanding and not our own. As a result, He'll help us learn to communicate better as we let Him take care of the details.

. . . speaking the truth to one another in love, we will in all things grow up into Him who is the Head, that is, Christ.

Ephesians 4:15

In order for you to speak clearly, state the most important point. If you add the details, choose them carefully and use only a few.

Weeds

JANE TOD JIMENEZ

Look within. Within is the fountain of good, and it will ever bubble up, if thou wilt ever dig.

Marcus Aurelius

Living in Phoenix, where summer temperatures once reached 122 degrees on June 26, 1990, I am a gardener who loves *anything* that grows. Absolutely anything.

This Arizona fried-brain attitude makes life very difficult in the garden. Seed packages tell you to place zinnias six inches apart. But when you look at a small seedling isolated on a patch of dry dirt, six inches is a long way to reach a fellow zinnia. This is also why it's very hard for an Arizonan to work up a hatred for weeds.

I remember the first Californian who walked through my lush green yard. "What's this?" she asked.

When I told her, she exclaimed in horror, "In California, Bermuda grass is a weed!"

"Well," I inwardly sniffed, "it's green. Besides, everybody grows Bermuda grass. And *double* besides, they sell Bermuda grass seed at the nursery." I didn't want her to know she hurt my feelings, but to call Bermuda grass a *weed* seemed a bit harsh.

Slowly, one question percolated up from inside of me, finally making its way to the surface. What is a weed? I began looking up *weeds* in every gardening book I could find. Most didn't tell you what they were. They only told you how to poison them.

Eventually, in my non-poison Rodale organic gardening "bible," I found what I had by now begun to suspect, "Weeds are simply native plants that happen to be growing where you would rather have something else grow." Webster's is even more to the point, "A plant that is not valued where it is growing." Further down, Webster leaves no doubt, "an obnoxious growth, thing, or person."

I've come to identify with weeds. Bermuda grass knows how to take advantage of limited water and soil conditions. It's willing to endure searing summer heat, giving us green grass by the swimming pool. That's enough to make me forgiving when it sneaks into the row of cucumbers. I still dig and pull at stray Bermuda strands, insisting they obey my boundaries. But I don't poison it. And I don't celebrate over its dry remains. I wish it well.

Weeds take me closer to God than almost any plant I know. In human terms they may be plants "not valued where they are growing," but I doubt God thinks that. He made weeds. And He made me.

Many days I feel like a human weed. There are people who have told me as much. But God made me. He doesn't make weeds. He makes plants that extend beyond their boundaries, and he makes people who goof up now and then. But God doesn't make weeds. He loves us. And He wants us. No matter what names people want to stick on us. There are no weeds in God's kingdom.

For you created my inmost being; you knit me together in my mother's womb. I praise You because I am fearfully and wonderfully made; Your works are wonderful, I know that full well.

Psalm 139:13–14

Each day, write one special accomplishment of that day on a 3 X 5 note card. At the end of seven days, choose a nickname for yourself based on your accomplishments. Post your nickname on the refrigerator . . . and smile.

Happy Birthday

BARBARA BRYDEN

Be adventurous, like those who accept the risks and reap the benefits of seaborne trade. Do not always play it safe.

NIV Study Bible

Sliding the check into the envelope, I thought about Charles and Gladys' upcoming trip. I had always wanted to be a missionary, but helping to send others seemed to be as close as I would get to my dream. Laying my hand on the envelope, I prayed, "Bless this trip, Lord. Keep them safe and give them whatever they need."

Instantly the thought came, "Send Gladys a birthday card and some money."

I hesitated briefly before asking, "How much, Lord?" Excited, I pulled out the checkbook and wrote another check. I made this one out to Gladys and wrote "Happy Birthday" on the bottom. Was it really her birthday? Would I

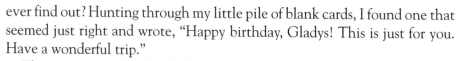

ever find out? Hunting through my little pile of blank cards, I found one that seemed just right and wrote, "Happy birthday, Gladys! This is just for you. Have a wonderful trip."

The next two weeks required some really inventive meals since a large part of my grocery money had gone to Gladys. More than once, I wondered if it was even close to her birthday. Every time the mail carrier came I ran to the mailbox to see if Gladys had written. Finally a little note came in the mail.

"How did you know it was my birthday?" Gladys wrote. "You will never know how much your card and check blessed me. I really had hoped to have just a little money to get some 'girl' things for the trip. I didn't feel I could ask Charles for the money. There are so many things he needs to buy for the congregation in Africa."

"Finally, I prayed," she continued, "and told the Lord I would like to have enough money to get my hair done and maybe even buy a new lipstick. I almost didn't pray. It seemed selfish to want things like that when the people in Africa need so much. I was so excited when your check came. You sent enough money to get everything I had on my little list. I could have made the trip without any of the extras, but it will be so much nicer this way. Thank you for listening to the Lord."

Which one of us was blessed the most? I think I was. He may not lead me across oceans or into native villages in Africa, but following where the Lord leads is always an exciting adventure.

What will your response be the next time the Lord prompts you to risk? I hope you'll obey and trust Him.

Cast your bread upon the waters, for after many days you will find it again.
Ecclesiastes 11:1

Keep five or six blank greeting cards with different kinds of pictures on the front and a book of stamps with your Bible. Then you'll be prepared if the Lord prompts you to write to someone.

Write When You Can

Delores Elaine Bius

If we discovered that we had only five minutes left to say all we wanted to say, every telephone booth would be occupied by people calling other people to stammer that they loved them.

Christopher Morley

In our local newspaper, I saw the picture of an elderly woman in a nursing home. The article told of many lonely residents such as she. I wrote the lady a note and enclosed a bookmark for her Bible, as the article indicated she spent much time reading it. I mentioned that although I did not have transportation to visit her, periodically I would drop in to "chat" via the mail.

In return, she wrote a lovely thank-you note, saying, "It is so encouraging to know there is someone out there who cares about a lonely old lady."

Remembering friends on the anniversary of their loved one's death is another way to bring comfort. I circle those dates on my calendar and send a note that will arrive on that day. It reminds the lonely mate or relative that someone else realizes they are sorrowing anew. It shows they are in someone's prayers.

Missionaries, too, welcome personal notes to brighten their day. They get lonely for news from home. One year I sent some missionaries in Africa a lovely, big, glossy Christmas card that showed a snowy scene. I later learned they had placed the card on their kitchen table and it helped Christmas seem more real to them, reminding them of past snow-filled holidays at home in Minnesota.

Neighbors who move away also face the loneliness of making adjustments. One couple from our block decided to move to another state when the husband retired. Both quiet people, they found it difficult to make new friends and felt isolated in their new community. Meanwhile they also wondered whether we, their former neighbors, had forgotten them. That fear subsided as they received letters from me every few weeks with news of the neighborhood and our family. They later confided that those tokens of care made it easier for them to cope and to develop new friendships.

New beginnings are difficult for anyone and the young people who go away to college or join the service are no exception. Of course, they will adjust, but we can help them by faithfully writing letters of encouragement. They look forward eagerly to mail call and how discouraged they must be if nothing arrives for them. It takes only a minute to mail a note or a postcard.

Several years ago, I received word that an uncle who had been like a father to me had suffered a stroke. When his birthday came, I made him a special card. In it I listed specific incidents from my childhood and thanked him for the many kindnesses he had shown me.

Less than a year later, he died. My aunt requested that no flowers be sent to the funeral. I was relieved to know I had already sent mine—in an envelope by mail.

Whom does God want you to remember through the mail or even through electronic mail? Either way, they'll be glad to hear that someone was thinking of them.

And do not forget to do good and to share with others,
for with such sacrifices God is pleased.
Hebrews 13:16

Write a note to someone today!

Summer's Best Picnic

FAYE LANDRUM

A man's fortune must first be changed from within.

Chinese proverb

Bright sunshine splashed shadows in the backyard when I brought out the early-morning trash. After I said "Hi" to my neighbor, we discussed the possibility of a picnic. She had a five-year-old daughter the same age as my older son. Along with my three-year-old, the kids loved picnics.

"I'll make some egg-salad sandwiches," my neighbor volunteered.

"I'll bring potato chips and bananas," I said.

We decided we would each bring our own soda drinks; she would contribute some pickles and I would furnish cookies. We agreed on high noon as the time for our adventure.

By eleven o'clock, gathering black clouds gave an ominous message regarding our picnic. By eleven-thirty the clouds had precipitated into raindrops. Our picnic looked like it was on hold.

"I've got an idea," my neighbor said. "Let's move the picnic table into the garage and we'll pretend we're eating outside."

I backed the car out of the garage and we brought in the picnic table. As we carried in sandwiches and other goodies, we told the kids about our plans for an imaginary picnic. We pretended we were eating in the country beside a rippling brook with shade trees protecting us from the hot sun.

"See the squirrels playing tag around the tree," my neighbor said. "And look at the deer coming down to the water for a drink."

The older children quickly joined in the pretense, but my three-year-old was a little slower in accepting the concept. "What deer?" he asked. "I don't see any deer." After we explained our imagery-tactics to him, he too joined in the fun.

Since then I have been to many picnics, but none do I remember like that one. With a malleable attitude, God can change many of our down experiences into pleasant ones.

The next time you're facing a disappointment, whether because of the weather or something—or someone—else, find something good in it and innovate!

And we know that in all things God works for the good of those who love Him, who have been called according to his purpose.

Romans 8:28

Make a list of how God has turned disappointing experiences into blessings.

"It's the Little Things . . ."

ALLISON PITTMAN

It belittles us to think of our daily tasks as small things, and if we continue to do so, it will in time make us small.

Laura Ingalls Wilder

I have an odd sense of priorities. I stand knee-deep in unfolded laundry, squint to watch *Oprah* through the layer of dust on my television, and iron the shirt my four-year-old is going to wear to T-ball practice. My husband comes in, takes quick inventory of the situation and says, "He's just going to get all sweaty and dirty," as if this fact hadn't occurred to me.

I never thought I would get to this place in my life. I don't recall oohing and aahing over babies and longing for one of my own. I spent more time scheming for my next date than dreaming of my forever mate. I never mooned over bridal magazines, baked batches of cookies, or listened to two consecutive "Hints from Heloise." When the man who would become my husband sat in my parents' living room and, in a sweet old-fashioned gesture, asked for their permission to marry me, their words were: "Sure! She can't cook. She won't clean. And we won't take her back." Boy, did I prove them wrong: I'm an excellent cook.

I'm not sure when I made the transformation from *That Girl* to *I Remember Mama*, but somewhere along the line I realized that sometimes you need to take your eyes off the big picture and focus on the details. Of course I'm still not to the point where anyone would confuse me with Martha Stewart. There are days when I consider it a culinary victory when I serve a vegetable other than canned green beans. And if cleanliness is next to godliness, the most you could say about my house is that it's really, really nice.

But if I do have stacks of junk mail balanced precariously on top of the wastebasket, it's only because buried within that stack is an envelope of coupons which my children love to pretend is money. And that may look like a pile of rocks on the bookshelf, but last Saturday afternoon, each pebble represented a piece of a pirate's treasure rescued from the ship in the playground and bundled in Grandpa's handkerchief. It might take hours of diligent searching to turn up my college transcripts or my teaching certificate, but I could unearth the rumpled card with the recipe for my husband's favorite carrot cookies from the jumbled mess I call a recipe drawer within minutes.

Yes, my house is a rumpled, crumpled tangled mess. Memories are piled into corners, tossed into closets, and stashed up on shelves. Milestones are tacked on walls, magneted to appliances, and nestled inside great big books. These are just as much my children's memories as they are mine, and they come about because of the little things I do. A crisp white shirt may not make it any easier for a four-year-old to trap a ball in an oversized leather glove, but it sure looks good against a new green field. And somewhere I have the picture to prove it.

If you have a house like mine, then enjoy! Don't let those who don't understand take away your delight in the most important things in life: people!

He settles the barren woman in her home as a happy mother of children . . .
Psalms 113:9

It's easy to let photographs pile up until the thought of putting them into a photo album seems positively daunting. Not every picture on the roll needs to be in the family album; choose three or four of the best ones to put in the album, and file the rest in a photo box.

Garbage Pickup At Your House Today
TIZIANA RUFF

My theology is simple. I can sum it up in four words...
Jesus died for me.
Charles Spurgeon, on his deathbed

Does anybody struggle to clean the house or am I the only one? When I speak of cleaning, I don't mean the regular every day "boring" stuff like making the beds, dusting, doing the laundry, etc, etc. . . . . I am talking about deep cleaning. Getting into all the corners of the house, washing all the windows, the walls and, of course, the closets. When I finally set my mind on looking into the closets, I am always amazed at the kind of junk I have been saving. Here's a belt from a dress that I used to wear twenty years ago. The dress is long gone, but for some reason, obscure to me, I had saved the belt. In one corner, a plastic bag contains a paper clip, a couple of safety pins, a bunch of expired coupons, ten-year-old receipts from the supermarket, some more paper clips, a dried-out pen, a handful of rubber bands that are now all fused to-gether, some pieces of material, a telephone cord, some buttons, a spoon . . . and so on.

Why was I saving those useless things? What was I thinking? Funny how we get attached to "things." Every time I clean the closets, I say to myself: "That's it, I've had it, no more. From now on, nothing goes into the closets or drawers that isn't absolutely necessary." But of course, the day after, I forget how much time I have spent cleaning, and "new stuff" will be saved until next time when I open the door to the closet and things drop on my head.

It is the same in our lives. We get "attached" to some of the garbage in our lives. Then we begin to "accumulate" some of those things: our past trans-gressions or the hurtful things others have done to us. Why not, instead, concentrate on today's blessings? If there's "junk" to deal with, instead of storing it in your "closet," leave it at the cross. "Garbage" pick-up is a never-ending service our Lord provides for us. You should see what He's accumu-lated over the last 2,000 years or so.

"Come to me, all you who are weary and burdened, and I will give you rest.
Take my yoke upon you and learn from me, for I am gentle
and humble in heart, and you will find rest for your souls.
For my yoke is easy and my burden is light."
Matthew 11:28–30

The next time you ask God to forgive you for something,
imagine that it's like throwing something into the trash,
never to be taken out again.

On Display

GIGI GRAHAM TCHIVIDJIAN

A Christian is not one who withdraws but one who infiltrates.

Bill Glass

"GIGI! ANNE! BUNNY! FRANKLIN!" they called to the four Graham children. Ned had not yet been born.

It was Sunday afternoon and once again the tourists had arrived. They came by the busload from the nearby conference centers and streamed into our yard, calling our names in the hope that we would come out and pose for pictures. We hid inside behind closed doors and pulled the drapes, peeking out every now and then to watch as they chipped wood from our little rail fence and snapped pictures of our home to take back as souvenirs. As children, we didn't understand all this intrusion and attention. To us, Daddy was just Daddy. But because he was well-known, we children were on display.

In looking back I realize that this was just another part of God's training program for my life. As Christians, aren't all of us on display before a watching world? We may not always relish the idea; we may find it at times to be inconvenient or burdensome. But we must always be conscious of the fact that representing Jesus Christ to others is a responsibility and privilege reserved for the children of the King.

Let your light so shine before men that they may see your good works, and glorify your Father which is in heaven.

Matthew 5:16

Look back on your life and pinpoint something that God used to make others notice Jesus in you.

Human Touch

J. A. STACKHAUS

I cannot believe that the purpose of life is to be "happy." I think the purpose of life is...to have made some difference that you lived at all.

Leo Rosten

As I packed for home after my internship in Washington, D.C., I pulled from my dorm's fridge the remainder of the sandwich fixings on which I had subsisted during my stay. I couldn't pack peanut butter and bread very easily, but I couldn't just toss them. The thought of the homeless people I had passed daily on nearly every corner came to mind. "Would they want the food?" I wondered.

I tried to talk myself out of the idea that nagged me, until I realized it was the Holy Spirit doing the nagging. "If people are hungry, and I have un-needed food . . . " Finally, the sandwiches were made, and, reluctantly, I headed up the road to Georgetown.

The trek from my dorm to the affluent shopping district was over a mile. "Great," I sighed to myself. "How many homeless have I seen down here, and now I can't find a one!" I walked alone on the sidewalk for some dis-tance before I spied a man sitting in an opening, waiting for a handout.

I deliberated about approaching him, even walked past him at first, but that blessed nagging returned. I turned around and made the offer of a mea-ger sandwich. The man accepted with such gratitude that it surprised me. Whatever doubts I may have had about giving out the sandwiches dissolved. I distributed a few more morsels that evening, and only one person declined the offer of food.

Of the homeless few I encountered that evening, what impressed me most about them were the looks of surprise in their eyes—not at the offer of food, but at the sound of my voice. I had seen my fellow interns throw spare change at folks asking for money in the streets of our Nation's capital. I had even heard curses hurled at them instead.

It hadn't occurred to me until my brown-bag excursion that so few kind words were ever spoken to the least of these. I spoke to a few of them personally and placed the sandwiches directly into their hands. Yet, all they were given were some skimpy sandwiches. Why did they react with such gratitude? But was that really all I had given them, sandwiches?

In reflection, I realized that the most powerful tool of Christ's ministry may have been His personal interaction with the people. Jesus didn't have to walk among the common people. He didn't have to speak to the outcasts of society, nor did He have to place his hands on the afflicted. But would we have understood His love for us if He hadn't? He touched people where they were. He went to the hurting within the context of their own realities. It was His simple, human touch that connected them, more than anything else to the eternal reality of His love.

When you next reach out to someone, don't just give them a "thing," but give them respect and dignity through kind words and a loving touch. It will communicate more than your simple gift can express.

A man with leprosy came and knelt before Him and said, "Lord, if You are
willing, You can make me clean." Jesus reached out His hand
and touched the man.
Matthew 8:2–3a

> Make a practice of saying hello each day to one person
> outside of your normal circle of friends.

Knock Knock . . .

CAROLYN STANDERFER

*It takes time and leisure, and minds not overburdened with cares,
to make beautiful dwellings.*

William Morris

How often do our good intentions come at too high a price? Take "Love thy neighbor," for example. Most of us desire to fulfill this command. But for the busy homemaker, mother, or possibly homeschool teacher, "neighbor" means all the little children who live on her street or in her apartment complex. For those of us like that, "Knock and the door shall be opened unto you," takes on a whole new meaning.

We appreciate neighbors who enrich our lives and give our children opportunity to grow socially while allowing us to be a witness for Christ. But for too many families that comes at too great a cost. Some homes end up busier than a train station, filled with noise and chaos.

Most mothers who expend themselves in such an environment day after day find themselves losing patience and ultimately don't have the energy they desire to invest in their own children. Worse yet, a frazzled, bedraggled, worn-out woman greets her husband at the end of the work day.

Balance, "the key to success," requires boundaries. Boundaries are a difficult issue for many women today. We struggle over when to say "yes" and when to say "no." How can we establish boundaries and how do we get neighbors to respect them?

I have found that a simple, friendly sign can alleviate a lot of front door inquisitions and minimize interruptions of family time, nap time, and important phone calls. At the same time it restores abundant peace and quiet on the days I need it most.

Simply purchase a pre-made, pre-strung two-sided wooden plaque which is available at most craft stores. Then, one bottle of acrylic paint, a child's paint brush, and a few colorful stickers are all you need. The cost will be about $7.00.

On one side the door sign should sport a friendly alligator and the phrase, "Let's Play Later Alligator." The other side shows a host of bright, shiny, happy faces and the phrase, "Welcome Friends."

Hang the sign on a nail on your front door just out of reach of small visitors. Take a few days to explain the new sign to neighbors who will learn to recognize the symbols of happy faces or the infamous "Alligator" that asks them to return later.

Even non-readers get the message. Just turn the sign as often as you need to. It's that simple!

> *Then they can train the younger women to love their husbands and children,*
> *to be self-controlled and pure, to be busy at home, to be kind.*
> Titus 2:4–5

Slow down your pace of life by not driving over the speed limit.

A Rabbit On The Swim Team

CHARLES SWINDOLL

He who is faultless is lifeless.
John Heywood

Having been exposed to a few of the "greats" in various churches and an outstanding seminary, I (like some of the other guys in the class) tried to be like *them.* You know, think like, sound like, look like. For over ten years in the ministry I—a rabbit—worked hard at swimming like a duck or flying like an eagle. I was a frustrated composite creature . . . like that weird beast in the second chapter of Daniel. And my feet of clay were slowly crumbling beneath me. It was awful! The worst part of all, what little bit of originality or creativity I had was being consumed in that false role I was forcing. One day my insightful and caring wife asked me, "Why not just be *you*? Why try to be like anybody else?" Well, friends and neighbors, this rabbit quit the swim team and gave up flying lessons and stopped trying to climb. Talk about relief! And best of all, I learned it was okay to be me . . . and let my family members be themselves. Originality and creativity flowed anew!

> *But he said to me, "My grace is sufficient for you, for my power is made perfect in weakness." Therefore I will boast all the more gladly about my weaknesses, so that Christ's power may rest on me.*
>
> II Corinthians 12:9

If you've been trying to be just like someone else, stop and realize that they have faults, too. Be yourself!

Homeless Sandwiches
Sharon Norris

I get by with a little help from my friends.
Paul McCartney

It's always a challenge for moms when the children are home for the summer. I find myself thinking, "Whatever shall I do to keep these kids busy during the waking hours of the day?" It was easier (although I didn't think so at the time) when they were infants and toddlers. Sure, I complained about little sleep, endless work picking up toys and washing dirty clothes, and thankless hours of tedium, but I got through it somehow. Now the kids are in school from 8 A.M. until 2:30 P.M., we only have the evenings to contend with, and they are filled with homework assignments, book reports, and science projects. The weekends are otherwise filled with sports practices, acting classes, and time at friends' houses. Although the routine is hectic, it doesn't take too much planning on my part other than working out the schedule.

But every year, without fail, summer vacation rolls around and I'm back in the dilemma again. Although we've managed to make each summer different and fun, I wanted my children to spend some of that free time doing some form of outreach. They spend so much time during the school year concentrating on themselves in the form of their grades and their activities, I wanted to find a way to get them to concentrate on others. I came up with a simple idea.

There are lots of homeless people in metropolitan Los Angeles where we live. We see them at the highway on-ramps, outside of public buildings, and sitting on (or under) bus benches. Even if summer activities find us running to and fro, we now take time to prepare our special "homeless sandwiches" before we leave the house most days.

We simply add a loaf of bread, a jar of mayonnaise, a box of zip-lock bags, and a large package of bologna to our personal grocery list. Then, each day before we leave our house for the various summertime activities, we prepare several sandwiches. As we go through the day, whenever we see a homeless person, we simply hand him or her a sandwich. We have also added a Christian tract with our church address and a juice box when we've had a little extra money.

We have not heard from any of these people yet. To our knowledge, they have not shown up at church, but my children feel good about helping someone who is so obviously in need. All we do know is that it is our job to reach out. It's God's job to reap the results.

The King will reply, "I tell you the truth, whatever you did for one of the least of these brothers of Mine, you did for Me."
Matthew 25:40

Once a week, decide to reach out in some small way to someone who cannot do anything for you in return.

Hush, Be Still

JUNE L. VARNUM

The spirit bloweth and is still,
In mystery our soul abides.

Matthew Arnold

Sunday morning, I knelt beside the couch to pray and shot a glance at the clock on the mantle. One whole hour before I needed to leave for church. Plenty of time to get through my prayer list. After all, it was neatly categorized in my mind.

"Father in heaven," I began.

Hush. Be still.

Startled, I jerked my head up and looked around the empty room. No one. Perhaps I'd imagined the voice. Bowing my head, I prayed, "Heavenly Father."

But again, *Hush. Be still.* Was God trying to get my attention? The Bible says He speaks in a still, small voice.

How could I pray if I had to hush? How could I be still while the clock's tick, tick, tick grew louder, like a metronome measuring off minutes of life? Precious prayer time was slipping away.

I decided to try again. "Lord," I started.

Hush! Be still. Know I am God.

This time the words smacked of a command.

Determined, I tried to listen to whatever God might be trying to tell me. Shifting on my knees, I caught the sound of a single birdsong. Through the window, I saw the small brown and orange singer perched on the deck rail. The notes swelled and trembled for a minute. Then quiet. "Lord, that was so beautiful. Thank You."

Anxiety about the time and not getting through my prayer list made me try again. But that little persistent Voice spoke once more.

Hush. Be still.

Frustrated, I sat on the couch. The cool morning breeze brushed my neck like a soft caress. I leaned back and closed my eyes. Our summer temperatures had galloped up to the low 100's, and the hot afternoon winds seemed to have dried up about everything. Was the heat drying up my spirit, too? Or was it the stress from additional care of my 87-year-old mother following major surgery? Also I'd been feeling a lack of insight to help a nineteen-year-old granddaughter living with me during the summer months as she worked two part-time jobs, took summer classes, and survived the breakup of a long-term friendship.

Resigned, I sat with closed eyes and bowed head. Soon my lips parted in a smile. From deep inside me a chuckle bubbled up into soft laughter. A great welling up of love flowed through every part of me, like clean, sweet water seeping up and filling a dry creek. I felt engulfed in a great cloud of happiness.

"You win, Lord," I sheepishly whispered. My prayer list, so neatly arranged in my mind, didn't seem important anymore. Because just then, for those precious moments, it was more important only to hush and be still in His presence.

When was the last time you just sat quietly in God's presence? Try it again and enjoy not having to say anything. Just "be," rather than "do."

> *My dear brothers, take note of this: Everyone should be quick to listen, slow to speak and slow to become angry.*
>
> James 1:19

Write a note to someone you've not talked with for awhile. Use plain paper and decorate it with crayon/marker drawings.

Simplicity Of Time

CHARLES E. HUMMEL

We all find time to do what we really want to do.

William Feather

In wartime the armed forces have top priority for use of the nation's resources. In World War II, facilities for manufacturing automobiles were converted to producing various kinds of military vehicles—from Jeeps to armored personnel carriers and tanks. Gasoline for civilians was tightly rationed. Yet there were extra allocations for special needs of the war effort; for example, a person driving to and from a defense job would receive extra gasoline coupons.

People were urged to make more efficient use of their cars by driving slowly and doubling up whenever possible. At the same time, across the country prominent posters urged everyone to ask the most important question: "Is this trip necessary?"

Drucker noted that by using a minimum amount of energy and time, we can be very *efficient* in performing a certain task. Yet our work is actually *effective* only when it contributes to our goals. *True effectiveness is not a matter of doing things right but of doing the right things.* For example, you may work out a very efficient, detailed procedure for keeping personal financial records. But before you congratulate yourself you should ask the basic question: Are those records necessary?

The effective person doesn't let the apparent success of being more efficient mask the mistake of performing an activity that is not important. The crucial question is not short-term efficiency but rather long-term effectiveness. In other words, how significant is the task at hand?

There is a time for everything, and a season for every activity under heaven.

Ecclesiastes 3:1

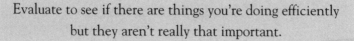

Evaluate to see if there are things you're doing efficiently
but they aren't really that important.

Protected Through The Storm

JANE E. MAXWELL

When the storms of life blow wildly, I will lock my feet of faith to
my Heavenly Father's promises.

Jane E. Maxwell

Crack! Boom! I cringed as bolts of jagged lightning flashed across the sky
followed by loud claps of thunder. I watched the white branches of the birch
tree sway in the wind. Leaves swirled in the air and tumbled to the ground.
Samantha, our calico cat, had sought shelter in her favorite chair. As I gazed
out the window, I wondered how the fragile songbirds I had enjoyed listening to that morning were surviving this fierce storm.

Early the next morning, the red-breasted robin's song drifted through my
open window. I looked out to see the chickadees, cardinals, and sparrows
darting back and forth looking as spry as ever. Where did these birds go
during the storm? No doubt some of them perched amid the inner branches
of the evergreen trees. Woodpeckers and bluebirds probably tucked themselves into tree cavities or nest boxes as the storm continued.

However, I learned that our Creator has provided the perching birds with a
wonderful special feature that helps them hang on to the smallest perch during high winds and heavy rains. He built a locking mechanism into their legs.
As the birds hop and settle on their perch, their ankles flex and the tendon
running down the back of their legs tightens and pull the toes around the
perch. As long as the birds are settled, their feet lock with their toes curled
tightly around their perch, even while they sleep. The storm continues, but

the tiny bird's locked feet prevent them from falling. As the thunder stops and the dark clouds disappear, the birds loosen their hold and freely fly away.

If God's abundant love reaches out to those tiny creatures, ensuring their safety, how can we ever doubt His abundant love and care for us in the midst of life's storms? Jesus asks us, *Are you not much more valuable than they?* (Matthew 6:26). Our Heavenly Father lovingly cares for all His creatures.

The storms may howl around us, but as long as we lock our spiritual feet to His promises, He will always provide a sure support. The storm will pass and the difficulty will be resolved. Yet when we are bombarded by the fierce winds of problems, we can stand firm in His power.

For great is His love toward us, and the faithfulness of the LORD endures forever. Praise the LORD.
Psalm 117:2

Look out your window today and gaze upon all of God's abundant creation. Find something in God's creation to teach you more about Him.

Surprise!
KATHLEEN HAGBERG

Life's disappointments are veiled love's appointments.
Rev. C. A. Fox

When my husband told me he had to be out of town on my birthday it was no big deal. That's how I thought I felt.

"We'll celebrate when I get back," promised my husband.

I awakened on my birthday, to a gray, overcast Sunday. As usual, my three teenage children and I attended church, returned home, and ate lunch. So far, no mention of my birthday. I tried to shrug it off. Surely they had not forgotten. Or had they?

By the time I began to prepare dinner, I realized my children *had* forgotten. My disappointment found its way to my tear ducts by the time I called my children to dinner.

"What's wrong, Mom?" my wide-eyed daughter asked as she caught "give-away" tears trickling down my cheek.

Feeling a strange combination of sadness, disappointment, and embarrassment, I wanted to minimize my hurt feelings but it was too late.

"I feel hurt no one remembered my birthday," I said. Attempting to assuage my disappointment, my children chimed in, "Happy Birthday, Mom!"

Their prompted acknowledgment made me feel even worse. I couldn't wait to leave my birthday day behind.

That night as I slipped into bed, I found an envelope resting on my pillow. It was addressed "Mom."

> Today is your birthday alright?
> Now let's not get in a fight
> I wrote this poem for you
> Couldn't figure out what else to do
> Although I forgot
> Unloving I'm not
> Happy birthday to you.
> Steffen

The poem's simple but direct message reminded me not to confuse forgetting with loving. I framed my "remembrance" and placed it in our family room where it remains to this day. Many family birthdays have come and gone. But the one birthday I'll always remember is the one almost forgotten.

Are you disappointed and missing out on God's abundance because you think someone's forgetfulness means a lack of love? We can't expect that everything that is important to us be important to others, even if they love us. Reconsider and realize they truly do love you.

Her children rise up and call her blessed . . .
Proverbs 31: 28a

If you've been putting off doing a chore or project, spend
just ten minutes working on it today.

Advertising For God

ESTHER M. BAILEY

*There can be no happiness if the things we believe in are different
from the things we do.*

Freya Stark

One of the perks of being a celebrity is the opportunity to endorse certain
products for a handsome fee. When a sports hero advertises tennis shoes,
stores stock up for expected sales.

Whether or not you are a celebrity, you too are in the advertising business. If you profess to be a Christian, you are making commercials that either
attract people to God or turn them away from Him. Your life may be the
only introduction to God that some people have.

Here are a few ways to make God look good through your life:

- Exercise patience and kindness when the waitress or waiter is ineffi-
  cient or mixes up an order.
- Return the excess change when a clerk makes an error in your favor.
- If you need to make a customer complaint, continue to be gracious
  even while you take a firm stand.
- Look for an opportunity to do something nice for a coworker who has
  ridiculed your Christian convictions.

- Yield your rights to a discourteous driver. Avoiding an accident will contribute greatly to the abundant life.
- Pledge your support to the new boss who got the job you expected to receive.
- Welcome the stranger who visits your church.
- Instead of taking offense at criticism, ask yourself what you can learn from the analysis of another person.
- Write a note of encouragement to someone who is sick or is in crisis.
- When a friend confesses a past sin that haunts her, emphasize God's love and forgiveness.
- Pray each morning for God to live in and through you during the entire day.

Advertising for God is one of your most important functions as a Christian. Very often non-Christians are looking for an excuse for not serving God. By setting good examples, you can take away the validity of their excuses.

In addition to showing the various aspects of God's love and integrity, you can also exhibit the joy of the Lord and the peace that the world does not know. Your responsibility is to produce a commercial that portrays the personality of God in such a way that anyone watching will say, "I want what you have."

We are therefore Christ's ambassadors . . .
II Corinthians 5:20a

Catch someone in the act of doing good and compliment them.

Going In Circles

Marjorie K. Evans

What a privilege to trust God for guidance.

John Hash

One Saturday afternoon my husband Edgar and I took our grandchildren to a children's park. First Charity and Cody rode on the Shetland ponies and the merry-go-round. After that the four of us had fun riding in an open car of a small train that encircled the park.

Later, as we ate snow cones and walked to a small lake to feed the ducks, the children asked, "Can we go in a boat? We want to row."

Grandpa questioned, "Do you know how to row?"

"Yes, we know how. Can we? Can we?" they chorused.

So the children sat in the middle of the boat; I sat in the front, and Grandpa sat in the back ready to direct the rowing.

But instead of dipping their oars into the water at the same time and pulling together like Grandpa told them to, Cody pulled his oar one way and Charity pulled hers the opposite. The boat went in circles. Several times Grandpa asked, "Do you want me to help you?"

"No, Grandpa, we can row the boat by ourselves," they adamantly insisted.

We continued to go around and around with the boat no farther away from shore than when we first got into it. Finally Cody pleaded, "Grandpa, will you help us?"

Grandpa changed places with Charity and showed Cody how they both had to dip their oars forward at the same time. They practiced until Cody knew how to row. Then Grandpa worked with Charity. Eagerly the children again took the oars. And, with Grandpa as coxswain, they slowly rowed the boat across the tiny lake.

In all our years of married life, there have been too many times when Ed and I have each "rowed" our own way and have gone in circles—getting nowhere. But when we remember to stop and ask God to guide and direct us, we go forward together.

So now our prayer is, "Dear Lord, before we start going in circles and become frustrated, help us to get our directions from You—the Master Coxswain. Amen."

If you are feeling like your marriage isn't progressing the way you want it to, could it be that you are each trying to do it your own way instead of working together with God's direction? Your spouse is not your enemy, but your fellow rower. Make a fresh start by seeking God's will and being willing to release your own desires.

Trust in the LORD with all your heart and lean not on your own understanding; in all your ways acknowledge Him, and He will make your paths straight.
Proverbs 3:5–6

Show your husband how much you love and appreciate him.
Prepare his favorite meal and serve it by candlelight.

Grace Happens
KATHLEEN HAGBERG

And here in dust and dirt, o here, the lilies of His love appear.
George Herbert

Two summers ago I planted morning glory seeds at the foot of a garden trellis. My efforts produced a single blossom.

This last summer I tried once again. I watched in wide-eyed wonder as my trellis exploded into a windfall of blossoms. I reveled in the profusion of lavender and crimson buds which appeared.

My delight, however, was dashed by my husband, Paul. "No dear," he insisted, "sorry, but those are not morning glories. They're the buds of the pole beans I planted in that row also." Since my husband is the faithful hobbyist while I only putter with gardening, I didn't argue. Still my eyes insisted that the blossoms were morning glories.

As summer began ebbing away I noted that I had not seen one pole bean. Reluctantly, after finding the evidence too persuasive, my husband conceded, "Looks like the flowers are morning glories after all."

"Aha!" I teased, "so the wispy blossoms did prevail over the mighty, mighty pole beans." Never mind that my husband had worked feverishly on his garden week in and week out. While I, strictly a lazy weekend gardener, had done little more than poke random holes in the soil and drop in the seeds.

It hardly seemed fair. I hadn't deserved the flowers and I knew it. Then it hit me. My gardening "lesson" loomed larger than pole beans and flowers. The morning glories illustrated God's grace. Like the undeserved flowers, grace breaks through not because of what I do or don't do but because of God's initiative.

Moreover, I was reminded that I don't deserve grace and I cannot earn it. That is why it's called grace. Grace overrides both our best and flimsiest efforts. If God's grace is manifested in the perishable flowers, which live today and die tomorrow, how much more is it available to me—and you.

. . . chosen by grace. And if by grace, then it is no longer by works, if it were,
grace would no longer be grace.
Romans 11:5b–6

Try planting some morning glory seeds and see what kind of results you receive. And let them remind you of God's grace.

Who Pushes Your Swing?

Max Lucado

When you cannot trust God you cannot trust anything; and when you cannot trust anything you get the condition of the world as it is today.

Basil King

Children love to swing. There's nothing like it.

Thrusting your feet toward the sky, leaning so far back that everything looks upside down. Spinning trees, a stomach that jumps into your throat. Ahh, swinging . . .

I learned a lot about trust on a swing. As a child, I only trusted certain people to push my swing. If I was being pushed by people I trusted (like Dad or Mom), they could do anything they wanted. They could twist me, turn me, stop me . . . I loved it! I loved it because I trusted the person pushing me. But let a stranger push my swing (which often happened at family reunions and Fourth of July picnics), and it was *hang on, baby!* Who knew what this newcomer would do? When a stranger pushes your swing, you tense up, ball up, and hang on.

It's no fun when your swing is in the hands of someone you don't know.

Remember when Jesus stilled the storm in Matthew 8? The storm wasn't just a gentle spring rain. This was a *storm*. Matthew calls the storm a *seismos*, which is the Greek word for "earthquake." The waves in this earthquake were so high that the boat was hidden. The Sea of Galilee can create a vicious storm. Barclay tells us that "on the west side of the water there are hills with valleys and gulleys; and when a cold wind comes from the west, these valleys and gulleys act like giant funnels. The wind becomes compressed in them and rushes down upon the lake with savage violence."

No sir, this was no spring shower. This was a storm deluxe. It was frightening enough to scare the pants (or robes) off of a dozen disciples. Even veteran fishermen like Peter knew this storm could be their last. So, with fear and water on their faces, they ran to wake up Jesus.

They ran to do what? Jesus was asleep? Waves tossing the boat like popcorn in a popper, and Jesus was asleep? Water flooding the deck and soaking the sailors, and Jesus was in dreamland? How in the world could He sleep through a storm?

Simple. He knew Who was pushing the swing.

The disciples' knees were knocking because their swing was being pushed by a stranger. Not so with Jesus. He could find peace in the storm.

We live in a stormy world. At this writing wars rage in both hemispheres of our globe. World conflict is threatening all humanity. Jobs are getting scarce. Money continues to get tight. Families are coming apart at the seams.

Everywhere I look, private storms occur. Family deaths, strained marriages, broken hearts, lonely evenings. We must remember Who is pushing the swing. We must put our trust in Him. We can't grow fearful. He won't let us tumble out.

Who pushes your swing? In the right hands, you can find peace . . . even in the storm.

You will keep in perfect peace him whose mind is steadfast,
because he trusts in you.

Isaiah 26:3

Enjoy a swing at a park and as you rise up into the air, throw a trouble out to the Lord to grab and take care of.

Turning To Him In The Small Spaces

KATHRYN HIGGINBOTTOM GORIN

Take advantage of any space that they leave you.
Grandad Savage

When I was learning to drive, I'd focus so carefully on what was right in front of me that I often completely missed the big picture.

Parking my car one day, I took the turn way too tight and tried, inch by inch, to maneuver into the spot. My grandfather let me try it my way a few times before pointing out all the room I had ignored on the other side of the car.

"You've got to take advantage of any space that they leave you," he said.

That advice keeps coming back to me. Balancing my job, my family, and my household responsibilities often leaves me completely overwhelmed and exhausted. Each day, I have an unending list of things to accomplish. Spending daily quiet time with God seems impossible.

But God is so faithful in meeting me where I am. I'm learning that He can turn the small spaces in my day into brief moments of refreshing in a realm of chaos. Something as simple as singing a worship song while doing laundry or whispering a word of thanks as I tuck in my sleeping baby draws me closer to Him.

As I use these small spaces to focus my heart on God, He is teaching me about His peace, His contentment, and His gentleness. My life may not be made simpler, but He quiets my heart and equips me for all of the challenges that lie ahead.

The next time you are feeling stressed or overwhelmed, stop and think of a single step to focus on God. It might be a worship chorus or an arrow prayer. Or maybe it will be a quick thank-you for something simple in your life.

Come near to God and He will come near to you.
James 4:8a

Instead of saving every piece of artwork your child does,
when the fridge door is full, take a photo of your child next
to their masterpieces. That way, you can save storage space,
while still showing your child that you value the work
that they do.

Spiritual Vitamins
DAVID HAUK

*A glutton is one who raids the icebox
for a cure for spiritual malnutrition.*
Frederick Buechner

These days, nutrition is a hot topic. People spend a lot of time worrying about eating the right foods, getting the proper amount of fiber in their diet, taking the right vitamin and herbal supplements. What about our spiritual nutrition?

The following vitamins are prescribed to supplement your spiritual diet. You are not restricted to one-a-day. In fact, studies have shown that the more you use, the better you feel.

Vitamin A—*Adoration*. Come before God daily with adoration and praise. As soon as you open your eyes, praise Him for another day of life to serve Him. This helps to start your day off right and relieve the daily stress of life. For extra measure, take another dose before bedtime.

Vitamin B—*Belief.* Believe God's promises. Trust that He will do what He says, and will provide all your needs. Another great stress reducer.

Vitamin C—*Confession.* Confess your sins before God and ask for forgiveness. This has the wonderful effect of cleansing the guilt from the arteries of your soul.

Vitamin D—*Dance.* Our faith should make us want to dance with joy and skip with delight, not make us dull and somber. A wonderful cardiovascular supplement.

Vitamin E—*Enlightenment and Edification.* Read God's Word daily to be enlightened and edified in your faith. This will help develop a strong spiritual body and promote growth from infancy to maturity.

Vitamin B-12—*Be Like One of the Twelve.* Follow Jesus' footsteps every day. Walk with Him. Talk with Him. Sit at His feet and listen to Him. Live as close to Jesus Christ and learn as much from His teachings as possible. Fantastic for opening your heart and mind.

Vitamin K—*Kiss.* Not literally, of course, but treat all people with love. Show kindness to everyone, even those you may not like so much. This has a magical way of multiplying the more it is used.

Do not work for food that spoils, but for food that endures to eternal life,
which the Son of Man will give you.
John 6:27a

Take as much time to exercise and feed your spiritual body
as you do your physical body.

Wacky Cake

LINDA HERR

Learning to cook can be an adventure—like exploring a new country,
with a recipe for your map.

"Betty Crocker" in *Betty Crocker's New Boys and Girls Cookbook*

My daughter Alice is eight and learning how to figure out recipes. I dug out a cookbook I had used as a child and was amazed to find that it encouraged using recipes as maps—because that is literally what I have been doing most of my adult life. Living in various cultures in Europe and the Middle East, I have found that neighbors' kitchens and farmers' markets, as well as written-down recipes, hold clues for finding my way in a new country.

My mother picked up the recipe for Wacky Cake from who-knows-whom and I learned to bake with it. When I was a high school exchange student surrounded by incomprehensible metric utensils, I could still make this cake! When I was working with a quirky little oven in Egypt, I forgot an essential ingredient. I took the cake out of the oven, stirred in the vinegar, returned it to bake—and it came out its usual dark, chocolate self. The ingredients are all nonperishable staples available everywhere I've lived. And now Alice is learning how to bake.

This is a firm cake, good for cutting into children's birthday or holiday shapes. A fifth birthday cake for Mary Ona, my middle child, was a square layer cake decorated as a castle with marshmallow turrets and a chocolate bar drawbridge pulled up with licorice strings. An Easter tradition in our house is a bunny cake made from a round layer cake. After putting the two layers together, cut off one third and put the large piece cut side down on a tray. Cut one third off of the smaller piece and prop the larger section against the side of the layer to look like the head and use the smaller section to make a tail. Cover with frosting or whipped topping and toasted coconut. Cut ears out of paper.

Wacky Cake (a.k.a. Goofy Cake)

Mix dry ingredients: two cups sugar, six tablespoons cocoa, two teaspoons baking soda, three cups flour. Add wet ingredients: ten tablespoons oil, two teaspoons vanilla, two tablespoons vinegar, two cups water. Mix well.

Bake at 350 degrees for 30 minutes. Makes two layers or one 9" x 14" cake.

Measuring rule of thumb: four tablespoons make ¼ cup. If using a soup spoon and drinking glass, choose items similar in size to measuring utensils, then *be consistent!*

"Cross-cultural" notes: If working in an area where vanilla sugar is available instead of liquid, add with the dry ingredients. If the oven temperatures are in an unfathomable system, use a moderate heat and test for doneness.

Cooking creatively does not consist of using new recipes from marketing departments and test kitchens. Creativity means you apply what you already have—staples in the cupboard, recipes in a basic cookbook, flavors from your life experience—in new ways.

Why spend money on what is not bread, and your labor on what does not satisfy? Listen, listen to me, and eat what is good, and your soul will delight in the richest of fare.
Isaiah 55:2

Post a kitchen math chart (16 tablespoons = one cup, for example) and a quick substitutions list (such as one square = one ounce unsweetened chocolate = three tablespoons cocoa) inside a kitchen cupboard door. This speeds measuring doubled or halved recipes and allows you to try new dishes without a special trip to the store.

Our Heavenly Father

KEN R. CANFIELD

An infinite God can give all of Himself to each of His children. He does not distribute Himself that each may have a part, but to each one He gives all of Himself as fully as if there were no others.

A. W. Tozer

A friend of mine tells me of a theology class he took years ago in seminary, where on the first day of the semester, the professor handed out a personal questionnaire. Many of the questions on the survey had to do with the student's perceptions of his father and the relationship he had with him. The surveys were collected and no more was said of it. The students forgot all about them during the rigorous months of studying about the First Person of the Trinity, His attributes, His work, and His words. At the end of the course, the professor handed out a second survey. This time the students were supposed to honestly record their perceptions of God and feelings about their relationship with Him. The questions, in fact, were the same as on the first survey they took, but redirected toward the heavenly Father, not their earthly ones. When the professor returned both sets of surveys, including the previously forgotten one, the students were astounded that even after a whole semester of studying about God, they still had trouble differentiating Him relationally from their earthly dads.

Here's the trick. We need to understand that when God reveals Himself as father, He is not simply using "father" as a metaphor. It is not that He is like a father; He is a father, and He is your father. In a deep and very real sense, God is a father. In fact, notice in the Scriptures that when God does relate Himself to earthly fathers, it is to show how much beyond compare He is. For example, when Jesus says, *If you, then, though you are evil, know how to give good gifts to your children, how much more will your Father in heaven give good gifts to those who ask him!* (Matthew 7:11).

God is a father, and He is your father.

The benefit of this truth—the way it sets us free—is that we can let God reveal to us what type of father He is. We don't have to assume that He is an inconsistent, distant, authoritarian figure. We can let Him show us who He is: compassionate, consistent, inclined to our good. I have encouraged many men to pray this prayer: "Heavenly Father, show me what type of father You are." God will answer this prayer. And your map will never be the same again.

If you, then, though you are evil, know how to give good gifts to your children, how much more will your Father in heaven give good gifts to those who ask him!

Matthew 7:11

Every day this month, focus on one attribute of God per day.
Find one verse to support the truth of that attribute.

Abundant Giving
SANDY CATHCART

A generous action is its own reward.

William Walsh

I stood in the Christian Bookstore searching through the rack of the latest CDs. I felt excited to at last be able to buy my favorite Eden's Bridge album. As I picked out my purchase and headed for the cashier, I overheard a conversation between the clerk and a young man. "Congratulations," the clerk said. "How many does this make?"

"This is our sixth baby," he said. "It's a girl."

"Six! How on earth do you take care of all those children when you work in a shoe store?"

"It's only one of my jobs," he laughed. "I have three altogether."

The clerk shook her head while the young father adjusted a pair of ear phones to listen to a demo CD.

"He comes in here on his lunch hour to get his Carmen fix," she said to me. "He never quite saves enough money to buy it."

"I raised five children of my own," I answered. "I understand."

I watched the father's face light with joy as he listened to the music. How well I remembered being a young mother and never being able to afford to buy anything more than necessities. Suddenly, the Eden's Bridge CD didn't seem so important. I turned to the clerk. "Do you know which CD the new father is listening to?" I asked.

"Sure do," she answered. "It's the same one every time."

"I would like to buy it."

She looked at me quizzically before filling my request. "That will be sixteen dollars."

I paid for it, then handed it back to her. "It's for the young man," I whispered. "Wait and give it to him anonymously."

She smiled. "That's very nice of you. He will be tremendously pleased."

I left the store without my purchase but feeling richer. I imagined how pleased the new father would be to know that God cared even about the little things in his life. Often, the abundant life is richer when you give things away.

> . . . *God loves a cheerful giver.*
> II Corinthians 9:7c

Keep a twenty dollar bill in your wallet. When you feel the urge, give it to someone without any thought as to how they will spend it.

All Fired Up

PAULINE RAEL JARAMILLO

There is nothing innocent or good that dies and is forgotten: let us
hold to that faith or none.

Charles Dickens.

My four-year-old son had invited a friend over for lunch. After they finished
their meal I sent them to play in his bedroom. As I was walking by the
opened door a few minutes later, I heard my son's raised voice and paused to
listen. I peeked into the room in time to hear him say, "You said a bad word,"
as he looked at his friend with a shocked expression.

His friend stared back wide eyed.

"Do you want to get all fired up?" my son asked.

After a slight pause his friend shook his head.

"Well, then you better tell God you're sorry so he won't fire you."

They bowed their heads and began praying.

I'm always amazed by the simplicity with which children interpret God's
word and the way they apply it immediately and without reservation. Perhaps that's what Jesus meant when He commanded us to retain a child-like
faith.

And He said: "I tell you the truth, unless you change and become like little
children, you will never enter the kingdom of heaven."

Matthew 18:3

Keep a loaded camera handy and catch those rare
and precious moments on film.

Chains Of Habit

MARILYN JASKULKE

The chains of habit are too weak to be felt until they are too strong to be broken.

Dr. Samuel Johnson

Every Sunday, as a young family, my husband, our three children, and I went to church. Same time, same place, without fail. When our fourth baby came along, a change began in the good habit we had exhibited to our older children. The effort it took to get three children, myself, and a baby ready for church became mammoth. Our pattern of going to church for our weekly worship service began a downhill slide. As we became more lax in our church attendance, it was easy to forget to pray before our evening meals. Another good habit we'd taught our children fell by the wayside.

One Sunday morning, our seven- year-old stepped from his room, wearing his best outfit. Marching through the house, he slammed his Bible on the kitchen table and demanded, "When are we ever going to church again?"

I shuddered in shame. Through a small boy, God yanked us from our retreat and scolded us for our weakness.

Since that day of long ago, the chains of habit and worship continue to be strengthened. We've made no excuses to stay home on Sunday mornings. For our daily meals, we gladly give thanks.

That same small boy is now a husband and father, with a son of his own. His family attends church every Sunday and prays before meals.

Teaching our children the importance of doing things, same time, same place, though sometimes flawed, produces faithfulness. Seeing this, we are blessed abundantly.

Discipline your son, for in that there is hope;
do not be a willing party to his death.

Proverbs 19:18

Write a letter to each of your children and tell them
how proud you are of them. We are never too old
to welcome words of praise.

Anise—A Gift From God's Garden

LORRAINE JENNINGS

God's gift of herbs benefits our health, beauty and well-being,
in addition to flavoring our food. Women everywhere
are becoming God's Herb Growers—and enjoying
the many benefits of His creations

Anne Morris

Herbs have been with us since the very beginning. In the sixth day of creation God said, *I give you every seed-bearing plant on the face of the whole earth and every tree that has fruit with seed in it* (Genesis 1:29, NIV). There are many Biblical references to food and herbs, all of which serve as reminders of God's provision for our earthly needs.

The use of anise is also recorded in early Roman documents, as well as those of Egypt and Greece. In pre-Christian times it was used for the payment of taxes. King Edward I of England was reputed to have levied an import tax in 1305 to help cover expenses to repair the London Bridge.

The Roman scholar Pliny once stated that "it removed all bad odors from the mouth, if chewed in the morning." In the Fifteenth Century, Edward IV ordered that his bed linens be scented with small sachet bags of anise seeds.

Anise was one of the first herbs planted in North America. Records of early colonial gardens contain many references to this herb. In fact, the State of Virginia enacted a law that every newcomer was required to plant six anise seeds.

The use of anise for medicinal purposes goes as far back as Hippocrates, who prescribed it for the relief of coughs. The inclusion of anise in today's cough drops and medicines bears out the importance of this herb.

Anise is widely recommended for improving digestion and preventing flatulence. A tea can be made by crushing the seeds and steeping 1 teaspoon in a cup of boiling water for about 10 minutes, then sipping it slowly to soothe the stomach.

Anise is extremely popular in cooking, and the licorice flavor can be added to some of your favorite recipes by simply including a few anise seeds or drops of oil. German Springerle cookies are a holiday tradition in many homes, and have a wonderful anise taste. Shoestring licorice flavored candy remains a favorite over the years, along with "Good & Plenty" sugar coated candy.

Fruit combines well with anise, and a simple way of enhancing a fruit compote is as follows:

ANISE FRUIT COMPOTE

1 cup sugar
¼ tsp. anise seeds
1½ cups water
Dash salt

Combine all ingredients in saucepan, mix, and cook 4 minutes, stirring frequently. Cool, strain to remove anise seeds, and pour over fresh fruit cubed to bite-size pieces (oranges, apples, grapes, pineapple, strawberries, bananas, mangos—whatever is in season at the time). Chill and serve in your prettiest dishes.

When you ask for God's blessing of the food, don't forget to thank Him also for the wonderful plants that He created for our use.

"Woe to you, teachers of the law and Pharisees, you hypocrites! You give a tenth of your spices —mint, dill [anise in KJV] and cumin. But you have neglected the more important matters of the law — justice, mercy and faithfulness. You should have practiced the latter, without neglecting the former."

Matthew 23:23

By simply adding herbs—anise, basil, thyme, cilantro, parsley, or rosemary, for example—an ordinary dish turns into a gourmet treat.

Turn Your Dreams Into Reality

NELDA JONES

We must not sit still and look for miracles; up and be doing, and the Lord will be with thee. Prayer and pains, through faith in Christ Jesus, will do anything.

John Eliot

I have always been somewhat of a daydreamer. As a child on my parents' farm, I spent many hours daydreaming about various things, including what I wanted to do when I grew up. I daydreamed about getting married and having a family. I daydreamed about someday being a writer. Later, I daydreamed about attending college and getting a journalism degree.

However, none of my daydreams came true—not until I quit just daydreaming and changed my dreams into goals, and my goals into plans and my plans into reality. Now, each of those dreams has come true, besides many others which I did not even know to daydream about at the time. God has abundantly blessed my efforts. However, we cannot just sit around waiting for our dreams to come true. We must plan and act.

First, you should prioritize your dreams, and evaluate which are the most important to you and which are the most attainable. Write them down in order of priority and attainability. Break them down into long-term goals and short-term goals. Pray over them and ask God to bless the dreams and goals that will glorify Him; also those that will bless you and bring you closer to Him. Then pray that God will block any plans which will not glorify Him and those that will not bless or benefit you; also any that will hinder your relationship with Him.

Then draw up a plan of action, using small steps that you can take in order to start turning your dreams into reality. Start with the most attainable steps first, so that you don't become discouraged. Then work on longer-term plans and goals.

Put your list in your Bible and continue to pray over it daily. You may need to reevaluate and revise your plan of action from time to time. (I've had to do this many times.) Then watch as God begins to bring your dreams and plans into fruition. As you take an action step by faith, God will take a step too and bless you and direct you to the next step. God will help you to turn your dreams into abundant reality.

Commit to the LORD whatever you do, and your plans will succeed.
Proverbs 16:3

Write down your dreams and goals, date them, and place them in your Bible. From time to time check your list to see how many of your goals and dreams have come to pass.

Tips From A Bunny

Ellie Kay

Treat your friends as you do your pictures,
And place them in their best light.

Jennie Jerome Churchill

Ever since she was old enough to hold a crayon and find an empty wall, Bethany's been a writer. We call her our "bunny" and she's composed some 5,247 works of art in her seven years on this planet. They're posted on our refrigerator, my husband's desk at work, my computer monitor, and the toilet seat cover. We've got our bunny's "cottage industry products" on the rear-view mirror in the car, the bathroom mirror, and my compact powder mirror. They are a reflection of her soul.

Sometimes she writes her feelings through pictures. As her language skills have progressed, she's written her thoughts in poems.

Here's a poem she wrote, when she was six, to a pair of sisters in our neighborhood.

> Friends
> A Poem
> No one is good as you two.
> No one has a Better Time,
> You two.
> And you two our the best ever.
> By Bethany Kay
> Bethany Kay ©1997

Yes, I suppose I'm biased, but I think this little girl has talent. She writes, colors, and pastes her way into the hearts of friends and family—even acquaintances. Bethany has a simple gift of seeing the best in others. She encourages people—when the world rejects them.

A couple of years ago, we were sitting in a doctor's waiting room with a very large woman. This lady would be clinically labeled as "morbidly obese." At the time, Bethany was only three and her older brother, Philip, was five. I imagined this woman had a life chock full of rejection and judgment. I was concerned about Philip's annoying verbal habit called *brutal honesty* so I gave him the family photos in my purse and asked him to rearrange them—a standing gag order for Philip. That left Bethany and me sitting by the lady.

While my "kindness" was to politely ignore the woman, pretending she wasn't there, Bethany talked to her. She soon discovered the lady's name was June. She told June about her doll, bunny collection, and Papa's airplane. Then Bethany looked into June's face and sweetly said, "You have beautiful hair."

June's countenance brightened, as she returned Bethany's smile. "Thank you, Bethany, my father always used to tell me that, too." There were tears glistening in June's eyes as she said, "He's been gone for fifteen years now."

Bethany's observation was true. June's one beautiful physical trait was her honey blond hair. My little girl can see beauty that escapes many of us. I wondered how long it had been since anyone paid this woman a compliment? Who knows? It could have been fifteen years.

Bunny has been given a simple gift that turns an uncomfortable situation into the divine. She shares the spontaneous love of the Father with those who are hurting. She lets people know, in her little girl way, that they are beloved of the Father. The bunny takes complex rejection and creates—simple acceptance.

What simple words can you write—or speak? By looking around us, we'll see that God has placed hurting people in our path who can benefit from a few simple words. The result of ministering God's love in this way is simply lovely!

A word aptly spoken is like apples of gold in settings of silver.
Proverbs 25:11

> When driving today, try taking a more rural route so that
> you can enjoy God's creation.

The Godly Pursuit

Marvin D. Lamb

*I've learned to hold everything loosely, because it hurts when God
pries my fingers apart and takes them from me.*

Corrie ten Boom

The most often (mis)quoted verse in the Bible seems to be *money is the root
of all evil.* The only verse that I can find that comes close to that is *For the
love of money is a root of all kinds of evil.* (I Timothy 6:10).

So money, itself, is not the root of all evil, but the love of money comes
close. God judges our hearts or motives in addition to our actions. I might be
a poor, homeless street person, and still have an inordinate love for money.
So, to say that the love of money is the root of all kinds of evil does not just
pick on rich people. It *picks* on anyone who has a love in his or her heart for
anything where the love for God must be.

It's not just money, but the desire for any *thing*, which we have to watch
out for. Money is just a good scorecard for how successful we are. When we
follow Corrie ten Boom's advice and hold things loosely, we can surrender
them with joy when the Lord nudges us to give something away or do something for someone else.

A grandfather was hoping to teach this lesson to his four-year-old grandson. As they parted in the church foyer, the grandfather gave a dollar and a
quarter to his grandson.

"What are these for, Grandpa?" the curious boy asked.

"You're going to Junior Church. They'll be takin' up an offering there. I want you to put whichever one you think you should in that offering. You can keep the other for yourself to spend after church."

As he picked his grandson up after the services, he wondered what lesson the young lad had learned. "Well, David," he asked, "what did you put in the offering?"

"Uh . . . Mrs. Johnson taught us a lesson on being a cheerful giver. She said that God loves a cheerful giver!"

Grandfather started to smile, thinking that his young charge had finally learned a useful lesson. Then his grandson continued, ". . . And I decided that I could be a whole lot more cheerful about giving that quarter than I could about giving that dollar bill!"

The Apostle Paul says that godliness is not a means to financial gain. He has expressed the secret. There are two ways to be rich. The one most people think about is having enough money to buy anything they want. The other way to be rich is in the few-ness of our wants.

Pray that the Lord will help you learn to be content with what you have. When you have *Him*, you have everything you need for successful living.

But godliness with contentment is great gain.
I Timothy 6:6

Videotape an elderly member of your family as they answer questions about their childhood.

Please Pass The Chow Chow

MARTY MAGEE

*I pray your children will be clutching the baton of faith the way a
three-year-old grasps her first cotton candy at the county fair!*

Dr. Joe White

"Three gallons chopped green tomatoes, three pounds sweet pepper, three small cabbages, one pound hot pepper, 2½ cups sugar . . ."

A friend brought back a piece of my childhood when she presented me with a Kerr fruit jar full of chow-chow like my grandmother had made forty-five years before. With it, she included a hand-written recipe.

When I told people about this rediscovered delicacy, several asked, "What is chow-chow?" I was able to give them a taste and a copy of the recipe.

Then I had a dreadful thought. This culinary legend could easily die out and nobody would know about chow-chow. This part of my past could have been lost forever.

But what else are we failing to pass on to our children and grandchildren? Maybe things more important than the relish we put on our pinto beans. Do our kids know common manners and courtesies? Is the Walkman out of their ears long enough for them to learn the art of conversation? What about respect for elders? Do our young ones realize the wealth of knowledge to be gleaned from their grandparents' years of experiencing life?

I wonder if we've instilled in their hearts God's simple principle of "Be ye kind." Do we show by our lives how to be "tenderhearted, forgiving one another?" Are we passing down quality music to our children? Do they know the old hymns of the faith? What sustaining power can be found in that "Blessed Assurance" and "Amazing Grace"!

I remember having fun quoting the books of the Old and New Testaments, memorizing verses and learning stories from the Bible. I didn't have an interpretation for all of the passages I learned, but one by one, many of them took on a real and lasting meaning for me. John 3:16 and several verses in Romans brought understanding of the living Savior and how He could affect my life. The prophet Isaiah made me see how this Redeemer was promised long before He came in the flesh. Isaiah 26:3 tells us we can have perfect peace by keeping our minds on God. The Psalms are full of praise and worship. The Proverbs are a practical manual for living life. Many of the Old Testament books are full of better-than-fiction adventure stories, like Jonah in the belly of the fish, Joshua and Gideon, great warriors for God. And where can we find a better love story than from the books of Ruth and Song of Solomon?

Eight gallons of Scripture, five quarts of music, six cups of laughter, a dash of good times. Mix vigorously with love.

Each family's ingredients and quantities may differ. They *must* differ to reflect such a creative God. But please, let's pass on to our children and grandchildren our experience-tested and proven recipes for living life to the fullest.

> *These commandments that I give you today are to be upon your hearts.*
> *Impress them on your children. Talk about them when you sit at home and*
> *when you walk along the road, when you lie down and when you get up.*
> Deuteronomy 6:6–7

Share an afternoon with your kids, making one of their grandmother's special recipes.

Words Of Life

JAN McNAUGHT

She [Ruth Bell Graham] carried her black leather Bible, dull and soft from use, with pages so swollen and fragile that she now bound the book with a black leather belt, her Bible belt, she jokingly called it.

Patricia Cornwell

I was an anemic Christian, with hardly enough spiritual strength to face my day, never mind enough to climb mountains or battle the Enemy. I regularly used the "I-Otta Bible Reading Plan": I "otta" read the Bible today. I don't really want to but I know I should. This plan was successful but only for making me feel guilty and defeated. I knew I "otta" read the Scriptures, but seldom did.

Then I heard a speaker say: "Be honest with God. Tell him you want to want to read the Bible." So, beginning with a scripture that came to my mind, I asked God to help me "want to want to" read his Word, hoping He would give me what I wanted. The scripture was: *Delight yourself in the Lord and He will give you the desires of your heart.* (Psalm 37:4).

I soon realized God was changing my heart. I no longer dreaded but instead longed to read God's Word. I admit I was surprised at first, then God gave me this insight: when God says He will "give" us the desires of our heart, He means: "I will *implant* and then *grant* my desires in and through you." He was doing both for me!

The first scripture I was drawn to was Psalm 46:10: "Be still and know that I am God." The result was a desire to act from a quiet heart and to know God in a personal way. This scripture became my focus that year. My journal reflected the changes in my desires as His purposes became my purposes. Quietness stilled my frantic pace. His love replaced much of the fear and anxiety I often felt. I had a Friend.

My appetite whetted, I sought God's appointed scripture focus the next year . . . and the next. Seventeen years have passed and a list of that many scriptures fills the back pages of my Bible, a spiritual autobiography of sorts. I call those verses "My Experience Scriptures" . . . verses God has made alive in my life. God continues to shape my desires and often gives me opportunity to make friends with others who are ready for God to implant and grant His desires in their hearts. Are you ready?

Delight yourself in the LORD, and He will give you the desires of your heart.
Psalm 37:4

Floundering for encouraging words to give a friend?
Write or pray with confidence those "experience Scriptures"
God has brought to life in you.

Constant Factor
JENNIFER ANNE F. MESSING

The best things are nearest: breath in your nostrils,
light in your eyes, flowers at your feet,
duties at your hand, the path of God just before you.
Robert Louis Stevenson

Last night I attended our weekly worship team rehearsal. Before opening in prayer, our pastor shared some distressing news. Two dear ladies in our congregation would soon lose their bank jobs because of a buy-out. They had both worked at that bank for many, many years.

While listening and praying, some sobering thoughts struck me. How quickly we can lose something that has been a steady, constant factor in our lives! Our jobs, spouses, family, or a comfortable home, for instance, are all things we could lose in a moment. Yet many times we take these precious blessings for granted and murmur instead, "If I only had a nicer car (or a higher paying job or that new dress), then I would really be happy and content . . ."

The pastor's news made me realize that I should be grateful for those constant factors in my life that have not changed nor been taken away, but which the Lord has graciously given for my happiness at this time. What are the constant factors in your life that you take for granted? How will you be grateful instead?

Keep your lives free from the love of money and be content
with what you have, because God has said,
"Never will I leave you; never will I forsake you."
Hebrews 13:5

Read entire books or novels aloud together as a family
by reading one chapter out loud every other evening.

God's Garden

ALICE KING GREENWOOD

We sit at the keyboard, willing to play the only song we know, only
to discover a new song.

Max Lucado

"Ooh! What beautiful tomatoes! Looks like they're fresh from the garden," exclaimed Mrs. Moore as she admired the plump, red fruit in her hands.

"They are," answered Gene. "Right out of God's Garden." "God's Garden" was a five acre tract of land lying like an oasis in the desert on the outskirts of a dry west Texas town. Gene Shoup had retired from his regular job, but he enjoyed raising vegetables and fruits, and this garden was his opportunity to do what he loved.

God had begun to speak to Gene and put into his heart a desire to serve Him. "What can I do for God?" he wondered. "What talents do I have?"

God answered, "You can raise a garden of vegetables and fruits." It was just that simple. When Gene and his wife Denevee dedicated this plot of ground to God and appropriately called it God's Garden, little did they know how prolific it would become.

While other local gardeners struggled to keep their plants from dying in the scorching sun and winds, Gene watched his plants thrive. He and God raised tomatoes, okra, squash, beans, sweet potatoes, blackeyed peas, canta- loupes, and watermelons. Not only did they produce one harvest, but all through the hot summer and fall, crop followed crop. Without doubt the Shoups could have sold this produce for a nice profit, but they felt that such a bountiful harvest should be shared. God had blessed the garden abundantly and they would spread around those blessings.

Each time they came to church, they brought boxes of vegetables and fruits to share with friends. They loaded their pickup truck with luscious cantaloupes, which were distributed to many families. Long after other gar- dens had withered and died in the near-drought, God's Garden continued to produce. As crops multiplied in a miraculous way, friendships grew, love multiplied, and praises to God abounded.

At the same time, God began working in the hearts of other couples. They began to deliver sacks of the produce from God's Garden to the elderly and homebound. How delighted these dear people were to receive fresh-from-the-garden fruits and vegetables, which not only provided them with healthful nutrients but also brought back happy memories of their days "back on the farm."

Because Gene Shoup dedicated his talents to God, he was blessed with a rich abundance of produce. But his greater blessings came in the joy of sharing with others. Perhaps God has given you and me a bountiful harvest to share, as well.

Like Gene, any service that you perform is not only supplying the needs of God's people but is also overflowing in many expressions of thanks to God.

Because of the service by which you have proved yourselves, men will praise God for the obedience that accompanies your confession of the gospel of Christ, and for your generosity in sharing with them and with everyone else.
II Corinthians 9:13

Volunteer to deliver Meals-On-Wheels. In ministering
to the physical needs of shut-ins, you will put smiles
on their faces and joy in their hearts.

Hidden Treasures
SUSAN WATERMAN VOSS

Contentment is not the fulfillment of what you want, but the realization of how much you already have.
Unknown

The nursery was full of flowers. Every imaginable color and kind seemed to be available. I was totally confused. My planting experience was limited and I had never done it alone before. Our new house had a bare and lonely stretch of earth, though. It needed brightness and beauty.

I spotted the bright red salvia. Perfect, the little tag indicated, for my hot and sunny yard. I planted them exactly according to the directions and watered them faithfully.

Then I waited. Surely the spiky red blooms would multiply—or expand—or something! Instead they just sat there. *No problem*, I thought. *They are pretty, regardless.*

But time and the summer heat took its toll. The beautiful scarlet flowers began to dry up and fade. Disappointed, I finally decided that cutting off the dead blooms was my only option. The plants certainly didn't look pretty anymore.

Pruning shears in hand, I sadly went to work. As I clipped away the first flower my hand brushed aside the spread of leaves. There, hiding underneath the thick foliage, were several tiny red buds. Beyond my view, they were there waiting. Trimming off the old growth gave them just the boost they needed to grow. Eventually, I ended up with the beautiful flowerbed I had hoped for. Actually, it had been there all along.

Sometimes in our lives, it is easy to lose our focus. We center ourselves on the things we perceive to be important, never stopping to think about God's will for us. We put our time and energy into things that have no real lasting benefit.

If we pray for God's guidance we begin to see the truly important blessings that He has given us. Like the tiny hidden buds on my flowers, we may even discover some wonderful hidden treasures in our lives. God will help us to appreciate the wondrous riches of His love as we seek His will. Sometimes we need to look beyond the obvious to find the glorious riches awaiting us.

Many, O LORD my God, are the wonders You have done. The things You planned for us no one can recount to You; were I to speak and tell of them, they would be too many to declare.

Psalm 40:5

> Sketch out the number and types of plants in your annual garden. It will help in planning for next year.

Catch Of The Day

GEORGIA CURTIS LING

Joy is a net of love by which you can catch souls.

Mother Teresa

I can't believe I'm saying this, but I felt like Jane Fonda, or at least the character she portrayed in the movie, *On Golden Pond*. Okay, that's as far as I'll go on that comparison with Jane, and I guess to tell the truth, it wasn't a pond, it was a lake—but it really was golden and tranquil.

Each summer, we leave Seattle and make our mecca back home for a visit in the bluegrass state of Kentucky. Our son Philip's favorite part of the trip is fishing with his aunt. This time was no different. In the cool of one early evening, Philip, my sister Sherry, and I baited up our hooks with those poor little slimy worms and began our sport of casting and reeling. Bored with not enough bobber action in our beginning location, Philip and Sherry headed to more promising waters and it proved to be a good move. Philip was the champion fisherman, as he pulled out a dozen or more fish.

I was content with the little activity my line experienced, so I stayed in solitude in my little cove, propped up my pole, relaxed on a patchwork quilt, and turned pages of a book that proved more interesting than fishing.

As the evening wore on, I took a break to give my eyes a rest and swat away some pesky mosquitoes. I began admiring my beautiful surroundings. The tall green trees that framed the lake reflected like a mirror on the opposite shore as the golden sunset danced like gold fleck on the sparkling waters. Something caught my attention, as so quietly two little colorful mallard ducks glided along the top of the water. They were no stranger to our party. We had shooed them away hours earlier when they invited themselves to our picnic. This time they seemed to be enjoying the sunset, minding their own business.

As they drew closer and closer I wondered about my line that lay still and almost invisible in the water. I contemplated reeling it in, but before I could the ducks came about an inch from the line and, immediately detecting danger, took a sharp left to avoid the snares and tangles of my dormant line. They floated along on their merry way.

I'm sure some of you might think that domestic ducks living a life on a lake have learned their lesson from previous entanglements with their cute little web feet—but no, I give them more credit for their natural instinct. Daffy Duck may be portrayed as a dumb duck, but I think he gives the duck domain a bad name.

We're no dumb ducks either. I think we instinctively know when to avoid the snares and tangles of the world. We just need to be more duck-like and take a sharp turn in the opposite direction of danger. It can really be that simple!

I didn't have much success fishing that night, but learning from the smart little ducks was definitely the catch of the day.

> "... *my God, in whom I trust." Surely he will save you*
> *from the fowler's snare and from the deadly pestilence.*
>
> Psalms 91:2–3

In your next conversation,
ask questions more than give opinions.

Simple Prescription

C. ELLEN WATTS

The only ideas that will work for you are the ones you put to work.
Unknown

The simple health rules Miss Bell taught her third grade class were easy enough to learn—and, for some, equally easy to forget. I was reminded of this the morning our elderly house guest (once a teacher of hygiene herself) complained of dizziness.

"I exercise and eat right and try to get out. And I never forget to take my pills," she explained to our doctor. He asked a few questions, examined her carefully, and handed her a prescription.

She grasped the paper between gnarled fingers. "No pills?"

"No pills."

I peered over her shoulder. "Eight glasses of water? Daily?"

Like many among her peers, to avoid drinking water meant (hopefully) never having to excuse oneself in the middle of a conversation or ask a driver to stop.

The doctor explained to her how necessary water is to the way our bodies work, then patted her shoulder and smiled. "Water is the best we can offer for the dehydration and pollution causing your current problems. Drink plenty and you should soon be fine. Water also acts as a preventative against colds and other simple ailments such as headache or stomach upset." He suggested she begin her day with two full glasses of water and warned her that coffee, tea and soda were not to be counted.

The prescription worked—for our visitor and for me. While water has long been my drink of choice, drinking two glasses before breakfast and making sure of the eight has had lasting benefits. After my husband decided to also increase his water intake, the two of us were soon put to the test.

We were enjoying a few days with our family near Lake Tahoe when the kids decided it would be fun to hike up a rocky hillside to a secluded lake. Being Mom, Dad, and grandparents to all the rest, we wondered how we would fare. On the day of the hike, we tanked up on water, donned proper gear, got to the foot of the mountain, saw pop cans and juice bottles sprouting from everyone else's pockets, and knew what we'd forgotten. While some offered to share, the climb had scarcely begun before most proved to be more needy than we.

At the top of the trail we looked back at the red-faced hikers lugging their empty containers and smiled. Our tanks had held. We did not feel thirsty!

Water, of course, is neither medicine nor cure-all. It is a simple blessing from God that tastes better and costs less than any other remedy or prescription. Further, like the spiritual benefits God lavishes upon His children, water is available to all who would drink freely.

". . . whoever drinks the water I give him will never thirst. Indeed, the water I give him will become in him a spring of water welling up to eternal life."

John 4:14

On hot days, place a pitcher of ice water and a glass where it will be handy for the person who cares for your lawn to enjoy a cool drink.

Boat Of Life
NORA LACIE ABELL

Let your boat of life be light, packed with only what you need—a homely home and simple pleasures, one or two friends, worth the name, some one to love and someone to love you, a cat, a dog, and a pipe or two, enough to eat and a little more than enough to drink; for thirst is a dangerous thing.

Jerome K. Jerome

"Those stupid people!" I shouted, "How could they have done this?"

Rain poured down my face, washing angry tears into my collar and down my chest. A sudden summer downpour interrupted our work at the landfill, where my husband, children, and I soggily sifted through the thirty-five years of accumulated treasures, garbage, clothing, furniture, memorabilia, assorted household items, and books, from my in-laws' recently emptied home. Everything was getting wet, ruining the stack of Bibles I had rescued and cradled protectively in my arms. Through blurry rage, I could see Mom's name blurring inkily down the front page of one of the Bibles. How could the housecleaners have thrown out Mom's family Bibles? Frustration from dealing with her death and the enormous task of cleaning out the house gushed bitterly from me like a cloudburst, and my furious remarks clapped like the thunder overhead.

Mom was a "clutterbug." She saved packets of old letters she thought she might reread. Cardboard boxes held reams of colored paper for craft projects. Baskets hid skeins of yarn. Carefully folded yards—maybe miles—of fabric stuffed closets. And chocolate bars and six-packs of Pepsi filled her pantry. She collected rocks, Irish crystal, silver dimes, antique bottles, children's books, tea, magazines, patterns, recipes, and linens. These "collections," a need from having survived the Great Depression, existed solely as comforting items that Mom imagined she might need "in the future." She knew her collections cluttered her home, but she fully expected to sell, give away, or dispose of them.

Except the Bibles. She needed them each day. She memorized Psalms and lived in the beauty of them. She practiced the Golden Rule, and never waited for others to "do unto her." She tended to the needs of her family, graced her community with her generosity, and encouraged discipline and wisdom in her children and grandchildren. She *used* her Bibles, dog-earing them, writing in them, toting them to and from our little country church, and praying over them. They filled her "boat of life" with the Word of Life.

The unsentimental, overwhelmed housecleaners gutted out the house, and thoughtlessly tossed everything, including the Bibles, into the dump pile. We rescued not only Bibles, but a few, treasured belongings: a small, chipped plate from the farm in Kansas, my husband's bronzed baby shoe, a cotton quilt, Grandpa's wooden leg (it just didn't seem right to leave it at the dump), and a lasso-printed, faded linen cowboy shirt Mom had sewn on her old treadle machine. The rest of the clutter was just wet junk.

Mom never de-cluttered her "boat of life," but I'm trying to de-clutter mine. It doesn't take a fancy house or an enormous wardrobe to "float my boat." I'm tossing my wet-junk gatherings of grudges and bundles of bitterness overboard! Through His Word, God abundantly supplies a modest collection of wisdom, graciousness, and patience. Like Mom's Bibles, those qualities take up little space, yet add bubbly buoyancy to my boat.

Is your boat of life overburdened? How about tossing some junk out?

In the beginning was the Word, and the Word was with God,
and the Word was God.

John 1:1

De-clutter your life! Once a month, fill a box or bag with
unused clothing, household items, etc., and take to the
Salvation Army, St. Vincent de Paul,
or other charitable organization.

Fall

Fall, or Autumn, beckons us to put aside our pride and jump into a pile of leaves. In the same way, God calls to His children, saying, "Come, stop your fretting and know that I can abundantly provide for all your cares."

This section of readings will include Christmas selections so that we end up the year focusing on God's greatest gift: His love through the birth of His Son, Jesus.

Victory Over The Concrete Monster

KATHERINE LUNDGREN

> . . . Abandon yourself with a generous trust to the good Shepherd, who has promised never to call His own sheep out into any path, without Himself going before them to make the way easy and safe. Take each little step as He makes it plain to you. Bring all your life, in each of its details, to Him to regulate and guide.
>
> Hannah Smith

Everyday, millions of peaceful suburbians like myself face the concrete monster snaking through the cities. From all walks of life we merge into crowds spending hours through the miles of the "commute." Many of us are on the road one to two hours one way to get to our jobs! The reason I say "monster" is because the drive can be a mental, spiritual, and physical battle.

When I'm in the middle of so many cars on the highway anything can happen! The many and varied driving situations represent the divergent ways people think and make life choices. I know there are good, safety-conscious people behind other steering wheels, but I am in danger of great harm from the careless, uninsured, unlicensed, chemically impaired, and above-the-law bullies. Speeders and tailgaters cause gridlock and deadly accidents.

I have left home, joyful and ready to work, only to experience commuters speeding right toward my rear bumper. Sometimes they drive so close I cannot see their headlights in my mirror. This isn't too bad at thirty-five miles an hour in town but when I'm in my little sports car at freeway speeds, I'm fearful! As a result, I stay to the right, going the speed limit, and I keep my distance from anyone in front of me. I tap the brakes to warn people of slowing. I sing and pray. I shake my head and my fist. The battles rage. I can be tempted to turn into the "Wicked Witch of the North."

The victory over my intense feelings is really only won when I am filled with God's Holy Spirit and think like He does. When I choose compassion, not anger, God helps me pray specifically for His mercy for that wayward driver and others endangered by him or her. After all, I have peace with the Lord, but that poor soul may not even be ready to stand before God's throne (and he or she seems to be approaching it fast!).

As I look at my commute with godly attitudes, my fear diminishes. Instead of focusing on potential danger, I thank God for all my blessings. My distress is replaced with peace. Coworkers ask me how I arrive at work so calm and I am able to share what my precious Jesus does for me. After all, doesn't that matter more than anything?

How is your commute these days? If it's getting to you, try focusing on God's hand of protection and the mercy He has extended to you. Then when the drivers around you make mistakes, you can be as forgiving as God is with you.

. . . Sing and make music in your heart to the Lord, always giving thanks to God the Father for everything, in the name of our Lord Jesus Christ.
Ephesians 5:19b–20

When you start getting angry, don't think about what someone else is doing wrong, ask Christ how to react like He does. Then find specific things for which to be honestly thankful in spite of the circumstance.

A Good Friend Speaks The Truth

LES PARRIOTT

If we let our friend become cold and selfish and exacting without a remonstrance, we are no true friend.

Harriet Beecher Stowe

"Les, you sometimes drive yourself so hard, pushing and pushing on an important project," someone recently told me, "that you sometimes place the same high expectations for driving hard on those around you, whether you know it or not." Ouch. Where did that come from? Talk about a zinger. Where did this guy get off telling me about how I treat other people?

Actually, he had every right to tell me what he thought. John was, and is, my friend. And he was right. I can focus in on a goal so intensely that I neglect other people's feelings in the process. We were on to a second helping of spicy chicken at our favorite Chinese restaurant when he gently lowered the boom. Truth is, John wasn't trying to berate or scold me—he was actually trying to save my neck. As a good friend, he cares about me and didn't want me to get into a sticky situation with the members of a committee I was working with.

Good friends are like that. They speak the truth. Honesty is a prerequisite to their relationship. "Genuine friendship cannot exist where one of the parties is unwilling to hear the truth," says Cicero, "and the other is equally indisposed to speak it."

As painful as the truth might be, good friends are obligated to speak it. Now, this does not mean they have license to insult, offend, and badger. The Bible talks about speaking the truth in love. And that's the goal of an honest friend. The question is, how does a friend do this? The answer involves a lot of respect. Without respect, honesty is a lethal weapon. Perhaps that's what caused Cicero to add, "Remove respect from friendship and you have taken away the most splendid ornament it possesses."

*Perfume and incense bring joy to the heart, and the pleasantness of one's
friend springs from his earnest counsel.*

Proverbs 27:9

Write down a list of the things you appreciate in a friend and
then examine how many of those qualities you offer to others.

Christmas Treats

Barbara J. Anson

He rolls it under his tongue as a sweet morsel.

Matthew Henry

"Ahhh . . ." The tantalizing aromas and delicious tastes of home-made Christmas specialties. Over the years, I've built up a recipe collection of personal favorites that began with my mother's recipes for cornbread stuffing, spicy pumpkin pie, and mouth-watering plum pudding. Of all the recipes I've tried over the years, some of the simpler ones are my favorites.

It's fun to try new recipes, but since the complicated ones no longer tempt me, I have a simple, yet rich, toffee recipe I want to share with you. It's easy to make, is rich, is abundantly satisfying, and makes an excellent gift. It epitomizes simplicity with only four common ingredients. Preparing for each step before beginning insures quick, foolproof results.

Enjoy this candy with tea or coffee and a selection of your favorite Christmas readings.

English Toffee

½ pound butter (don't use margarine!)
1 cup brown sugar, firmly packed
5 or 6 1½-ounce milk chocolate bars (a little more or less is okay)
½ cup finely chopped filberts, almonds, or macadamia nuts

Butter an 8- or 9-inch square baking pan and set aside. Unwrap the chocolate bars and also set aside, along with the nuts, after chopping. In a deep saucepan, combine the butter and sugar. Cook over medium high heat, stirring constantly until the mixture reaches 300 degrees on a candy thermometer. Then immediately pour it into a buttered pan. Lay the chocolate bars evenly over the hot candy; and when soft, spread into a smooth layer. Then sprinkle the nuts over smoothed chocolate; press in gently with your fingers. Chill until the chocolate is firm. Invert the candy on a flat surface and break into small pieces. Finally, store in an airtight container.

Enjoy!

How sweet are your words to my taste, sweeter than honey to my mouth!
Psalm 119:103

Set out a basket of nuts in the shell for fun and easy snacking.

Whose Birthday Is It Anyway?
Mary Bahr Fritts

We may face situations beyond our reserve,
but never beyond God's resources.
Unknown

As our sons grew, so did their love for the "giving" of Christmas. But as they grew and grew, their bank accounts didn't. College does that to families. It all began like this. "I know you're strapped this year, guys. Don't spend lots. Just stick something special in your brothers' stockings." They did. And a tradition was born.

I watched with joy as each Christmas the stocking gifts grew, not in price tag or size, but in personalization and fun in the hunt. There were only two rules. Rule 1: Gifts must fit the stocking and the budget. Rule 2: Holiday visitors receive their own stocking, which they can take home. (During this time we welcomed a new daughter-in-law into the family. This is her favorite tradition.)

What's fun is the sneaky shopping, wrapping, hiding, and eavesdropping for new ideas. When Bill lost his ¼" socket, he got one. When I mentioned a pen with purple ink, it was mine. When the boys received drivers' licenses, they got their own sets of keys for house and car.

College sons receive stamped postcards, food vouchers, calling card credits, and quarters for laundromats. When funds are really low, coupons abound, like "good for three car washes" for those who drive; "good for two trips to the mall" for those who don't. There are keychain flashlights, teeny colognes, gift certificates, movie passes, luggage tags, and much more.

What's fun is personalizing the gifts.

What's fun is watching the faces.

What's fun is knowing our sons will pass the tradition on to their own families.

New traditions are begun for many reasons. But I think more than anything, this was God's way of reminding us Whose birthday it is in the first place.

Every good and perfect gift is from above . . .
James 1:17a

When budgets are stretched, gather the family around the dinner table to discuss birthdays and ask for suggestions on new ways to celebrate them, not *spend* them. Be sure to include Jesus' birthday in your discussion.

Me? Memorize?

Erma Landis

The devil is not afraid of a Bible that has dust on it.

Unknown

Is scripture memorization important? Can just anyone do it? I was convinced I was too forgetful or unable to benefit from it, so for the first forty years of my life I didn't attempt anything so mentally demanding.

My forgetfulness as a child was a frustration to my mother and to me as well. I had managed the verses for Bible School and Sunday School, and the poem or two a year required in school, but to memorize more than a couple verses in succession was out of my realm.

Then one day I was challenged by a Bible speaker who said, "You can memorize anything. If you can find your way home tonight; if you can find your way to work, to the grocery store, to church, the shopping center or a dozen other places, you can memorize scripture."

I didn't believe him, of course. But he continued, "Only two things are necessary to memorize something. First, you must repeat it often enough, and second, it must be important to you."

The Bible important to me? Repetition was within my ability I knew, but it was difficult to convince myself I hadn't memorize scripture all these years because the Bible wasn't important enough to me.

I knew he was wrong but the only way to prove it was to give memorization a try. So I chose the Sermon on the Mount from Matthew 5–7. To my amazement I had the entire portion memorized within a few months.

But I wasn't convinced—yet. After all, those were all familiar verses, I just had to learn them in their proper order.

So I set out again to prove that speaker wrong. This time I chose something less familiar, the book of I John. When I actually had it memorized in less than six months, I admitted defeat. I knew the speaker had spoken the truth. You *can* memorize anything if you repeat it often enough and it is important to you.

To change my old attitude, I chose a simple method. I broke up the passage in manageable portions, from five to seven verses. Each morning I read that portion three to five times, slowly and meditatively. In the evening I repeated the process. Usually in a week that part was memorized and I moved on to the next portion. When I had a chapter memorized, I gave as much time as necessary to reviewing the whole chapter until it was word perfect. Then on to the next chapter and the process was repeated; and so forth until the book was completed.

I have memorized numerous lengthy portions of scripture and a number of books since then and I am delighted to say I was wrong. The speaker was right.

But maybe you should try to prove him wrong.

I have hidden your word in my heart that I might not sin against you.
Psalm 119:11

If you become bogged down with your memorization,
take a short recess, but come back soon!

Beyond Childish Ways

PATTY STUMP

Little faith will bring your souls to Heaven, but great faith will bring Heaven to your souls.

Charles H. Spurgeon

As a child, one of my favorite television programs was a CBS show entitled *Kids Say the Darndest Things*. I can recall listening attentively as the host, Art Linkletter, conversed with his guest panel of young children on an assortment of topics including parents, pets, siblings, school, and chores. As each child responded to the questions that were posed, it was apparent that they hoped their answers would accurately and wisely represent how things should be, would be, or had been based on their life experiences! Obviously, their childish perspectives revealed a mixture of innocence and ignorance, as well as tidbits of truths amidst mounds of misinformation.

It's been years since I've seen that show, yet because it was a childhood favorite I was delighted to recently have an opportunity to meet Mr. Linkletter. With a twinkle in his eye and a well-worn smile, he glanced in my direction and asked an interesting question: "Do you know how to make God laugh?" Not wanting to respond with the "wisdom" of a child, I declined guessing and cautiously waited for his response. "Tell Him your plans!" he responded. As Mr. Linkletter headed on his way I quietly chuckled to myself, struck by the element of truth in what he had shared.

In my relationship with the Lord, there have been times I've approached God with my plans and perspective. In those moments, I, too, can say the darndest things, often failing to see the big picture.

If you and I are to experience the fullness of God's abundance in our lives, we must mature beyond our childish viewpoints and look to Him for His wisdom and will. As we do, He'll reveal the plans He has in store for us, inviting us to grow in faith and spiritual maturity as we adjust our hearts toward Him.

A simple step that will allow us to more fully experience God's abundance is to take time each day to P.L.A.N.

P Prioritize time with God on a daily basis through reading His Word and spending quiet moments in prayer.

L Lay aside any thoughts, feelings, and behaviors that prevent you from walking in His power.

A Actively apply His Word to your life and circumstances.

N Note on a daily basis at least three delights/blessings He has brought your way. You'll be amazed how this will change your outlook!

It's refreshing to encounter the innocent perspective of children and their creative outlooks. Yet, just as the passing years are supposed to bring increased growth and maturity in children, so should the passing of time result in increased spiritual growth and maturity for us. Take time each day to P.L.A.N. your steps in such a way that you draw closer to God; as you do, you'll experience the abundance He has in store for you.

When I was a child, I talked like a child, I thought like a child, I reasoned like a child. When I became a man, I put childish ways behind me.
I Corinthians 13:11

If you are interrupted by a call from a needy friend, look at it as a blessed time to put up your feet and relax.

Be Anxious For No Thing
MARGARITA GARZA DE BECK

During our flight of life our attitude is most critical during the "tough times." That is when we are tempted to panic and make bad attitude decisions.
John C. Maxwell

We were all seated at the dining room table helping the kids do their homework—all except Josh, my eight-year-old grandson, who was upstairs working on his multiplication tables on the computer. All of a sudden we heard him running from the bedroom to the top of the stairs, yelling, "Mom! Mom! Mom!"

Being the closest to the stairs, I jumped up from the table, papers and pencils flying everywhere, and ran to the hallway. I called out, "What's the matter?"

He yelled back, "What's seven times seven?"

What's seven times seven? He had scared us out of our wits for such a silly question! But of course, it had not been a silly question to Josh. It was a matter of great concern to him for he was trying to beat the computer and for a moment, he was afraid he was going to lose. To him, he thought he had an extremely good reason to be anxious.

1 guess we all at times seem like that, thinking we have good reason to worry and fret. We cry out, "Lord! Lord! What shall I do about this? What shall I do about that? What's going to happen?" We probably run around helter-skelter sometimes, as though we did not have any sense of direction nor an ounce of peace about our situation, in the small things and the big.

Josh's "panic attack" reminded me of the wise counsel I heard in church one Sunday morning. The preacher told us that each time he was tempted to worry about anything, he would write that concern down in his appointment book on the days he always reserved just for worrying: the last two days of each month. He said that always, without question, when he came to the end of the month, the situation he'd been so tempted to worry about had already resolved itself (with Divine intervention, of course!)

I thank God for His admonishment that we shouldn't be anxious, worried, or full of care about *anything*. He promises that His peace will preserve our hearts and minds through Jesus Christ as we make our requests known to Him.

Do not be anxious about anything, but in everything, by prayer and petition, with thanksgiving, present your requests to God.
Philippians 4:6

Write out Philippians 4:6 on an index card and carry it with you so that you can prevent worry from seizing your mind.

Laughter

JANIE LAZO

Love and laughter hold us together.
Ingrid Trobisch

Our home was filled with the mouth-watering aroma of the two deep-dish pumpkin pies that were baking in preparation for our Thanksgiving dinner. My daughters anxiously waited as they peered through the oven's glass door and frequently checked the timer. Finally, the long hour had passed and the pies were ready. The children stood back as I donned oven mitts and opened the oven door. Their eyes lit up in anticipation as I gingerly reached in and began to remove the cookie sheet on which the pies had baked.

Unbeknownst to me, the oven mitts were damp. The searing heat permeated the mitts and I instinctively jerked my hands back in response. I dropped the pies! I stood bewildered, unable to move. The children looked on in horror. Then I began to cry.

With the utmost of sincerity, my nine-year-old daughter sheepishly asked, "Can we still eat it?"

Suddenly, my tears changed to contagious laughter. Soon we were all laughing! And we continued to laugh as we ate the pie right off the kitchen floor.

During my stint as wife and mother, I've learned that things seldom go according to plan. Life is always throwing you a curve—interruptions, last minute schedule changes, unexpected visitors, mishaps, and forgotten deadlines, just to name a few. I try to find the humor in every situation and it helps me to keep things in perspective.

Over the years I've baked many pies, but none as memorable, nor as special as the two that spilled. Through this small catastrophe, God blessed me with a beautiful memory of a special time shared with my daughters, a time filled with love and laughter.

When you have your next disaster, laugh! If you can't rewind time and make it turn out differently, then enjoy the moment. At the least, it'll be fuel for a future memory.

He will fill your mouth with laughter and your lips with shouts of joy.
Job 8:21

Record funny happenings on index cards and store them in a recipe box. In the future, you'll have a humorous collection of precious memories.

Traditional Terrific Coffee
GOLDEN KEYES PARSONS

The best of all gifts around any Christmas tree: the presence of a happy family all wrapped up in each other.
Burton Hillis

A scrawny tree with a few ornaments, a string of popcorn, and a paper chain was about the extent of Christmas decorations at my house when I was a child. Holidays and birthdays came and went without much fuss. They simply reflected a sadness which permeated my family. I diligently prayed for a happy, Christian family someday.

The first time I visited my fiancée's family during Christmas holidays, I was overwhelmed. A sparkling eight-foot tree, heavily laden with beautiful decorations, shimmered in the corner of the living room. Brightly wrapped gifts were stacked high on all sides of the tree. Every room of the house was decorated with twinkling lights, ribbons, candles, and wreaths . . . even the bathrooms! Laughter rang throughout the house. Christmas carols played on the stereo and a fire crackled in the fireplace.

There was abundance every place one looked in the house. But the abundance was not only in the decorations and the gifts. The abundance was in the love shared by the family. Love and acceptance were expressed in hugs and smiles and laughter.

And the food! The dining room table was replete with turkey and ham, dressing, steaming vegetables, homemade yeast rolls, and colorful salads. One could choose from an assortment of cakes, pies, cookies, and candy. I sampled them all, but my favorite was the toffee . . . crunchy and buttery with a touch of chocolate on top.

The toffee became a tradition as we established our family and now our girls make it for their families. We make literally dozens of batches each year to give as gifts. Some years we have even packaged it up to sell. The yummy confection doesn't stay around very long. It disappears as fast as we can make it. The recipe is very simple:

Traditional Terrific Toffee

In a heavy saucepan, melt one stick of real butter together with one cup of sugar, ¼ cup water, and a dash of salt. (Do not substitute margarine.) Bring to a boil over medium high heat stirring occasionally. Add ½ to ¾ cup chopped pecans. Boil until dark brown and smoking. (Don't take off of heat too soon. It needs to be a dark carmel color.) Pour onto an ungreased cookie sheet. Work quickly and spread as thin as you can. Cool. Melt one package of German sweet chocolate and pour on top. Add more finely grated pecans on top of chocolate. Cool. Break into pieces and enjoy!

To this day, every time I stand over that pot of boiling butter and sugar and the aroma fills my senses, I think of the abundance of that first Christmas with my soon-to-be husband. As my daughters prepare the toffee every holiday season, I pray they remember joyous, happy Christmases filled with laughter and an abundance of love. I trust that someday our grandchildren will have the same warm memories. As you prepare this recipe, celebrate the bounty and abundance God has poured out on your family.

The grace of our Lord was poured out on me abundantly,
along with the faith and love that are in Christ Jesus.

I Timothy 1:14

Free yourself from having to do everything the same way
every year at Christmas. Be creative.

Don't Blow Out The Candles

WILLIAM COLEMAN

There is no more lovely, friendly, or charming relationship, commun-
ion or company, than a good marriage.

Martin Luther

At a recent wedding I wanted to stand up in the middle of the ceremony and shout, "Stop! Stop!" Fortunately, I restrained the impulse—even with my primitive social skills I knew better than to do that. But I wanted to.

The service had reached the point where the bride and groom lighted a tall, white "unity" candle to demonstrate that they are now one. So far so good. Being one is an excellent idea. But then they blew out their individual candles, as though they were puffing themselves out. It gave me the jitters.

Can't the bride and groom become one person without extinguishing themselves? Can't there really be three people in a marriage? You, Me, and Us?

Love at its best should allow Me to become a better Me. That same benefit should be afforded to my spouse. Love does not squelch, shrink, or diminish either of us. And the better the You and Me are, the better the Us will be.

True love demands sacrifice on the part of each. However, love also stimulates and invigorates. Love promotes dreams. Love sets us free. Love dares us to stretch our wings and fly. Love was never designed to snuff anyone out.

Love frees us up to give, to help, to provide, to care, to share who we really are. Love will expand our possibilities and allow our personalities to ride new waves.

Who wants to snuff out the candle? No loving husband wants his wife to become less. No loving wife wants her husband to stop being him. Love gives life. In marriage two people do become one flesh, but they remain two people. When they get up in the morning, one can still choose pineapple juice while the other pours grapefruit.

At the next wedding the bride and groom should be a bit nervous. I might be sitting in the congregation. And when they light the unity candle and bring their own candles up to their lips, I just might forget my inadequate manners.

> . . . and live a life of love, just as Christ loved us and gave himself up for us
> as a fragrant offering and sacrifice to God.
>
> Ephesians 5:2

Put peanut butter on an apple and then cover with birdseed.
Put it out for the birds to enjoy.

Living and Giving Tree
KAYLEEN J. REUSSER

If I can stop one heart from breaking, I shall not live in vain.

Emily Dickinson

If your church is looking for a way to share Christmas with members experiencing tough times, create a "Living and Giving Tree." Unlike traditional

Christmas trees, a Living and Giving Tree doesn't sit in a corner. It's made up of people (living) who are helped by brothers and sister in Christ (giving). Here's how it works.

A Living and Giving Tree coordinator makes a list of people in the church who could use encouragement of some kind—single parents, shut-ins, the unemployed, those who have lost a loved one or who are experiencing a long-term illness. A staff minister or someone on the benevolence committee can help create the list.

The coordinator then contacts each person on the list, explaining that the church has organized the special program of caring during the Christmas season and asking if he or she would like to be included as a recipient.

Those reluctant to accept help can be told that the Living and Giving Tree was created out of love, not pity. No pressure should be applied however—the choice must rest with the individual.

The coordinator then writes the person's name in a notebook, along with phone number, address, and suggestion for assistance. Helping buy groceries, having dinner out, or simply spending an evening in someone's home are possible ideas, as well as financial assistance. All information should be kept confidential.

Once the coordinator has the final list of people, the names are written on small pieces of paper, which are then folded and stapled shut. While others could decorate the outside of the papers with festive stickers or symbols, only the coordinator should know the names inside. The "ornaments" are then attached to a paper or artificial tree positioned somewhere in the church so it can be easily seen.

People in the church who wish to participate pick one card from the tree the first Sunday in December. They then report the name they received to the coordinator, who stands next to the tree.

There's one unbreakable rule: No trading of names is allowed. This not only avoids confusion, but it encourages contact between people who might otherwise never cross paths. Those with the cards promise to contact the person whose name they picked before Christmas and arrange a suitable time for them to get together for their assistance.

We have seen many lives blessed and given a burst of encouragement during a potentially difficult season. Maybe your church would like to try it this Christmas season.

Carry each other's burdens, and in this way you will fulfill the law of Christ.
Galatians 6:2

> If a distant relative sends a gift for a child, put a picture of that relative on the gift so that the child can picture who it's from.

Hassle-Free Shopping
NAOMI WIEDERKEHR

The greatest use of life is to spend it for something that will outlast it.
William James

Do you dread Christmas shopping? Do people on your list have everything? Here's a suggestion.

As the holidays approach, send a note to each person on your list explaining your plans. Instead of buying a present, tell them you are going to give a gift in their name to a charity, an organization or needy person. Invite them to suggest something if they have a preference. Then later send a Christmas card telling which organization or need you supported in their name. Suggest that they put this card under their tree and open it Christmas morning.

When the day is over, others will have received gifts that warmed their hearts (and yours) in a special way.

Think of a persecuted Christian hugging his own Bible, of the hungry at a local mission eating a warm meal, of battered women and children at a shelter warmed with hope, of encouragement given to a new missionary seeking financial support or of an orphan feeling love by receiving one gift.

Can anything compare to this kind of Christmas giving and Christmas joy?

. . . if it is encouraging, let him encourage; if it is contributing to the needs of others, let him give generously; if it is leadership, let him govern diligently; if it is showing mercy, let him do it cheerfully.
Romans 12:8

When you see the stars in the sky, think of the Christmas candles you have lighted around the world through your giving this year.

Cinnamon Christmas Ornaments
CHRISTINE R. DAVIS

Remembrance like a candle, burns brightest at Christmas time.
Charles Dickens

One of the busiest months of the year is December, and even though there are hundreds of things to do to prepare for Christmas, I still enjoy making hand-crafted gifts for family, friends and co-workers. A handmade gift is heart-felt and shows the recipient he's remembered and special.

One of my favorite crafts is making cinnamon Christmas ornaments. These are made from easy-to-find ingredients and are fun for children or adults to make. These ornaments can be cut into any size or shape and fashioned into tree ornaments, strung on garlands or swags, or tied on packages and wreaths. They will last for years, but if they should lose their scent, a drop of cinnamon oil can be added to the back of the ornament. The "recipe" for these ornaments is as follows. Please note, however, these ornaments are *not edible* and are intended for crafting purposes only.

¾ cup applesauce (drained)
¼–½ cup Elmer's glue
1 cup cinnamon
2 tablespoons cloves
2 tablespoons allspice
2 teaspoons ginger
2 teaspoons nutmeg

Mix the ingredients together and knead well on a surface sprinkled with cinnamon until the consistency of cookie dough. Roll to ³/₈ inch and cut with cookie cutters. Make a hole in the top with a skewer or straw if you want to hang them.

Dry on waxed paper for seven to ten days, turning at least once daily to prevent the edges from turning up. Acrylic paints can be used to decorate or personalize. Use narrow ribbon or thread to hang.

Decorate your Christmas tree with these beauties or wrap some up as last-minute gifts for unexpected visitors. Most of all, enjoy!

On coming to the house, they saw the child with his mother Mary, and they bowed down and worshiped him. Then they opened their treasures and presented him with gifts of gold and of incense and of myrrh.
Matthew 2:11

Why not make lots of these little ornaments for sale at your church bazaar, along with instructions on how to make them?

The Value Of Rebounding

TONY EVANS

Today's mighty oak is just yesterday's little nut that held its ground.

Unknown

To professional basketball players, rebounding is an art form. Some players are considered highly valuable for their rebounding ability alone.

Why is rebounding such a valuable art in basketball? Because those guys miss a lot of shots! The ball doesn't go in the hoop. It bounces off the rim or caroms off the backboard. The winners are those who get the rebound and take another shot.

That's true in the Christian life, too. All of us take bad shots. We know where the hoop is and we have the ball, but somehow the two don't meet. The issue I'm concerned about is not so much the missed shot, but the rebound: what you do to get up and get back in the game.

Let me put it in other terms. If you have allowed something to replace your first love for Jesus Christ, there has been a missed shot somewhere. But the game isn't over. You can rebound, you can regain that first love for Christ and still come out a winner in the game of life. That's what Christ wants you to do.

Jesus replied: "Love the Lord your God with all your heart and with all your soul and with all your mind."

Matthew 22:37

Who do you admire that has persevered? Write them a note of thanks for their example.

Christmas Without Him?

SHERRIE WARD MURPHREE

They were looking for a king to slay their foes and lift them high.
God came, a little baby thing, that made a woman cry.
Unknown

One Christmas Sunday morning a visiting preacher at my church illustrated the need for us to keep Christ in Christmas in a way that I'll never forget. Before church began he removed, at random, a number of our hymnals from the book racks. The congregation wasn't aware of the removal.

As the worship song service began, I noticed others beside myself looking around for a song book. I stumbled along trying to sing without any words before me. I felt incomplete.

Then toward the end of the sermon the preacher said, "You may have noticed some books missing from the pews today. Is Christ's absence that noticeable when he's missing from Christmas celebrations? Just as you can't sing a song without the words, neither can you 'have' Christmas without Jesus. Receive Him today."

Sometimes we aren't even aware when Christ has been taken out of Christmas and then we begin to feel restless and dissatisfied. It happens so subtly. To fight that happening, we must consciously and specifically take steps to keep our focus on Him and make Him the center of everything we do.

Seek the LORD while He may be found; call on Him while He is near.
Isaiah 55:6

> If you need to travel on Christmas day, make it fun and special.
> Take your presents with you (the children won't mind being
> crowded with presents) and open one every fifteen miles,
> depending on the length of the trip. Savor the Christmas story
> from the Bible, reading and discussing one verse at a time.

Twelve Ways To Simplify Christmas
LETTIE J. KIRKPATRICK

*Even minor adjustments in how you celebrate the holidays can have
a major impact on how you feel about Christmas.*
Alice Slaikeu Lawhead

Since we all know Christmas can become a very busy time that can diminish our joy in the good news of Jesus' birth, here are a dozen ways to simplify.

1. Practice early giving. Baked items might be enjoyed more in early December. Christmas-oriented gifts such as ornaments, candle arrangements, Christmas books, seasonal jewelry or clothing, or advent calendars can be given ahead of the hectic holidays. Tickets to an upcoming Christmas event would be a considerate present.

2. Be alert and maintain an ongoing gift list throughout the year. When someone mentions a need, want, or interest, jot it down. You know what to buy and they are surprised at your thoughtfulness.

3. Budget for Christmas monthly and buy as you go!

4. Don't feel compelled to use *all* decorations every year. Alternate or downsize to favorites.

5. Buy in multiples when appropriate. Calendars, socks, lotions, and candles all make simple but appreciated small gifts for teachers, co-workers, or friends.

6. Prepare Christmas cards throughout the year. Fill a basket with cards, pens, address labels, and address book. Work on a few at a time in spare moments or while watching television. This even allows time for a short note and doesn't absorb a large block of time in an already hectic schedule.

7. Bag most gifts for quick wrapping. Gift bags now come in all shapes and sizes and can be purchased economically by good bargain shoppers.

8. Practice late giving! A neighbor put an after-Christmas poem in our mailbox and it was a day brightener. A platter of homemade goodies on New Year's Eve is a wonderful contribution to the celebration.

9. Consider theme gifts:
   • Fill an angel bag with an angel calendar, an angel mug, angel stickers, and angel notes.
   • Personalize for people according to their specialty. Give a cookbook, fancy paper towels or napkins, cookie cutters, and perhaps some chocolate chips or pecans to someone who enjoys baking. Follow this same line of thought for people who like to garden, do carpentry work, spend time on cars, etc.
   • Fix bath baskets with fragrant soaps, bath gel, lotion, and a scented candle. For more elegance include a lovely bath towel.

10. Bake ahead. Most cookies, candies, and breads freeze well.

11. Force yourself to think "Christmas" on December 26th and purchase discounted wrapping paper, napkins, cards, candles, and items which you'll need for the next year. This will save money and time next Christmas.

12. Set aside moments of quiet. Contemplate the babe in the manger and find the true wonder of the season.

Teach us to number our days aright that we may gain a heart of wisdom.
Psalm 90:12

> Evaluate your family's Christmas traditions. Take courage
> and discard or replace those that are stressful or
> have been outgrown.

Ho-Hum Christmas Morning

SHEILA RABE

*Many people miss Christmas, even though they celebrate parties,
decorations, and gifts...*

William Goetz

The lights from the tree cast a rainbow glow on the presents piled under it. Carols rang out from the stereo. Steaming mugs of cocoa scented the air, and a plate of breakfast pastries tempted our palates. The family perched on the sofa, swathed in warm bathrobes and smiles. Everything was perfect, and so . . . boring.

Where has the excitement of Christmas morning gone? I wondered. *I love gifts, I love my family, and I've got both right here. I should be ecstatic. What's the problem?*

It certainly wasn't that I was a female Scrooge. Every year I decorated, baked, shopped, and entertained. I had Christmas down to a system.

But this year, as the music leader at our church, my focus had centered on organizing a Christmas program for our community as well as our Christmas Eve program. And as I became immersed in focusing those events on the greatest gift in history, I found myself feeling a joy that had nothing to do with the boxes of decorations I'd hauled down from the attic or the tons of calories I'd been baking. The night of the program, our church's musicians never sounded better, and the drama had us alternately laughing and crying. On Christmas Eve, we gathered to read Luke's account of the Christmas story. We sang "Silent Night" by candlelight and pondered the meaning of the words: "Son of God, Love's pure light."

No wonder my Christmas morning seems anticlimactic. It is, I realized. The true celebration has already taken place. I have attended the real party and met the guest of honor, something with which the morning ritual around the tree just can't compete.

It dawned on me that I had long forgotten an important birthday principle. When I go to a birthday party, all I am required to do as a guest is enjoy the event and pay attention to the guest of honor. But all those Christmas mornings when we commemorate that most important of birthdays, I had been doing things backwards. I had shifted the focus from the One being honored to myself and the other guests. Like a child, I had been preoccupied with the party favors.

This Christmas, I will put things back in their proper order. I will go to the party and focus on the guest of honor. Granted, Christmas morning won't be as exciting as those in the past, but the season, itself, will be more meaningful. I will dig below the presents and tinsel and focus on what makes my soul rich. I will celebrate Christmas on a deeper level this year, and I'll finally understand Tiny Tim's famous words: "God bless us, every one." I don't need the big Christmas morning. I have already been blessed.

Thanks be to God for His indescribable gift!
II Corinthians 9:15

> Find one activity that will point your family to the real reason for Christmas and focus on that.

A Helpful Game

LINDA GILDEN

*In every job that must be done there is an element of fun. You find
the fun and snap! the job's a game.*

Mary Poppins

With Christmas just around the corner, my pre-Christmas chores seemed insurmountable. But I developed a plan for our family that allowed us to accomplish several of these tasks at once.

"C'mon everyone. We're going to play a game."

"Mom, I've got lots to do. Do we have to play?"

"Yes, this is a family game."

As soon as we finished with the supper dishes, I called everyone to the table. I produced a basket containing little pieces of paper. Each slip of paper described a job. After each person drew a job and understood their instructions, I set a timer.

For twenty minutes, each person worked at their first job. When the bell sounded, it was time to come back together and "draw" another job. The process continued until each person had done three different jobs over an hour's time.

Our jobs were things like:

1. Put candles in the windows—electric, of course.

2. Wrap presents. This is self-explanatory. Just be sure to have the presents and wrapping supplies in one place.

3. A smile face. This slip is important and necessary in every round of the drawing. His or her job is to "float" from job to job and make sure everyone is having a great time. Sometimes this means serving iced tea or hot choco-

late. Sometimes it means lending a hand for a few minutes to make someone else's easier. Sometimes it means sharing a smile or singing a carol.

4. Decorate the front porch or some specific area.

5. Make "rocks," our favorite holiday snacks.

The list could go on and on.

Our hour began with a reluctant crew of borderline Scrooges. When the last bell rang, the house was filled with a busy band of happy elves, each taking pride in how well and quickly he or she completed the assignment.

We gathered in the kitchen for a final sample of rocks. The smiles on the faces of our family elves said volumes. Our "game" had been a success!

How about putting your elves to work this holiday season? And as you do, here's the recipe for "Rocks."

2 cups chocolate chips
½ cup peanut butter
1½ cups dry roasted peanuts
1 12.3-oz. box Crispix cereal
Confectioner's sugar

1. Melt chocolate in a large bowl in microwave oven. Heat on high for 1 minute. Stir well. Heat 30 seconds more or as needed to melt chocolate. Stir until smooth. (Note: Chocolate may also be melted in a double boiler over low heat on the stove.)

2. Add peanut butter and stir until well blended.

3. Add peanuts and cereal and mix until thoroughly coated. A wooden spoon works best for this.

4. Put confectioner's sugar in a plastic bag. Add cereal mixture, close bag tightly, and shake gently until mixture is coated with sugar. If you do a third of the mixture at a time, it is easier to handle. Store in airtight container.

But as for you, be strong and do not give up, for your work will be rewarded.
II Chronicles 15:7

To eliminate procrastination, divide up tasks
into twenty minute segments.

The Early Bird
SANDRA PALMER CARR

Schedule your pleasure
Schedule your fun
Roast Mr. "T" early
And enjoy everyone!

Chuck Carr

Every Thanksgiving, magazine covers are graced with the golden brown turkey on a lovely glass platter. Mouth-watering recipes surround the bird with fancy napkins, candles, silver, and china plates all in a row.

Somewhere, perhaps out of sight, is the family turkey carver: Grandpa, Dad, or Uncle Tim. Maybe he's on the cover, poised with large fork and carving knife, wearing something too nice to stain. The apple cider has been poured into the crystal goblets. Dinner is ready.

But carving a turkey at the table is not as easy as it looks. Even without feathered wings, this bird could fly, given a loose fork, a slippery plate, and Aunt Carla's ready lap. It's a lot of work and clean-up before dirty dishes ever enter the picture.

My husband, Chuck, and I have found a simpler way. We cook the turkey about a week before Thanksgiving. He carves and I package white meat, dark, soup-size bites, and dressing into various sizes of plastic bags. Everything goes into the freezer, except the broth, which is refrigerated until the fat rises to the top. The fat is spooned off and the jelled broth is divided into snack-size plastic bags, and put into the freezer. Some will be used to add moisture to the meat when it is re-heated in the microwave on Thanksgiving Day. The rest is saved for soup broth.

Now I have several days to clean house, plan dessert, and the rest of the menu. Among my favorite dishes is Make-Ahead Mashed Potatoes. Here's the recipe:

MAKE-AHEAD MASHED POTATOES

8 large potatoes, pared
1 (8-oz.) package of cream cheese
1 (8-oz.) carton of sour cream
Salt and pepper to taste
Butter
Paprika

Boil potatoes until tender. Drain and mash. Add cream cheese, sour cream, salt, and pepper, mixing well. Pour into greased, 2-quart casserole. Top with pats of butter (optional). Cover and store in refrigerator several days or sprinkle with paprika and bake uncovered 35 minutes at 350 degrees (or cover and heat in microwave for 5 minutes or until heated through). Serves 8.

Add your own special family favorites, and dinner can be served before the children or grandchildren have finished off the olives and pickles.

A few extra hours on Thanksgiving Day might calm everyone's nerves a bit, making a better memory for the whole family. And that's another thing to be thankful for.

. . . he provides you with plenty of food and fills your hearts with joy.
Acts 14:17b

Buy a plain paper tablecloth and let your children or
grandchildren draw decorations on it. Help them design
matching name cards for each guest.

Eternity In Our Hearts

JOSEPH M. STOWELL

*I thank Thee, O Lord, that Thou hast so set eternity within my
heart that no earthly thing can ever satisfy me wholly.*

John Baillie

Paul Azinger was at the height of his professional golf career when the doctor told him that he had life-threatening cancer. Up to that moment he had not given much thought to dying. Life was too all-consuming for him to stop and consider the reality of the grave and all that is beyond. But that encounter with the inevitability of eternity was an abrupt reality check. His life would never again be the same. Even the $1.46 million he had made as a professional golfer that year paled to insignificance. All he could think about was what the chaplain of the tour had said: "We think that we are in the land of the living going to the land of the dying when in reality we are in the land of the dying headed for the land of the living."

Embracing the reality of the world to come radically alters everything in this world. Our values are prioritized and purified. Money, things, time, friends, enemies, family, and life itself are all adjusted to their appropriate worth and place.

If anyone should express the reality of eternity, it's those of us who have been guaranteed safe passage to the other side through Christ, our divine passport. Yet, interestingly, we who are marked with heaven in our hearts usually live as though it were real but irrelevant. We are consumed with the tyranny of the temporal, and both the character and power of a life with an eternal focus are traded for the ordinary.

We are not unlike the average person on the street who lives out his existence in the limited confines of a one-world point of view. Blinded to the reality of the world beyond, his all-consuming expectation is to experience maximum pleasure and prosperity here. Quality of life is measured in terms of accumulating stacks of stuff and ascending to platforms of power and position. Life is defined by eating this world's best food and drinking its best wines. Leisure and large doses of comfort shape the pursuit. Finding maximum peace and the thrill of maximum pleasure become an illusive quest—illusive because ultimately this world is, at best, a hollow experience and, at worst, leaves us disillusioned and in despair. When eternity is off the screen, all of life is compressed into the distorted assumption that this is all we have. And, frankly, it's never quite enough.

Why? Because we are built for eternity. We are built for an eternal, unhindered relationship with God, who created us to know the deep pleasure of His companionship.

> *He has made everything beautiful in its time.*
> *He has also set eternity in the hearts of men . . .*
> Ecclesiastes 3:11

Write down five things you're looking forward to
when you get to heaven.

Watch Out For The Snakes

Martha B. Yoder

The Christian life is one of sharp focus on Jesus.
Raymond P. Brunk

Recently I was impressed with how ridiculous the order from Moses to the Israelites must have sounded. "Look up to this brass snake as God commands. You will be healed of your snake bites and you will live," Moses pleaded.

That is not sensible. Snakes need to be killed! Shut up their holes! Treat those bites immediately!

What good comes from looking to a pole draped with a brass snake? And Moses was saying it was God's remedy! How incredible!

But those who obeyed Moses' pleading received instant healing. It did work! Looking in obedience to that raised snake brought life!

"Just as Moses lifted up the snake in the desert, so the Son of Man must be lifted up, that everyone who believes in Him may have eternal life" (John 14:15)

When "snakes" of depression begin to tangle around, causing my spirit to fall from joy, I must look up to Jesus, to see what He has done for me. Then I sense healing.

When "snakes" of self-pity bite painfully, nothing brings relief until I focus on Jesus. He gives me a new song and self is dethroned.

When "snakes" of frustration for work not completed because of overwhelming fatigue come, I must look up to Jesus. He lifts my fatigue while I lie on my bed. He gives gifts of peace and rest as I thank Him for His goodness.

When "snakes" of retaliation come, wanting to take revenge for how I'm hurt, my focus must shift from self to Jesus. He reminds me He suffered much. Should I expect to be free from suffering if I am truly His child?

What "snakes" do you have to fight? Do you keep using your own remedies? Or have you learned to look up to Jesus? He is our true Remedy!

He will call upon me, and I will answer him; I will be with him in trouble, I will deliver him and honor him.

Psalm 91:15

Fold a paper towel and place in the resealable plastic bag before filling with freshly washed and drained leaf lettuce. It will soak up remaining moisture, lengthening the freshness of the lettuce.

Pick Me, Pick Me!

KELLY BELL

God does not ask us to understand His ways in order to accept them, He simply asks us to say yes to Him.

Cynthia Heald

Remember back when you were a kid, and it was time to pick teams? Some kids just sat quietly, silently, hoping that their name would be called. But then there were other kids who just couldn't sit still. They would jump up and down, yelling, "Pick me! pick me!" at the top of their lungs! I was one of those kids. I was ready, willing, and very eager to play, and I couldn't wait to be picked.

In the Old Testament, there was a prophet named Isaiah. God was looking for a servant who was willing to be His mouthpiece. Isaiah reminds me of one of those kids who would scream, "Pick me!" Isaiah didn't wait to be chosen, he said, "Here am I. Send me!" (Isaiah 6:8). He wasn't waiting passively to be picked, he asked to be chosen for the job. (I can just see him jumping up and down.)

How willing are we to be used for God? How excited are we to do His work? Are we waiting passively to be picked, or are we asking to be chosen?

Next time you see two teams choosing up sides, think about their response. When God looks for a player, will you be first in line?

Show me your ways, O LORD, teach me your paths.
Psalm 25:4

Find practical help for getting organized from *Clutterology* by Nancy Miller, available through www. roundsmiller.com.

It Helps, Girl, When You Read The Instructions

JERI CHRYSONG

Personally, I'm always ready to learn,
although I do not always like being taught.

Sir Winston Churchill

As a legal secretary, I am bombarded with rules. Rules of the Court, Local Rules, subsections to Rules, and individual Judges' Rules. So when faced with a six-inch list of rules and instructions on the back of a new shower cleaner, I balked. "How difficult can this be?" I asked myself. Just "Spray On and Wipe off," the perky housewife on TV told me.

So, I grasped my newly purchased bottle of the fresher smelling shower cleaner, unscrewed the safety valve, stepped into my shower, and sprayed with a vengeance. I marveled at how quickly the shower cleaned itself. I knew I was dealing with a dangerous chemical so I closed the bathroom door, shutting out my children and dogs.

I began vigorously scrubbing the more difficult areas and soon my shower was gleaming—but I was gasping for air! I stumbled out into the fresher air of my bedroom to take a deep breath but the burning sensation in my chest cut short any deep inhalation. Alarmed, I fled the death chamber, closing the door behind me, sealing the fumes in my bedroom and shower.

The toxic punch which jarred me awake early the next morning was the first clue that I should have opened a window or two before going to sleep. The fumes had permeated my sinus cavities during the night and it seemed that a layer or two of the protective lining surrounding my lungs had corroded.

A shaft of early morning sunlight reflecting off the faucet penetrated my thickened eyelids. My neck snapped when I jerked my head back at the unexpected brightness. Yet these discomforts were forgotten when I saw my sparkling shower. The end did justify the means, it seemed, until the steam from my shower reactivated the toxic cleaner. I began to feverishly rub my eyeballs with the heels of my hands and the energy of a runaway train.

When the burning subsided, I finally read the bottle's instructions. Had I done so first, I would have known to properly ventilate my bathroom and that opening a window the size of a ship's porthole is not considered proper ventilation. I would have known I was working with a powerful eye irritant—if I'd read the instructions.

But I don't like countless rules and there seem to be so many these days. But Jesus makes everything simple. He says there are really only two rules: love God first wholeheartedly, then your neighbor as you would yourself. You won't go wrong if you do—or lose your ability to breathe!

Jesus replied, "'Love the Lord your God with all your heart and with all your soul and with all your mind. This is the first and greatest commandment, and the second is like it: 'Love your neighbor as yourself.'"

Matthew 22:37–39

As you clean house, thank the Lord for each item you clean.
It makes the task "friendlier."

The Whole Armor

HELEN LUECKE

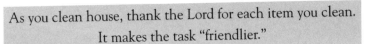

One reason sin flourishes is that it is treated like a cream puff instead of a rattlesnake.

Billy Sunday

I glanced out the front door and saw a jumbo grasshopper eating on my yellow rosebush. Armed with only a pencil, I raced out to shoo the pesky insect away. He looked at me and continued to chew. I pounded on his skinny legs with the pencil but he only looked annoyed. I thumped on his head and beat on his legs. Finally, he loosened his hold, jumped off, and vanished behind a tree.

I thought of the many times Satan and I had met on the battlefield. Unarmed and unprepared, I was no match for the prince of darkness. How he must have laughed as I tapped in a halfhearted attempt at my large sins and thumped on the small ones.

Like that pesky grasshopper, sin can grab hold of us and hang on. If we fail to fight, it soon becomes a part of us and no longer seems like sin.

As we battle Satan, our strength must come from the Lord's mighty power within us. Each day we must put on the whole armor of God so that we will be able to withstand all the tricks, schemes, and stumbling blocks Satan hurls at us.

Our armor should consist of:

- believing the truth about God and His perspective of life
- knowing my standing with God is based on Jesus' death in my place

- being prepared to offer the gift of salvation to whomever God might lead me to
- trusting that God is completely in control and I can trust Him
- being assured that nothing will separate me from God's love
- studying the Bible so that I can grow in my faith.

Is your armor shiny or rusting? Get it sparkling clean today.

Put on the whole armor of God so that you can take your stand against the devil's schemes.

Ephesians 6:11

If you have pets, consider a pet supply organizer called "The Pet Pockets" from Together Enterprises (800) 746-9604.

"They're Little Kids, Gram"

JUNE L. VARNUM

In the fragileness of childhood, a piece of candy ranks right up with teddy bears and one-of-a-kind blankets.

June L. Varnum

"They need some candy," Crystal called as she tossed a small sack of gummy bears into the partially filled box of food. "Here's a bag of Tootsie Rolls for the family you have, Gram. Don't they have three children?"

Two afternoons a week for three hours, my teenage granddaughter and I filled requests for food at the community food bank. Basics included food for the evening meal and breakfast the following morning. Depending upon the needy person's situation, lunch items often were included. After boxing the usual staples, we helpers were free to add extras as available.

Relying on my grandmotherly "wisdom," I had been bagging only nourishing food stuffs. After all, nutrition was important. Empty stomachs surely needed to be filled with those vital vitamins and minerals. However, I'd overlooked one important fact: the joy a piece of candy gives to a child.

Quickly checking off the requested items on my list, I hurried to the waiting area. I nudged the bag of candy onto the top of the food items and gave the box to the clerk. Stopping just inside the warehouse door, I peeked out. The dad's tired face seemed to light up. Mom smiled and slowly held up the candy as three pairs of little hands reached. "Oh, Mommy! Candy!"

Often we can't right the wrongs in our world. But sometimes we can ease the hurts and hardships with a little kindness—a little "sugar," especially for the children.

Behind me, Crystal whispered, "They're little kids, Gram. They need some candy."

Even a child is known by his actions, by whether his conduct is pure and right.
Proverbs 20: 11

Invite a young child to make candy or popcorn balls with you.
Package them and deliver to a homebound person.

It Doesn't Matter
MARILYN NEUBER LARSON

We don't solve our problems, we simply learn to live with them.
Unknown

In my years of teaching fourth grade in public school, I learned an important lesson. It came from a wise old sage who served as substitute custodian for a short time. One Wednesday afternoon while he emptied the wastebaskets, I complained about a classroom incident.

He looked at me and said, "Will that matter next year?"

I shook my head.

"Will it matter next month?" he asked.

I shrugged and answered, "Absolutely not."

He smiled and asked another question. "Will it even matter tomorrow?"

"No," I admitted with a giggle. "It doesn't even matter now."

He picked up his broom and said, "Then just remember to tell yourself 'It doesn't matter.' Life is filled with insignificant trifles to worry us, but analyze them and you'll see, they just don't matter."

I needed to apply this lesson when my life turned so hectic and frantic that it became a monumental task to make the bed or dust the furniture. It taught me to focus on true priorities. The dust really didn't matter. When it did, I dusted.

It was also applicable when friends needed encouragement and lifting up more than I needed sleep. And it pertained when forgiveness and reconciliation became even more urgent than my selfish pride.

As a result of concentrating on this simple, yet significant principle, I've discovered some meaningful truths. People and relationships are important, not which person is in control. True friendship is more valuable than possessions. Children are precious; the messes they create can be cleaned up.

Think about it. Some issues can upset us if we let them. Yet we can choose how to react when we don't get our way, when people are grouchy, or when we're shoved and jostled on someone else's agenda. In many of these instances we can choose to reply, "It doesn't matter."

But some things *do* matter. Jesus said, "I have come that they may have life, and that they may have it more abundantly." God created us to have a relationship with Him. Our first priority should be to love Him and to invest our time to know Him in a personal way.

Let's face it. This life will never be perfect. The next time you're confronted with an insignificant problem that threatens to drag you down or steal your joy, you can choose to say, "It doesn't matter."

*I will instruct you and teach you in the way you should go; I will counsel you
and watch over you.*

Psalm 32:8

Make a list of things that interfere with God's abundance
in your life. How many of them really don't matter?
Pray and ask the Lord to diminish their importance
in your mind and heart.

A $100 Gift

Edwin Louis Cole

Liberality consists less in giving much than in giving
at the right time.

Jean de la Bruyere

I learned my lesson years ago. A pastor friend named Gerald and I were
crossing the Puget Sound on a ferry, going from his hometown of Port Orchard to Seattle, to attend a gathering of men and ministers. In the throes of
the final week of a forty-day fast, sensitive to God's Spirit, I felt a strong urge
to give Gerald the one hundred dollars in my billfold. It was the only money
I had. With the action came a surge of well-being, expansiveness, completeness, from both the obedience of the act and from the generous nature of it.
I felt a great sense of accomplishment in my obedience.

Going home from the meeting, Gerald said, "Ed, it's good you gave me
that hundred because I gave it to the minister in the meeting who fell off his
ladder, broke his arm, and didn't have money for doctor bills. I figured he
needed it more than I did."

As he spoke, I became upset with him. No, I was mad. That was my last
hundred, and when I gave it to him, I never expected he would give it away.

185

My expansiveness, well—being, completeness shrank to nothing because he gave my money away. How dare he?

About the time I thought all this, I heard the still, small voice of the Holy Spirit in my mind and heart bringing me the words of Jesus.

"Did I tell you to give it?" He asked.

"Yes, Lord," I answered in my mind.

"Did you give it to Me?"

"Yes, Lord."

"Your reward is in your obedience to Me and does not rest on what others do with what I tell you to give!"

Okay, that was it. Once given—out of my control.

From that moment to this, I have never worried concerning contributions. I don't worry about what others do with what I give. At times I even give with the smallest urging to those I am not sure will deal righteously with my gift. They will give an account to God for their disposition of the monies, not to me.

Jesus answered, "If you want to be perfect, go, sell your possessions and give to the poor, and you will have treasure in heaven. Then come, follow me."
Matthew 19:21

When talking with friends or new acquaintances, try using their name frequently. You'll make them feel special.

Let Us Hasten To His Throne

Avis McGriff Rasmussen

O God, whose throne is heaven, whose footstool is the earth below, whose arms enlace the firmament, nothing is hidden from thy sight . . . in the deep recesses of the human heart, thou see'st every secret thought. O God, my Savior, I turn to thee.

Margaret of Navarre

Today is another opportunity to seek God's face. What will we choose? Will we rush into the day, relying on the spiritual reserves from yesterday? Or will we hasten to the foot of God's holy throne, to be prepared for this new day?

It's easy to begin the day on our own; after all, we are a resourceful people. We hit the alarm snooze button a few times, then climb out of bed and begin a new day. Of course, only after we have a jolt of caffeine, or perhaps exercise, do we feel able to take on the world. We may even convince ourselves that we'll be "okay," if we just keep moving. But we can't function at our best without heeding God's daily guidance. And only He knows how to prepare us for what the day will bring.

We are God's creation; only He truly understands our thoughts and desires. If you could spend unlimited time with your dearest friend, would you hesitate? How would it feel for you to pray, cry, or sing, with someone who truly knows your heart's desires, your life-long dreams? Would you feel refreshed after having such meaningful, caring interaction with your friend? Would you adore that friend? Consider your time with God as a visit with your closest friend—your soul mate.

Yes, I know what it's like to be busy. And I have missed many opportunities to worship at my Master's feet. When I rush into my day, driven by "things to do," God gently reminds me that He is my first priority—my first love. Have you heard His reminder to pause and rest at His feet?

As you kneel before Him, ask Him to warm your heart with His love and equip your mind with His truth. He is your dearest Friend. He loves you unconditionally. Don't wait for a time of crisis to hasten to the throne. Enjoy a daily time of worship, seeking His wisdom.

"For I know the plans I have for you . . . plans to prosper you and not to harm you, plans to give you hope and a future. Then you will call upon Me and come and pray to Me, and I will listen to you. You will seek Me and find Me when you seek Me with all your heart."
Jeremiah 29:11–13

Choose a consistent time to meet with God each day. Keep a journal of any special insights the Lord shares with you.

The Apple Of My Grandmother's Eye
KATHLEEN HAGBERG

Music, when soft voices die, vibrates in the memory—odors, when sweet violets sicken, live within the sense they quicken.
Percy Bysshe Shelley

Forty years later I can close my eyes and return to my grandmother's mahogany dressing table for our Saturday night ritual. The tools for our ritual are spread out on a doily: comb, brush, hand mirror, and china bowl brimming with pins.

"Now, Petty, you hand me the pins."

"Petty" was my grandmother's choice term of endearment for her loved ones. Facing the smoky oval mirror, I remember my grandmother's attention to each curl. The last pin curl set securely in place, she drew a scarf from her bureau to secure her handiwork. Later, my cheeks relaxed into a feathered pillow as I drifted off to sleep, inhaling the lilac scent permeating her scarf.

My comb-out in the early Sunday dawn completed our ritual. As my grandmother unlocked the bobby pins, a cascade of ringlets bounced upon my shoulders. Lucille brushed out the tightly wound spirals, blending them into layers of waves. Bright morning sun peeked under the window awning, then flooded her bedroom, spotlighting the gold and red highlights of my hair.

My approval of her work generated a smile on her face as wide as the brim of the hat she placed upon my head. Our ritual completed, I slipped on my white cotton gloves for church. We posed silently for one last second before the mirror's eye, my cheeks tingling from the afterglow of our ritual.

Over the years, memories of our ritual aged like wine stored in a cellar made more valuable for the fermenting. As my grandmother's grandchild, I knew I was loved. But only as an adult would I see that it was her delight in me which characterized our relationship. To be loved is to taste of grapes. To be delighted in is to taste vintage wine.

Whom do you love? Do you also delight in them? How can you express both your love and your delight today?

Children's children are a crown to the aged . . .
Proverbs 17:6a

You don't really need negatives of photographs since reprints can be made from the printed picture.

Home Is A Place In The Heart

KATHLEEN HAGBERG

Home is where you hang your memories.

Charles Angoff

Long before my husband and I moved to the country I dreamed of owning a vintage house. As the realtor walked us through the "handyman special," I knew I had found the house of my dreams. It had several fireplaces, wide pine floors . . . charm to boot. Just like my heroine, Laura Wilder from *Little House on the Prairie*, I dreamed of wearing long skirts to decorate our antique home, bake bread, and make jam using the wild blackberries growing out back. Our rolling parcel of land, once a grazing field, would render a bountiful vegetable and flower garden for dining by candlelight. Dreams and ideas by the dozen made me giddy with anticipation.

What I had not logged into our plans was the birth of our colicky first son, Paul, who arrived nine months after we moved into our handyman special. Our second child, Steffen, was born two years later. He learned to climb before he learned to walk. Our pint-sized gymnast forced us to barricade our two steep staircases with double-decker gates.

That old house never had a chance. Long flowing skirts never escaped the closet. The only candles we lit were for frequent power outage. As for the garden; the few perennials found themselves in the path of my two active boys and the groundhogs ate the veggies.

My dreams of renovating that old house didn't die quickly or easily. Only in retrospect would I learn that dreams create possibilities, not memories. Life creates the memories.

Ten years into our second house, these are the reminders of our first home which remain: snapshots of two sons returning home hand in hand with their father from a "bear hunt" in the woods, knotty pine floors swallowing up our boys' marbles, blackberries picked fresh—more eaten on the spot than we could ever save for making jam.

I had to let my dreams die before they could return to me as something better . . . memories.

Are some of your unfulfilled dreams an obstacle to appreciating the memories? If you harbor disappointment because your dreams weren't accomplished, try focusing on the abundance of the good memories and allow those to replace the disappointment.

> *As for the saints who are in the land, they are the glorious ones*
> *in whom is all my delight.*
>
> Psalm 16:3

Need help dealing with clutter? Contact Messies Anonymous:
(305) 271-8404.

Comforting New Babies

JEANNE ZORNES

Life is made of simple days, pieced together with love.
Seen on a gift plaque

I love babies, and I love baby showers. But I also know our budget means I can't afford many of the ready-made clothes and baby gadgets usually given at showers. Instead, I give a very special item, something which is unmistakably "me" and thoroughly used: a patchwork baby blanket. My total cost, depending on the sales at the fabric store: between $6 and $10. Time involvement: two hours.

People who know I sew often give me their fabric scraps, providing me with a colorful, generous supply from which I cut five-inch squares. I sew them together—eight across, ten down—with no regard to pattern except to have as colorful an arrangement as possible. A yard and a half of packing fabric (often I'll ask the mother-to-be for her preference for color or pattern), a layer of batting (I wait for half-price sales), and a session of tying each square with yarn brings each blanket to completion.

I tell the young moms the colorful side gives baby something interesting to look at. But it also quietly conveys a number of messages.

One is that "frugal" doesn't mean ugly. We've lived so long with a throwaway mentality that everything has to be brand-new or "match"—or it's not wanted. There's beauty in second-chance—whether a refinished chair, a remodeled house, or a patchwork blanket.

The other message is that God delights in variety. No baby is like another. Some may have dark sides to their temperaments, like that navy corduroy left over from sewing a toddler's pull-up pants. Others may be sunny and fun, like the cotton scrap of big daisies that came from a little girl's play dress.

Though my pace of sewing has slowed in recent years as I focused on other ministries, I've probably sewn 200 patchwork baby blankets over the past two decades. It's fun to walk through our church foyer and see babies wrapped in these one-of-a-kind blankets. Or to notice a grim-faced toddler clutching one of my blankets, now very chewed and fatigued. One little girl "loved" her blanket so much that it eventually became a foot-square rag!

God has supplied generously for my blanket projects, even with gifts of batting and backing fabric. In gratitude, I made some blankets I dropped off at the hospital and pro-life ministry for their layettes for the needy—trusting He knew just which babies should have them.

At times I wondered if I was wasting time on these home-sewn gifts. But I've gained much pleasure in using what might otherwise be thrown away. And the hour or so it takes to tie the blankets has become a sacred time for me. While I sit at my kitchen table pulling a needle in and out of squares, I pray for the baby, its family, and others God brings to mind. Sometimes I turn on the

Christian radio station and let its music fill my heart with worship.

Every baby comes as God's reminder that He has not yet given up on man. He blankets us with His love. I find that truth quite, well, comforting!

He gathers the lambs in His arms and carries them close to His heart;
He gently leads those that have young.

Isaiah 40:11b

Patchwork blankets do not take a great deal of sewing skill; neither does another very handy baby item: burp cloths. Simply sew together two pieces of flannel, big enough to amply cover a shoulder (about 12x18 inches).

Needless Worry

VEDA BOYD JONES

I am an old man and have known a great many troubles,
but most of them never happened.

Mark Twain

When my oldest son left for college, I lay awake at night worrying about him. Had he gone to class? Did he have enough money? Was he driving safely? Was he in his dorm room? Did he like his roommate?

For two weeks I couldn't take his place mat off our round kitchen table. When I did, the four placemats that were left looked as lost as I felt.

I played "what if." What if his car broke down? What if he didn't pass his classes? What if he got sick?

One day I looked at the answer to all those "what if" questions. If something bad happened, I would be notified. If something bad happened, God would give me the strength to deal with it. But most important: what if I quit trying to predict my son's life and let him live it? What if I simply had faith in him to make good decisions?

Now when I think of my son, I think positive thoughts. What if he has a wonderful day? Just like mine.

Do not be anxious about anything, but in everything, by prayer and petition, with thanksgiving, present your requests to God.
Philippians 4:6

When you plan an event, think of several ways of doing it. Then if something doesn't go exactly as it should, you can fall back on an alternative plan.

Finishing Well

JERRY JENKINS

The future is purchased by the present.
Samuel Johnson

I find it amusing when the eyes of people born in the '60s glaze over at the mention of the assassination of John F. Kennedy, the Beatles phenomenon, Vietnam.

Do you realize that Watergate is three times as long ago to our kids than World War II was to my generation when we were in grade school in the '50s? Think of that! When my father spoke of Pearl Harbor, of Iwo Jima, of Hiroshima, of the end of the war, he was speaking of something more than three times as recent to him as my high school graduation is to me now. World War II was fewer than ten years old.

Thirty-two years ago I graduated from high school. Twenty years before then, the war had just ended. Skeletal survivors of the Nazi death camps had just been freed. Twenty years before that, Babe Ruth hit sixty home runs, and the stock market hadn't even crashed.

It was so recent. So recent. And it's worse heading the other way, isn't it? High school graduation seems like yesterday, and thirty-two years from now I'll be in my 80's. I hope. My three boys will be grown, likely married, fathers. I'll be married to a grandmother.

Someone explained to me once that time accelerates as you get older because each succeeding year is a smaller fraction of your total. Makes sense. Remember how a school day seemed like years and a school year seemed forever? Such nine-month segments now simply cause people to say, "Seems like yesterday was New Year's. Here it is September."

Here it is September. People older than I think I'm silly for feeling old, when they'd just as soon trade places. In many ways, I still feel like a kid, still getting to know my wife after nearly thirty years of marriage. But I'm no kid anymore. The mirror doesn't lie.

Life is fun and funny, but melancholy when it breezes by. When I shake my head at the vapor that has already appeared for half an instant and is beginning to fade away, all I want to do is to remind myself that I could very well live again as long as I've already lived.

And I want above all else to redeem the time.

Let us not become weary in doing good, for at the proper time we will reap a harvest if we do not give up.

Galatians 6:9

Purchase inexpensive baskets for grouping items together, thus adding beauty and organization.

The Palace And Pumpkin Pie Cake

LYNN D. MORRISSEY

You do not have to be rich to be generous. If he has the spirit of true generosity, a pauper can give like a prince.

Corinne U. Wells

During overwhelming pressures of writing my first book, my husband, Michael, and I escaped to a private piano recital in a thirty-five room mansion—a stone labyrinth sprawled atop bluffs overlooking the Mississippi. I thought this simple excursion would offer soothing respite when I needed it most. Instead, I fidgeted in the palatial surroundings, afraid to breathe, lest I collide with the abundance of ivory, silver, marble, and china that filled every cranny.

After savoring a five-course repast around an elegant dining table, I hesitated to approach the hostess, awed by her wealth and prominence. I wanted her recipe for Pumpkin Pie Cake, the luscious dessert I'd just enjoyed. She asked me to wait, then casually talked to her other guests. I found her delay intimidating and wanted to leave. Fortunately, I had no recourse but to wait.

After the final guest had departed, she invited Michael and me to her kitchen, took off her shoes, and set a tea kettle to boil. She also sliced up more of the delectable dessert. We sat, sipped, nibbled, and chatted long into the evening.

My feelings of intimidation soon turned to captivation. She had a warmth and down-to-earth homeyness, and shared her recipe with me. I realized that I had wrongly judged her, assuming that someone owning such opulence would also own a pretentious spirit. Instead, she was simply charming and generous, opening her home to share her possessions, talents, and time.

Now, whenever I make her scrumptious Pumpkin Pie Cake, I am amazed that such an extraordinarily simple recipe can yield such an abundantly rich dessert. And I am reminded of the gracious hostess who shared her recipe from the simple abundance of her heart.

Pumpkin Pie Cake

1 regular can unsweetened pumpkin
1 can evaporated milk (11 or 12 oz.)
1 tsp. salt
2 tsp. cinnamon

1 tsp. pumpkin pie spice
1¾ cup granulated sugar
4 eggs

Topping:
2 sticks butter, melted
1 box yellow cake mix
    (dry–straight from the box, unprepared)

1 cup pecans, chopped

Mix first seven ingredients in mixer, pour into 13 x 9 ungreased baking pan, evenly sprinkle dry cake mix over mixture, then pecans, then melted butter. Bake in preheated oven at 350 degrees F. for 1 hour and 15 minutes, or until inserted knife comes out clean. Cut into preferred-sized squares. Refrigerate or serve warm. Garnish with whipped cream, if desired.

Command those who are rich in this present world not to be arrogant nor to put their hope in wealth, which is so uncertain, but to put their hope in God, who richly provides us with everything for our enjoyment. Command them to do good, to be rich in good deeds, and to be generous and willing to share.

I Timothy 6:17–18

In the autumn, when pumpkins are in season, cut off their tops, scoop out the "insides," and use the shells as tureens for serving soup or a casserole contents.

Color Blind

MARILYN J. HATHAWAY

I do not understand Your ways, but You know the way for me.
Dietrich Bonhoeffer

There was no denying that I was worried. It was a clear sunny day in Utah, but it was raining in Iowa. I wasn't surprised. It was always raining in Iowa.

Jim and I had moved to Salt Lake City with our three children in 1968 and annually cruised Interstate-80 on the two-and-a-half day journey from Utah to Northern Ohio to visit our families. Four out of five trips it was raining across Iowa. Not a misty drizzle, but a torrential downpour. The kind where the visibility is so poor you are afraid to keep going, but reluctant to pull onto the side and park for fear of being hit by another car.

But this time I wasn't worried about us driving, it was my parents who would be traveling to visit us. The weather service had issued tornado warnings for Iowa and I was worried.

All I could do was pray. As I beseeched God for their safety, a strange picture flashed into my mind. I saw a tan car speeding along a highway in a driving rain. Over the car and moving with it was a giant hand, stretched out like an umbrella. I was shaken by the image; however, since my parents owned a dark blue car I continued to worry.

The following afternoon as I stood in the sunny front yard watching for the blue car, I heard the honk of a horn behind me. Turning, I was shocked to see the car that had just passed the house pull into the driveway. It was a shiny late model tan car with my beaming Dad at the wheel, delighted with his surprise.

"Lord, forgive me for doubting You," I prayed, as I rushed to greet my safe and happy parents.

In light of all my past blessings, I cannot understand why I still doubt God so often. My life could be so abundantly simple if I would ignore my earthly "wisdom" and learn to just trust.

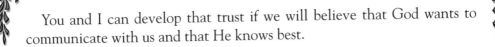

You and I can develop that trust if we will believe that God wants to communicate with us and that He knows best.

Even after Jesus had done all these miraculous signs in their presence,
they still would not believe in Him.

John 12:37

Never shop when you are depressed. You will buy too much.

Motivation During The Golden Years
LEEANN S. YAMAKAWA

Today is all you have, so live each day to its fullest.
Mamie Mucullough

My 89-year-old grandmother lost her "wheels" when she was 87 because of a mild stroke that took away her peripheral vision. She was always active in church and community activities, even up until the time of her stroke. Her activity suddenly became extremely limited, and she had to give up a great deal of her independence. In many ways, it has been a difficult adjustment for her to make. She can no longer minister to others in the way she has in the past and wishes she still could. She cannot go wherever she wants whenever she wants.

However, God is using her in a unique way. She prays every day for every member of our extended family as well as a myriad of others. Once when she told me that she didn't feel very useful anymore, I assured her that there was nothing that could be more useful than her intercessory prayer. I'm thrilled to know that she prays for me every day.

It can be very easy for any in their golden years to lose motivation for serving the Lord because their capabilities may be diminished. They could become discouraged. However, God still has every person here for a purpose. He still has work for each of us to do, regardless of our age.

We have a great example as we view the apostle Paul. He was an older man who was physically worn out and had suffered greatly for the cause of Christ when he wrote, "For to me to live is Christ and to die is gain" (Philippians 1:21). Then later he says that he would like to see Jesus in heaven but that he also wants to be available to help his fellow Christians here on earth.

Why could the apostle Paul say this? Because he had a spirit of selflessness. He was more concerned about what was beneficial for the sake of others than his own comfort. He didn't allow himself to wallow in self-pity.

Chuck Swindoll has said, "Please don't forget. God has decided to let you live this long. Your old age is not a mistake . . . nor an oversight . . . nor an afterthought." In other words, don't lose your motivation in your golden years. God still needs you!

God never considers you a nobody no matter what your age!

And whatever you do, whether in word or deed, do it all in the name of the Lord Jesus, giving thanks to God the Father through Him.
Colossian 3:17

Write down ten characteristics you want to have in your life in your older years.

True Riches

VIVIAN LEE BANIAK

There are two ways of being rich. One is to have all you want and the other is to be satisfied with what you have.

E. C. McKenzie

When our grown son was about five years old, my husband and I discussed whether he was ready to begin receiving an allowance. To determine this, we tried a little experiment. My husband called our son aside one night after dinner and gave him 20 pennies. He hold him they were his. Two or three days later, my husband asked our son to account for the pennies. Our boy raced into his bedroom and brought back seven or eight shiny pennies.

"Where are the rest of the pennies I gave you?" inquired my husband.

"Oh," he replied, "I gave some to my friend Josh across the street, I threw some over Grandpa Thomas' fence next door, and I think some might still be under my bed."

After this encounter, it seemed obvious to us that our son was not yet ready to handle an allowance. He had not yet learned several things: to keep money in a safe place, to use it wisely, and to account for what he had been given. This scene with our son seemed disturbingly familiar to me. Could there be a parallel between how we decided whether our son was ready to handle money and how our Heavenly Father determines whether or not we are able to handle more money than we have now?

God entrusts to our stewardship a certain amount of money and waits to see what we're going to do with it. As described in the parable of the talents in Matthew 25:14–30, we are entrusted with material blessings according to our ability. Will He find us faithful and handling what He gives us according to Biblical principles of financial management? Will we be able to give an account to Him for what He entrusts to us? Or will we be like our son at age five who really had no concept of stewardship and accountability?

God uses the test of how we handle our money to determine whether we are ready to handle true riches. Material riches are for this lifetime only, but true riches go on with us into eternity. True riches are things like deeper spiritual insight into God's Word, understanding Him on a more intimate level, wisdom in handling material wealth for eternal purposes, peace of mind and generosity. Ask God to show you which riches you are seeking after.

So if you have not been trustworthy in handling worldly riches,
who will trust you with true riches?

Luke 16:11

Make a goal to begin paying cash instead of using credit cards for your purchases and set up a plan to pay off your credit card debt.

I Quit!

KELLY BELL

It doesn't take much to say, "I quit."
It takes a lot more to say, "I'll try."

Thelma Wright

Once upon a time, long, long ago (twenty years to be exact), I quit while running a race. I can still see it like it was yesterday. The place: El Dorado Park in Long Beach, California. The event: a cross-country meet. The reason . . .

Usually I do well under pressure. It was my first year running cross-country at Long Beach State. Actually, it was my first year to run cross-country at all! My parents usually didn't come to my meets, but this time they did and

I was nervous! I wanted so badly to impress them. I wanted them to be proud of me. But I wasn't doing well in my running that season. In cross-country, you have some good days and some bad days. Well, this day wasn't a good one.

During the race, a jumble of thoughts tumbled through my mind. What will my parents think? Will they be embarrassed? What if they think I always run this slowly?

So . . . I did the unthinkable. I quit. I didn't just stop and say, "That's it." I pulled up lame. My leg was a little sore, so I blamed it on that. "I might as well save face," I thought, "then they won't be embarrassed about me."

I don't think I ever got over that because I am not a quitter, by nature. I believe in doing your best and persevering to the end. And never, ever quit. I believe that quitting once makes it easier to quit again.

As Christians, we can be tempted to quit. The apostle Paul often compared our walk with the Lord to running a race. Paul was not a quitter. In fact, he told us that he wanted to finish the race and complete what God had given him to do. He also said He knew how important it was to persevere and to endure.

We will experience many trials and hardships in life. We know we will face hard times, painful blows, and things we just can't understand. But we cannot quit! We must persevere, trusting in God's strength, knowing that Christ will give us all we need to make it through victoriously.

Are you going through hard or painful times? Are you contemplating quitting or throwing in the towel? Don't do it! God is there with you and for you. He has all the grace, strength, wisdom, and peace that you need As we continue to run, He will continue to pour it in! He is all that we need, so don't quit! Call upon His strength instead.

I press on toward the goal to win the prize for which God has called me heavenward in Christ Jesus.

Philippians 3:14

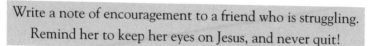

Write a note of encouragement to a friend who is struggling.
Remind her to keep her eyes on Jesus, and never quit!

Unlikely Philosopher

DONNA GARRETT

This ministry of consolation and encouragement is not to be re-
garded as inferior and of secondary importance... Did we but
discern it, we are daily surrounded by lonely, aching and sometimes
broken hearts.

J. Oswald Sanders

"How old are you when you die?" my five-year-old grandson asked. He was twirling around and around on the stool in his pediatrician's office, waiting to check whether the ten day antibiotic had cleared up an infection. It wasn't a life-threatening illness!

"Oh, maybe eighty or ninety," I replied.

"But you come back to life again."

"No, Brandon," I gently begin, "but if you are a Christian you get to go to heaven and be with God."

"I don't get to go to church much," precious, blond Brandon said. "But I believe. I haven't seen God before," he stopped, "but I have seen Jesus. He's white."

I thought of telling my darling that God and Jesus are one and that Jesus isn't necessarily white but I opt for the simpler, what-I-feel-he-can-handle-at this-time response.

"Yes, Brandon, there are pictures of Jesus that artists have painted, but we don't know exactly what Jesus looks like."

His simple, "I believe," gave me enough hope to not continue our philosophical discussion at the time.

Grandmothers have the joy and sometimes the awesome responsibility to teach what might be left undone in a schoolroom or at home. I am privileged to be in a position to take most all our grandkids to the doctor when they are sick or to a haircut. This allows some super quality time.

My son calls it "building up memories." He once commented, "The children don't realize it now, probably, but later on, these times with their grandparents will be very special to them."

Kids turn to their grandparents because of the undivided attention they receive. There is always time to stop and chat, whether in person, or by phone. Grandparents never appear to be bothered or in a rush to get back to what they were doing.

In the next few years, I hope to have lots of conversations with Brandon—and all our grandchildren. Some may be simply like, "When are you going to make us some more peanut butter fudge again?" or some may be of eternal importance!

Are you a grandparent? If so, plant the seeds. Someone else may have to water them or reap the harvest, but that's alright. What greater task could you have performed and spent your time and effort on?

If any of you lacks wisdom, he should ask God, who gives generously to all without finding fault, and it will be given to him.

James 1:5

As you think of the qualities of your own grandparents, write down the ones you want to emulate and which ones you want to avoid.

Envelopes Of Encouragement

LeAnne E. Benfield

Every charitable act is a stepping stone toward heaven.

Henry Ward Beecher

Think about the last time you received a card or letter in the mail. Sifting through the pile of bills and junk, you saw the envelope addressed to you and no one else. Maybe you opened it right away or saved it for later when you could savor it. Either way, didn't it feel good knowing that someone took the time to send it to you?

You can send that same good feeling on a regular basis without writing letters or even buying cards. For just a few minutes and little more than the cost of a postage stamp, you can lift people's hearts and share God's love.

It's simple. Ask God to guide you to people who need encouragement. Then, jot down a favorite or relevant Bible verse and tuck it into an envelope along with one of the items below (or come up with your own):

Things that are free:

- A funny cartoon to your stressed-out co-worker.
- A snapshot of your family and short note to a missionary family your church supports.
- A coupon to a nice restaurant for the young parents down the street.
- A list of some of God's promises with Scripture references to a new Christian.
- A magazine article about kids' crafts to a preschool teacher.
- Your favorite cookie recipe to the new bride.
- A list of things you love about your church to your pastor.
- Small, inexpensive gifts (these might require extra postage)
- A bookmark with a Scripture verse or inspirational poem on it to your neighbor, the bookworm.

- A tiny, decorated note pad to a secretary.
- A pinch of confetti to the recent graduate.
- A get-well balloon (deflated) to a sick friend.
- Brightly-colored stickers to your child's best friend.
- A flower seed packet to your aunt with a green thumb.
- A colorful, unsharpened pencil to your niece, who's learning to write her name.

Keep items like these on hand at work or at home, next to your envelopes, stamps, and address book, so you'll be ready to send encouragement on a moment's notice. Not only will you lift someone's spirit, you may help bring them closer to God.

Therefore encourage one another and build each other up,
just as in fact you are doing.
I Thessalonians 5:11

If you have shelves overflowing with books, cut down on the clutter by giving books you've already read to your friends. Choose titles based on your friends' interests. They'll appreciate the thoughtful surprise, and you'll be glad you did it.

Here, All The Time

JOAN RAWLINS BIGGAR

Faith is the inborn capacity to see God behind everything.
Oswald Chambers

Every art student knows that the negative spaces surrounding the main elements of a picture are as important to the impact of the picture as are the positive shapes.

Some years ago, my friend Mary mounted a new plaque on her wall. Raised white lines formed an intricate design against deep-toned wood. Were those angular shapes letters from some foreign alphabet? *Perhaps,* I decided, *the plaque was just a bit of abstract art meant to complement the other objects grouped on the wall.*

On my next visit, the plaque again caught my eye. This time the name "JESUS" leaped out in bold dark letters against a white background. The name had been there all the time but I'd been concentrating so hard on the surroundings—the negative spaces—that I'd missed what was now easy to see.

What a lesson! Jesus is *here,* all the time. If we concentrate on the details that clutter our lives, we'll miss Him. If we focus on worries or fears, they'll block Him out. But He's here, in the center of the clutter, in the midst of the cares, if we'll look for Him.

Only Jesus can make sense out of the puzzles of our lives. He's able to make the "negatives" and the "positives" of our lives come together into a beautiful, integrated work of art.

Where can I go from your Spirit? Where can I flee from your presence?
Psalm 139:7

> Keep a journal of your prayers and God's answers.
> See how He uses both negatives and positives to shape
> the masterpiece of your life.

Am I Good Or Am I Good!

INA MAE BROOKS

When you learn to keep your perspective and to stay loving toward yourself, even when you prove you are human, you'll be well on your way to a happier life.

Richard Carson, Ph.D.

They sounded like gun shots—bang, bang. I jumped as the power hammer reports rattled my nerves. Carpenters were partitioning my office. The noises, smells, and interruptions they made tested my concentration.

The carpenter's helper, a muscular youth, avoided my gaze when he moved about the room. Dark curls stuck out from under his cap. Working with him was an older fellow who was pleasant and cheerful. They worked side by side without talking.

When the young man entered the room carrying a large piece of wall board, I was studying the papers in front of me. He tacked the board in place and stepped back. It fit perfectly.

"Am I good or am I G-O-O-D!," he crowed at the top of his voice. He glanced my direction, blushed, and grinned; he had forgotten he was not alone. Without a word to me, he picked up his hammer and finished the job.

Looking up, I laughed in spite of myself. Here was a fellow who loved his work, was proud of doing a good job, and had the self-confidence to praise himself when praise was due.

I often think of this young man's positive attitude. He was not looking for other people's praise; he knew he was good and that was sufficient. I worry and fuss about what others think of me and my work. But God gave me skills and talents, too. With confidence in my own ability and faith in God, I can stop worrying and find pleasure in a job well done.

. . . and do it, not only when their eye is on you and to win their favor, but with sincerity of heart and reverence for the Lord."

Colossians 3:22b

Keep a record of how "good" you are at obeying God, and be sure to write down how God blessed you for it.

No Perfection Expected

GAYLE CLOUD

Our children make us grow up.

Kevan Cloud

In hindsight, my eldest son was not THAT difficult to guide through the pre-school years: I just assumed he'd be perfect. After all, I had read lots of books. My husband and I were firm Christians and I had inherited a lot of common sense from my mom. Nevertheless, I had some problems.

Sam spoke early, was insatiably curious and had some idea of what *he* wanted out of life—and it wasn't always what I wanted! I wanted him potty trained early. He decided on late. I wanted him totally obedient. He liked partial. I wanted him actively engaged in life. He chose to be a dreamer. I liked to snuggle up. He was independent.

In other words, he didn't quite fit my mold. Oh, I truly enjoyed him. In fact, he was the joy of my life. But he also caused me to struggle with my parenting skills. I really thought that if I followed a common sense child-raising plan (A), and considered his personality (B), that I would come out with a pretty near perfect child (C). You know, A + B = C! It wasn't that easy.

In the midst of my frustration, I got involved in a women's Bible Study. It was there that the Holy Spirit began to renew my mind. I learned that perfection isn't measured in getting everything right, but rather in doing a task to the best of my ability. Perfection was maturity. I began to mature. Sam was just acting like a child. And I learned to let him.

As a wiser friend shared with me one day, "If we were perfect parents, our children wouldn't need a Savior." My burden of perfectionism was lifted. I was no longer under a cloud of guilt for my son's childish misbehavior. He still frustrated me at times, but I realized he, like I, was not perfect.

Sam was our guinea pig but he came through our uncertain parenting and overbearing manner remarkably well. He is now in medical school and causes his father and I little ill will. And the parenting experience he gave us prepared us for the five more unique and wonderful children God gave us to raise. God had clearly showed me a remarkable lesson, one that has served me well all of these years. He does not expect us to be perfect. He loves us. And He can enable us to mirror that message to our children.

Fathers, do not exasperate your children; instead, bring them up in the training and instruction of the Lord.
Ephesians 6:4

Make a study of the temperaments by reading *The Personality Puzzle* by Florence Littauer and Marita Littauer.

Better Than This

EVA MARIE EVERSON

Follow your bliss!

Joseph Campbell

I couldn't believe my eyes! In less than a half an hour, my friend had not only mixed and baked a chocolate cake, she had frosted it as well. When I sampled a square (it was baked in a sheet pan), I pounced for the recipe. After all, nothing is better than chocolate cake . . . except, perhaps an *easy* chocolate cake!

Within a woman's lifetime—especially if she has an active church/social life—are dozens of times when "quick foods" are needed. Not only is this cake scrumptious, it's easy!

Cake:

2 cups sugar
2 cups all-purpose flour
3½ Tbsp. cocoa
½ cup butter
½ cup oil

1 cup water
2 eggs
½ cup buttermilk
1 tsp. baking soda
1 tsp. vanilla

Sift sugar, flour, and cocoa into a large bowl. In a saucepan put butter, oil ,and water. Bring to a boil. Pour over dry ingredients. Blend well. Add eggs, buttermilk, soda, and vanilla. Pour into an 11 x 16 greased pan. Bake at 400 degrees F. for twenty minutes.

When the cake has been in the oven fifteen minutes, begin to prepare the frosting. In a saucepan combine:

½ cup butter
3 Tbsp. cocoa

1/3 cup milk (can be buttermilk)
Bring to a boil. Remove from heat and add:
1 pound confectioner's sugar
1 cup chopped pecans
1 tsp. vanilla

Stir. Pour over warm cake.
Enjoy!

> *Then I realized that it is good and proper for a man to eat and drink, and to find satisfaction in his toilsome labor . . .*
> Ecclesiastes. 5:18a

To encourage journaling your prayers, buy a beautiful journal and enjoy writing your prayers to God.

Make A Prayer Calendar
MARILYN NEUBER LARSON

There is no more significant involvement in another's life than prevailing, consistent prayer.
Charles Swindoll

A friend told me of an upcoming traumatic incident and I promised to pray. But somehow I forgot the date and time. The day passed and I failed to stand in the gap to uphold my friend. The embarrassment taught me to keep a prayer calendar. In doing so, I entered God's plan for a more abundant life. I learned what a privilege it is to pray for others. I also discovered that prayer has the power to impact dramatic changes in lives—even people I've never met.

When a friend or acquaintance tells me their parent is having surgery on the twenty-second of the month, or they have a court hearing on the eighteenth, or their brother has an important job interview on the seventh, I can promise to pray for them and know I'll do it. That's because I use a small calendar to remind me.

You can do the same. Slip a small calendar into your prayer notebook or Bible, or keep it on the desk or night table. Log each entry on the correct date. Check it daily to pray for friends on moving day, final tests for kids at school, or an unusual doctor's appointment. You could also keep track of birthdays or other special dates and telephone numbers, or send a note to let them know you remembered the anniversary of a death, or other important milestones in their lives.

Write the concern in black on the date of the request. When God answers that prayer, write the answer in red. Years ago I heard Dr. Charles Stanley say that if we record our answers in red, it's proof positive that God hears and answers our prayers. Later on, even years later, we can flip through those pages and the red proves that God loves and cares about us. It builds our faith.

Praying for others gives us a vested interest in their lives, and certainly their eternity. It can strengthen our friendship and deepen our relationship with them and with our Father. Praying for others takes the focus off us and our problems, and gets our eyes back on Jesus. The privilege of praying for others comes back to bless us. As a matter of fact, it blesses our lives abundantly.

Therefore confess your sins to each other and pray for each other so that you may be healed. The prayer of a righteous man is powerful and effective.
James 5:16

Record God's answers to your prayers in a notebook.
Be sure to include the date and a brief description.

Resting In The Lord

LINDA CUTRELL

Every morning I open the window for my King's grace, and every evening I sleep upon the pillow of his love and care.

Celtic Saint

One Sunday night as I opened my Bible Study lesson, I realized that six days had passed and I had not studied one hour. How could I let the busyness of every day life interfere with my daily Bible study time? I became very frustrated and horribly guilty. *Where do I begin? How can I make up for lost time?*

Still feeling confused, I picked up my Bible and opened it to the lesson for that week: Hebrews 4. As I began to read, the words seemed to jump out at me: "Entering His rest."

As I read further, I felt God's nudge with an answer. It became very clear to me that I had too many irons in the fire and was not doing any one thing well. I really was not even taking seriously the commandment of keeping the Sabbath. Hebrews 4:9 tells us, "There remains, then, a Sabbath-rest for the people of God; for anyone who enters God's rest also rests from his own work, just as God did from his. Let us make ever effort to enter that rest . . ."

Once I recognized the problem, I took a good long look at where and how I should spend my time. Then everything seemed very clear and God gently walked me through some suggestions.

Here are some ideas for you to consider so that you can rest in the Lord in the midst of a busy schedule.

- Ask God for permission before saying yes to an opportunity.
- Commit to spending a specific, even if small, amount of time with Him in prayer daily.
- Give up unrealistic expectations that everything you'd like can be done.

Instead, trust that God knows the right things to be done each day as you obey Him.

As you put these ideas into practice, you'll find God's wonderful peace surround you, as I did. Give up those "too many irons" and commit to a few things done well.

Therefore, since the promise of entering His rest still stands, let us be careful that none of you be found to have fallen short of it.
Hebrews 4:1

When was the last time you visited a museum?
Take some time to visit one soon.

Winter

Although the analogy of Winter is often used for the later part of a life, it need not be a season of discouragement or disappointment. Winter is that gift from God of snuggling up before a blazing fire and remembering the times when God demonstrated His abundant love in our lives.

Though there's a chill in the air and our activities might even be hampered, we can know each day that God's faithful provision and protection will always sustain us. The promise of His perfect work in us will fan the flames of warmth, knowing He is guiding us even more than we realize.

The Crystal Storm

DONNA J. ADEE

Surely praise and thanksgiving are ever to be the great characteristics of the Christian life.

Martyn Lloyd-Jones

The thermometer read ten degrees, after freezing rain most of the night in our part of Kansas. I wanted to stay inside but someone had to care for our flock of ten ducks. Reluctantly I pulled on my warmest winter wear, planning to make a quick dash to the duck shed with water and feed. Cautiously, I opened the front door to step out on the ice-covered step. My boots crunched along the ice-covered snow. Tree branches hung low with ice; the water bucket left full overnight was one solid chunk of ice as was the duck's feeding pan. That didn't improve my attitude.

"Why couldn't God ease us into winter more gracefully rather than the sudden drop of sixty degrees within two days?" I kept wondering. I grumbled as I walked, "God, I don't like your choice of weather today."

Gradually it dawned on me: This really isn't so bad. There isn't any wind and the sunshine is making the ice sparkle. As I turned from feeding the ducks, I noticed the lilac bush completely encased in crystal ice. I gazed around the rest of the yard with a different attitude.

The storm had left everything beautiful by crystallizing every grass leaf, weed, rock, and tree. Often ice storms coat the trees and electric lines, breaking them and causing damage and loss of power. This storm was different, it transformed the drab winter scene into a magical world of crystal.

Taking the frozen water bucket inside to thaw, I grabbed the camera. Touring the yard, looking for unusual scenes in this magical kingdom, I spotted the red barberry bush, which had become a masterpiece of art. With my camera, I began to capture God's handiwork. With the sunshine streaming through the branches of the trees, the whole country took on a breath-taking wonderland.

The cold that I'd feared wasn't there. With no wind and a little sun, it seemed almost spring-like as I rushed to catch another scene. God was showing me another side of problems. There could be beauty in even seemingly difficult situations. I had almost missed God's blessings by my pre-determined aggravation at the sudden onset of winter.

Why do we often see only the problems and miss the blessings and lessons from a loving God?

"For I know the plans I have for you," declares the LORD, "plans to prosper you and not to harm you, plans to give you hope and a future."
Jeremiah 29:11

Take a CPR class. You never know when you'll need that information.

I Am No Longer Afraid!

KATHERINE LUNDGREN

. . . All things need God. To God alone nothing is necessary.
A. W. Tozer.

One of the most amazing transformations of my thoughts and feelings came about as I concentrated on the awesome power and love of mighty God. Before I was reconciled to Him, I was a bundle of fears. Being an artist with a highly exercised imagination, I sometimes had difficulty even knowing for sure what was real and what was not. I had no measure or standard by which to judge what was truth or a lie, so my own thoughts became my tormentors.

At an early age I had been sick with a high fever and dreamed nightmares of spiders or bugs crawling on me. A child of a military family, I was moved often and had no lasting friends. I felt sure that everyone talked badly about me. Since I have very sensitive hearing in quiet nights, every scrape of a branch against the wall or a cat jumping on a fence would turn into a lurking enemy. By the time I was an adult and choosing a sinful lifestyle, guilt added to my already growing mental and emotional weaknesses. I was afraid of everyone and every thing.

Fortunately, some loving friends kept praying for years that I would open my heart to the King of the Universe. Once I did and began to learn of His mighty power, my life was never the same. Just because I cannot see in the dark does not keep Him from seeing all things. If there is any threat to my safety He already knows it would happen. I am protected far more than I could ever desire. Though I may feel inadequate compared to someone else, they also will stand before God. Therefore, we are on level ground and I am not less than they. No one is greater than He is, and it is He who has suffered for me!

If you struggle with fear—fear of the unknown or fear of comparisons—focus on these important truths. God loves and protects you. He loves you unconditionally and doesn't compare you with anyone else. Let God's peace take away your fears.

My help comes from the LORD the Maker of heaven and earth . . . indeed,
He who watches over Israel will neither slumber nor sleep.
Psalm 121:2, 4

Search the Scriptures for the verse God has written
that deals with your specific fear. Memorize it
and use it as often as needed.

Life Is Short—Celebrate Now!

Barbara Johnson

Joy is a necessity, not a luxury.

Harold F. Leestma

One of the reasons we should celebrate more is that life goes by faster than we can imagine. Before we know it, we've missed out on enjoying so many wonderful things because we feel we should save them for "Sunday-best." Or perhaps we wait for that special occasion that never seems to arrive.

Like me, you may have read more than one report of how someone dies and the surviving relatives find all kinds of beautiful things that were never used. Furniture in a front parlor may never have been sat upon. New baby clothes might be forgotten in a drawer because they were too nice for a baby to spit up on, and of course, the baby outgrew them. Beautifully embroidered towels may be hidden in another drawer, obviously saved for that special occasion that never seemed to come.

It may be this way throughout the house. The dear person who passed on had saved all her beautiful things for special occasions that never came.

Whenever I read or hear stories like this, it reminds me that it's easy to deny yourself many of life's simple pleasures simply because you want to be "practical." That's why I'm such an advocate of having a JOY BOX, which, in my case, has grown into a JOY ROOM, twelve feet wide and sixty feet long.

For years I've urged folks to become "joy collectors." It doesn't cost much, if anything, to start. All you need is a shoe box decorated with bright, shiny paper and filled with simple little things—cartoons, poems, and quips or quotes cut out of newspapers or magazines.

Special cards received for Mother's Day, birthdays, etc., are also naturals for your Joy Box. Your Joy Box collection doesn't have to be expensive. The only requirement is that everything in your box be a SPIRIT-LIFTER—something that encourages you and makes you smile.

Splendor and majesty are before him; strength and joy in his dwelling place.
I Chronicles 16:27

Make a Joy Box for you and a friend.

The Tree That Wouldn't Die

DONNA ADEE

Though every believer has the Holy Spirit, the Holy Spirit does not have every believer.

A.W. Tozer

A Golden Rain tree that I dug up as a tiny plant from my aunt's farm fifteen years ago had grown to six feet tall, but more sideways than up. My husband told me it would not live after our farm cats tore deep cuts in the bark. It gradually went downhill, looking more and more unhealthy.

After soaking it with water and giving it the best fertilizer I could, it did leaf out the next spring and even put on the yellow flowers before the lanterns. But then the hot summer winds pounded it day after day and a large crack developed in the weak trunk. My son and I even wrapped the trunk together tightly with my old nylon hose and poured on the water.

One morning I looked out to find the whole tree flat on the ground. I asked my husband to help me stake it securely. Instead, he told me to cut it off and to not put a tree in that location as the evergreen trees sapped the soil so heavily. Sadly, I cut it from the trunk and put the little tree in the trash to be burned.

Three weeks later, I was surprised to see new leaves coming from that old trunk. Before long, it's new growth sprung up much faster than the old tree had ever grown. I had intended to saw off the old trunk but had been too busy. Today, it is a ten-foot tree blooming every year and bearing the little lanterns.

My reactions to the Golden Rain tree's problem is how I react to life problems. I want God to solve my problems in my time and in my way. I try to prop up the situations, fertilize, and water with my weak efforts, only to find my way won't work. Once I quit trying and allow God to work by giving up my self-dependence, He brings something worthwhile and strong that will bring glory to Him.

But blessed is the man who trusts in the LORD, whose confidence is in Him. He will be like a tree planted by the water that sends out its roots by the stream. It does not fear when heat comes; its leaves are always green. It has no worries in a year of drought and never fails to bear fruit.

Jeremiah 17:7–8

For all of today, if you think of someone, pray for them.

All Those Lights

SHARON NORRIS

She would rather light candles than curse the darkness and her glow has warmed the world.

Adlai E. Stevenson (written of Anna Eleanor Roosevelt, Nov. 7, 1962)

My friend Molly once said, "God looks down and sees us as His lights. It's like looking down from an airplane at night." Since I have occasion to fly across the country every now and then, my mind began to race with this image. I could see Jesus flying on a 747 jumbo jet at night and looking down at the earth. There are huge patches of darkness, a light here and there, then all of a sudden, a cluster of brightness comes into view. A city. How brilliant those areas are. Even from thousands of feet above, you can sense the warmth. There must be lots of activity, growth, encouragement, and relationships going on because of those lights. The light really looks good.

However, just as quickly as they appear in the outline of the airliner's tiny window, the lights of the city are gone and you can see nothing but darkness again.

I can imagine Jesus seeing the Church as those patches of light like those cities. What's His perspective? When He looks down, does He see the light reaching out into the darkness to brighten it, or does He see the darkness encroaching upon the light? Do the suburbs represent the Church reaching into the darkness, or do they represent the ways of darkness creeping in and being accepted inappropriately into the Church?

What are you doing with the light God has made you to be?

You are the light of the world. A city on a hill cannot be hidden.
Matthew 5:14

Whenever you see a lamp or light bulb, let it remind you
to let your light shine in some way today.

Avoiding Stress Fractures
H. Norman Wright

It matters not how great the pressure is, only where the pressure lies. If we make sure it never comes between us and our Lord, then the greater the pressure, the more it presses us to Him.

Hudson Taylor

Athletes know what stress fractures are. Little microscopic cracks in bones that start from the pounding we give our body. In time they enlarge and begin to hurt.

You may think stress fractures are limited to the bones, but they're not. We pound our bodies in other ways. Our schedule begins to pile up, as do the bills; we take on a coaching job, learn to eat on the run (usually junk food), try to satisfy the boss, spouse, and church. Before long our nerves have these microscopic cracks beginning. We're on edge like a tightly wound rubber band just ready to snap at whatever gets in our way.

Your spirit and your heart can be stress fractured as well. It comes from taking on and doing too much by yourself. Whoever said we were called to go through life alone? That approach will fracture your life. There's a Shepherd waiting to help you. Why don't you let Him?

Do not be anxious about anything, but in everything, by prayer and petition, with thanksgiving, present your requests to God. And the peace of God, which transcends all understanding, will guard your hearts and your minds in Christ Jesus.

Philippians 4:6–7

Take a walk today while listening to a praise tape.

Praying With Child-Like Faith

BEVERLY J. ANDERSON

After all, prayer is conversing with God. To converse with someone we must be with that person.

Rosalind Rinker

"I don't just pray, I talk to God all the time. We even play together," declared nine-year-old Rachel when I gathered children in our home group for a prayer time. While requests came for kitties, mothers, fathers, and less homework, I wondered if I could pray with the child-like faith they exhibited.

God hears and answers the prayers of His children no matter their age but it probably helps to come in simple, child-like faith rather than flowery language. This is like approaching a much loved parent. We come in confidence of love but also in recognition of their authority and wisdom. The centurion who came to Jesus at Capernaum asking that his servant be healed of paralysis and pain exemplified this when he said, "Lord, I do not deserve to have you come under my roof. But just say the word, and my servant will be healed. For I myself am a man under authority, with soldiers under me. I tell this one, 'Go,' and he goes, and that one, 'Come,' and he comes. I say to my servant, 'Do this,' and he does it.'" (Matthew 8:8–9). Jesus responded to his unlimited faith by healing his servant from afar.

"I want to pray for my kitty," Rachel's sister Clara requested. Others in the group echoed her.

"Yes, we pray for fathers, mothers, and homework," I thought, "but we also pray for kitties if they are important to us." Ignoring thoughts of some who might wince at such prayer, we asked God to be with each kitty and to give them long, healthy lives.

Before I learned anything about science and the limitations of man, I knew God could do anything. Later, as I found out people could not do everything they wished, I also put limits on God's powers.

I must again be the child who believes God is able to do whatever He chooses. He can answer any prayer no matter how hard it seems to my human understanding. However, I've learned He may answer it in a way I'd never imagine and accomplish even more than I ask—much like a parent adding an ice cream cone to a day at the amusement park.

When nine-year-old Rachel described a continual conversation and interaction with God, she was describing the way our prayers should be. Let's resist putting prayer in one of many short time slots in our busy adult lives like so many of the other things we compartmentalize. Mixing prayer with life does work. We don't have to stop the flow of living to pray. Walking and talking with God through the day will be our key to returning to child-like faith.

I am the LORD, the God of all mankind. Is anything too hard for Me?
Jeremiah 32:27

> What is your God-given purpose for life? Write it down
> and share it with someone.

Being Or Doing?

CHERYL BRASUELL

What then shall we be? That each will answer for himself. But for
myself and to myself I say: Though stripped of every armor; be a
warrior—a warrior of the spirit, for what, the spirit knows.

Dorothy Thompson

The church I have attended since high school has closed its doors for the last
time. I am not serving in any church. I don't have a position of leadership
and my job at our Christian school has just ended. Additionally, my Bible
Study group ended with the close of our church ministry. My life has changed
dramatically and I feel useless and depressed.

People have been trying to comfort me by telling me that I just need to sit
back and relax and enjoy the break from all my responsibilities. Yet, I don't
want to rest and I liked all my responsibilities! I liked being needed and
wanted. Now I feel as though I am nothing because I am doing nothing.

In teaching Bible studies for years, I cannot count the number of times
I've talked about significance and how it can only come from God. I cannot
count the times I've shared that *being* is more important than *doing*. Somehow, those things were easy to teach when they did not apply directly to my
life. They sounded great at the time when my time, talents, and gifts were in
constant demand. Now that story has changed and I don't feel in control of
my life anymore.

I suppose control is the key. But I must remember that I am not in control of my life, God is. I'm not in control of my circumstances, God is. However, I do have control over my actions, attitude, and will. I have the ability to learn from Him what is best for me and to listen to His direction for my life. I know that as He makes those truths more real in my life during this time of transition and change, I will recognize His hand of faithfulness. And I'll be able to truly know I'm worthwhile, whether or not I'm *doing* anything.

Do you find your significance more from your performance or your position in Christ? Don't let a time of a lack of ministry opportunities reveal the truth. Know now that you are valued because of who you are in Christ.

"I am the LORD your God, who teaches you what is best for you,
who directs you in the way you should go. If only you had paid attention to
My commands, your peace would have been like a river, your righteousness
like the waves of the sea."
Isaiah 48:17b–18

Enjoy looking at your wedding photos with your spouse
and share your memories of that day.

Let Go And Let God
LIBBY C. CARPENTER

Little is much when God is in it.
Kittie L. Suffield

"Honey, I think you should quit your job." My husband's words seemed to resonate across the room. Peering at him from behind a stack of my third-grade students' spelling papers, my mouth dropped in utter shock.

I understood Hugh's perspective. Our hectic lifestyle of balancing dual careers while attempting to keep pace with two small children often left us exhausted and irritable. We had the life we planned, but lacked the fulfillment we'd anticipated. Still, I hesitated to sacrifice my teaching career.

"What about my college education?" I quickly countered. "Won't it be wasted? And how will we pay back my school loan?"

In our five years of marriage we had tithed our income and sought to put God first. "Now is the time for us to let go of our plans," Hugh reasoned. "Let's see what God has planned for us."

Reluctantly I agreed to finish that year of teaching and then resign. My income would pay back my loan. We were both nervous about the sacrifices we were making; however, as I yielded to my husband and he yielded to God, something wonderful happened. God changed our desires and I experienced a joy and contentment that working had never provided.

The days and years quickly flew by as I eagerly planned special activities with our daughters, Lisa and Amy. We spent hours in the public library, enjoying story hour together, and checking out stacks of books we could barely carry home. I helped them identify shapes and colors and taught them both to read before they started school. At night, we read Bible stories and said bedtime prayers together.

Camping, nature hikes, summer picnics, and cookouts of hamburgers instead of steak, even living in a small mobile home for seven years, stir fond memories and laughter today. Amy still talks about the TV dinners we had on Sundays—they were special treats!

As a family, we prayed together for each need and watched God answer. From handling our family transportation needs to providing scholarships for the girls' college educations, God always answered just in time. Once when we responded to an advertisement for a second-hand van, it was no surprise that its color was "Hawaiian Blue"—just what the children had prayed for!

Recently I overheard Lisa, now with four small children of her own, telling about our two-week camping trek from North Carolina to Canada. "We slept in the van, three in the back, with little Amy between the front seats," she chuckled.

Today, after thirty years, I look back and see that as we sowed seeds of complete trust, God produced an abundant harvest of blessings too numerous to count!

Won't you begin this walk of total dependence today? You'll find when you give up your will, God gives back abundantly more than you could ever ask or dream!

> *So do not worry, saying "What shall we eat . . . drink . . . or*
> *wear?" . . . your heavenly Father knows that you need them. But seek first*
> *His kingdom and His righteousness, and all these things will be given unto you*
> *as well.*
>
> Matthew 6:31–33

Scan the newspaper or check with your local library, parks, or museum for free fun. Create a memory today.

Bogged Down Thinking
W. Phillip Keller

God takes life's broken pieces and gives us unbroken peace.
Wilbert Donald Gough

By nature I am one who enjoys variety in life. If, therefore, I set out to travel to a remote spot which I have visited many times before, I always try, if possible, to find a new and different way to go. I will take special pains to choose a route that offers a fresh view of the countryside and adds pleasure to traveling by taking me into new territory. If perchance I traveled a rough country road full of ruts and potholes before, then I am doubly delighted to find a better, smoother road. I am not at all keen to plow my way through the same old ruts and mudholes every time. I have been that way before. I have been bogged down too often to want a repeat performance. There is nothing very heroic about going into a situation where I am sure to hit bottom again.

Precisely the same applies to our thought life and thinking behavior. Again and again we allow ourselves to travel down the same old rutted road of muddy thinking that we have been over a hundred times before. Simply for lack of determination we wallow through the same old worries and stumble over the same old troubles. We torture ourselves with the stress and strain of struggling through the sloughs and swamps of depression and despondency in which we were bogged before.

Most of us simply submit to the tyranny of our thoughts, shrug our shoulders in despair, and say, "I just can't help it." This is delusion. We can change all this if we want to. The question is, "Do we want to?"

If so, what is required is a bit of dogged determination. We must make a positive decision to switch our thinking, to change the route we will take, to set our minds on other matters, to become masters of our own thoughts and where they will travel.

We demolish arguments and every pretension that sets itself up against the knowledge of God, and we take captive every thought to make it obedient to Christ.

II Corinthians 10:5

Choose something that happens frequently throughout your day, like a telephone ringing, and when it happens, stop and ask yourself, "Have I been letting my thoughts go into a muddy swamp?"

Portable Hospitality

LETTIE J. KIRKPATRICK

Hospitality is caring. We can entertain all we like, but not until we care does it become hospitality.

Emilie Barnes

For many of us, the pace of our lives makes it very difficult to offer hospitality in a leisurely manner or with great frequency. Still, women need to nurture friendships with one another. Even in a busy season, we should not eliminate this ministry of encouragement altogether. One alternate possibility is "portable hospitality." Consider these variations:

1. In pretty weather, pack a picnic basket with matching cloth napkins and place mats. Add cookies and fruit, a refreshing drink, and pasta or salad from a local restaurant. Pick up a friend who needs to talk and drive to a nearby park. These simple preparations and focused attention can be a real blessing.

2. Meet on the lunch hour. Again, pack the basket and meet in a convenient place. I have taken one friend to a quiet church prayer tower that has a small kitchen. Even an hour can be an energizer and full of encouragement.

3. Reload the basket for a precious break for preschoolers and their stay-at-home mom. Last fall, I loaded the youngest of my five children into our van, picked up another friend with her two preschoolers and headed for a local apple orchard. In this peaceful setting out came my basket, a sunflower tablecloth, and delicate disposable tableware. I had packed simple lunches for the boys in individual bags and prepared an easy chicken salad for us. We shared apple turnovers from the orchard bakery. It was a lovely afternoon that required little, but fed our spirits.

In hectic holiday seasons, like Christmas, practice creative ways of transporting hospitality. Perhaps my most ambitious undertaking was done as a

Christmas gift to my class at church. I taught adults and wanted to honor them during the season. Hectic schedules and lots of children made an extra evening hard to find. So I simply prepared several tins of finger foods and an easy drink. I decorated a small table, set out throwaway holiday table wear, and treated them to a brunch at the beginning of class.

Special times will not occur if we wait until we are able to prepare gourmet meals in spotless, quiet homes. We mustn't postpone reaching out until the circumstances are perfect.

Ask God to reveal ways to reach out to your friends. Let's not allow the "tyranny of the urgent" to rob us of relationships that strengthen us or the opportunity to be a blessing to someone else. Portable hospitality just might be the solution for many of us.

Offer hospitality to one another without grumbling.
I Peter 4:9

Prepare a quick, attractive, and delicious juice drink
for entertaining by mixing equal parts any juice
(I recommend cranapple, white grape, or purple grape)
with diet lemon-lime beverage. Children love it, too!

Growing, Instead Of Growing Old

Lea C. Tartanian

"I love life."

Ninety-four-year-old Elise Curran, my seventh grade teacher, who died at age 100

At the Bible Study meeting one of the participants shared a story about a positive gathering he had enjoyed with a group of acquaintances. However, he ended his tale with the following words, "It felt good that they spent time with an old antique like me."

Recently a family member invited a lady close to her out to dinner. The woman's reply was, "You don't have to do that. You're just doing it because I'm old!"

I wonder if people who are approaching their senior years realize the uncomfortable position they put others in when they make negative comments about their age? Everyone begins to age the minute he or she is born.

God did not create us with the intention that we dread each birthday or decade of life on the earth. Birthdays are a positive celebration of the gift of life. We are meant to be here. All human beings are on this planet to fulfill His purposes. However, those who focus on aging rather than the pleasure of utilizing the talents and abilities God has placed within them rob themselves of the joy of living.

How wonderful it would be to say each morning, "I am growing!" rather than, "I'm growing old." Every day is an opportunity for new beginnings and fresh choices. Yesterday is gone, never to return. We have several hours to learn more, be more, and continue to live in a spirit of gratitude for each breath that we take.

Therefore, it is not necessary for those approaching their golden years to remind others they are "old." Age does not concern our Creator because each minute of life is under His control. All we need to do is to trust Him.

Is not wisdom found among the aged? Does not long life bring understanding?
Job 12:12

Begin a fun project today that you have been putting off,
such as purchasing unique frames for your priceless photos
and placing them in full view.

Serving The Master

KAREN TAYLOR

Life is worth living when you find a God that's worth serving.
Robert Schuller

I swallowed back the unexpected lump that crept into my throat as we watched the yellow Labrador retriever guide his blindfolded master safely through the obstacle course. When the demonstration was finished, he sat obediently at her feet, seeking signs of approval with adoring brown eyes.

As a spectator at the first real dog show I'd ever attended, I was amazed and moved by the talents displayed by these furry friends.

Next came the obedience trials. Although these dogs were also well trained, I noticed that some of the handlers continually rewarded them with tasty morsels throughout their performances.

I couldn't help but observe that the animals who were motivated by a desire to please often spun joyful circles or leapt into the arms of their trainers following the exercise. Those who focused on the reward were preoccupied with sniffing the ground and seemed to still be looking for something after the event was over.

The experience prompted me to stop and examine my own motives with regard to serving. When my time here on earth is finished, will I still be searching for some elusive material reward after wallowing in the shallow waters of self-gratification? Or, will I feel the satisfaction of knowing my performance was based on my desire to please the Master? Watching the actions and reactions of these humans and animals reminded me that obedience and devotion are the keys to living a fulfilling and joyous life. Who could ask for a better reward than that?

So if you faithfully obey the commands I am giving you today—to love the LORD your God and to serve him with all your heart and with all your soul . . .
Deuteronomy 11:13

Enjoy a board game with your family members today.

Cat Parable
LORI WALL

As a friend, I can't heal or change a painful situation. But I can listen . . . with ears that open into my heart.
Carol Kuykendall

"All right, I hear you. I'm coming," I said loudly enough for my precious "alarm clocks" to hear one Saturday morning when they were meowing at the back door. Whether my two cats are in the house or outside, they make sure I hear them when they want to be fed. Yet on this particular morning, one of the meows sounded like a howl.

Pebbles quickly scampered in when I opened the door. Her black and gray tail fluffed up, she jumped up onto the kitchen counter ready to eat. However, something was not right with her mother, Tierna.

Tierna's long gray and black striped tail hung limp between her back legs, and her ear was scraped and bleeding. I attributed everything to her having been in a fight during the night. But when she didn't eat, I knew something more was wrong.

I quickly set up a bed for her and gave her some water. When I lifted her tail to try to clean her, she hissed at me and bit my hand before scurrying under a dresser.

Immediately the worst thoughts flashed through my mind. *Is she hiding so she can die?* I quickly grabbed her by her front paws and pulled her out to continue to clean her. Again, she hissed and crawled under the dresser. Now I had to make a choice.

After some phone calls, I decided to take her to the vet. I tried again to drag Tierna out from under the dresser but gave up when she scratched and bit my hand.

After watching me, my son, Jeffrey, volunteered, "I'll do it, Mom. I'm used to her scratching and biting me."

Jeffrey pulled her out with great success and accompanied me to the vet. There we discovered Tierna's wounds were due to her having been hit by a car. We were then faced with the decision of whether or not to amputate her broken tail. We decided to wait.

When we brought the cat home later that week, Jeffrey took on the role of administering her medicine to her. I avoided the tail issue for a time, while my friend Michelle prayed for it to be healed. Over a short period of time, God healed Tierna's broken tail.

Another friend pointed out how we can be like animals when we have been hurt. It's much easier to run and hide in dark places than to come out into the light to get bandaged up. Sometimes God has to send someone like my Jeffrey, who is willing to withstand the biting and scratching, in order to pull us out from our hiding place so we can be healed.

When you're hurting, allow God's gentle hand to repair the damage. It might hurt initially, but His healing touch will bring renewed joy and peace.

Two are better than one, because they have a good return for their work: If one falls down, his friend can help him up . . .

Ecclesiastes 4:9–10a

> A person going through a hard time will usually "bite
> and scratch" a loved one or good friend instead of a stranger
> because he or she knows they will not be rejected.

Priorities

PATRICK M. MORLEY

*Some men see things as they are and say why. I dream things that
never were and say why not.*

Robert F. Kennedy

Almost everyone has gone grocery shopping on an empty stomach and without a shopping list. Everything that tastes good looks especially attractive, and the shopping cart ends up filled with too many snack foods and not enough nutrition.

When the cashier rings up the final total and announces the bill, you are in a state of shock at the cost of your unplanned shopping spree! The worst part may not be the cost, but explaining to your wife how you spent so much money and still didn't get what the family needed!

The object of grocery shopping is to purchase a nutritionally balanced diet for the family. Shopping without a list risks spending your time and money on the wrong food.

Life's many options compete for our priority just like the well-stocked shelves of a grocery store. To have any control over our lives whatsoever, we must decide in advance what we will give ourselves to.

The object of setting priorities is to allocate limited amounts of time and money where God directs us. But too often we choose our priorities with the same foresight as our trip to the grocery store, and the things we give priority to are simply not what our family needs or God wants.

According to Webster's Dictionary, a priority is something which we give precedence by assigning a degree of urgency or importance to it.

What is important to God? The answer reveals what our priorities ought to be. Priorities help us narrow our focus.

Wake up! Strengthen what remains and is about to die, for I have not found your deeds complete in the sight of my God.

Revelation 3:2

If you've never done so, write out your Mission Statement.

The Mirror Doesn't Lie

CASSANDRA WOODS

Everyone thinks of changing the world, but no one thinks of changing himself.

Tolstoy

Which of us would dare wake up, dress up, and go out without ever looking in a mirror? Not many of us, I'm sure. For a long time mirrors have played an important role in our society. They come in all shapes and sizes, from compacts to the full-length types. They can be found in bathrooms, bedrooms, halls, and more. In pockets and purses, and hanging on doors. Yes, they're everywhere.

We use them to evaluate our appearance, to test the need for a tuck here or a dab there. We want to present a good image.

But who is taking care of the inside, the heart? I am convinced that we must practice regular self-evaluation, in order to live out God's purpose for our lives. After all, we're told, the pure in heart shall see God.

So why not tape a Bible verse to your most frequented mirror? Then you can get twice the bang with only one look.

Anyone who listens to the word but does not do what it says is like a man who looks at his face in a mirror and, after looking at himself, goes away and immediately forgets what he looks like.

James 1:23–24

Place an encouraging Bible verse in places that will remind you to read it throughout the day. Then ask yourself if you are exemplifying a Christ-like attitude concerning your situation.

Multiplying The Loaves
ALICE KING GREENWOOD

A dewdrop acts out the will of God as surely as the thunderstorm.

God's Tender Promises For Mothers

What could be a more perfect ending to a Thanksgiving feast than an old-fashioned pumpkin pie? From childhood I have relished the taste of this spicy dessert. But the value of a lowly pumpkin skyrocketed when I discovered the delights of pumpkin bread. Now I immensely enjoy making this bread as well as pies. The recipe I use makes the most moist, delicious bread I've ever tasted. Its mouth-watering aroma fills my house while the bread bakes and I anticipate with sheer pleasure the eating of it.

However, God has opened my eyes to see that this bread can have a more important role than bringing pleasure just to myself. Many of my friends are elderly, some frail and weak, others unable to leave their homes. Their lives tend to get very lonely, and they long for social contacts. To them, a short visit from a friend is a wonderful blessing. But you should see the smiles on their faces when I also hand them a plastic-wrapped loaf of pumpkin bread, perhaps with a perky red bow on top!

Rather than waiting until Thanksgiving, I now make this treat all through the year and give the loaves to three persons each time. This is my recipe:

Pumpkin Bread

2 cups white sugar
1 cup brown sugar
4 eggs
1 cup salad oil
2 cups canned pumpkin
2 teaspoons soda dissolved in
    ²/₃ cup water

2½ cup flour
1½ teaspoon salt
1 teaspoon cinnamon
1 teaspoon cloves
1 teaspoon nutmeg

Mix sugars and eggs. Add wet ingredients. Sift together and add dry ingredients to the first mixture. Pour into three small ungreased loaf pans. Bake at 350 degrees about 1 hour. Test as for cake.

A boy's small loaves in Jesus' hands fed thousands. My loaves of pumpkin bread are just small things, too, but given in Jesus' name, what large blessings they bring.

"Who despises the day of small things? . . . "
Zechariah 4:10a

Occasionally put a loaf of pumpkin bread in your freezer
to serve at tea or when unexpected guests drop in.

Watching With Jesus

ESTHER M. BAILEY

*You cannot do a kindness too soon because you never know
how soon it will be too late.*

Ralph Waldo Emerson

One of the saddest scenes from biblical history happened at Gethsemane. There Jesus agonized over events to come at Calvary while His disciples slept. Peter, James, and John gratified their tired bodies at the very time when their Lord needed them most. No one shared His suffering. No one watched with Him for even one hour. There was but one opportunity to tenderly touch Jesus and gently wipe the blood-stained moisture from His brow. There was only one occasion in history for such action, but the disciples failed to meet the challenge.

Sometimes I picture myself at the scene. I believe I would have done better than the disciples, but do my actions support my opinion?

If I really want to watch with Jesus, I can do it today. Vicariously I can watch with Jesus by what I do for others. Perhaps you would like to join me in selecting a course of action from the following list:

- Bake cookies for a working mother who has no time to bake.
- When you're stressed out with your own work, take an hour to help the new employee. Don't be surprised when your stress melts away and you receive renewed energy to cope with your job.
- When legislation that involves right and wrong is pending, write to your government official with a Christian voice.
- Volunteer to work in the church office. You may need to spend more than an hour to be really effective.
- Contact the youth pastor of your church and offer to mentor a troubled teenager.

- Make it a habit to be pleasant to the check-out clerk. You can probably do this all year for an hour.
- Drive a shut-in to the doctor or grocery store.
- Call, visit, or write to someone who is discouraged.
- Make a list of twelve people who need your prayers. Pray five minutes for each one.
- Read Scripture to someone who is sight impaired.
- For an entire hour concentrate on making your spouse, parent, child, or friend feel special.
- Teach a skill to a young person or help a child with a homework project.
- Without interrupting, listen while a friend unburdens her soul.
- Come up with a creative idea of your own to surprise someone with a favor.

You can please the Lord today as you reach out to others in His name and for His glory. Which of those ideas will do you today?

> . . . *"I tell you the truth, whatever you did for one of the least of these brothers of mine, you did it for me."*
> Matthew 25:40

Go to your pantry, pick out six items, and take them to a food bank.

Have You Any Wool?

Liz Curtis Higgs

*No cord nor cable can so forcibly draw, or hold so fast,
as love can do with a twined thread.*

Robert Burton

As a woman who lives in a nineteenth-century farmhouse and loves the country look in decorating, I always thought sheep were cute. After all, the ones I usually see are made of pure white fluffy wool with round wooden legs and little button eyes. They cost about $34.95, unless you want the full-size model for $59.95. I've never succumbed (bad stewardship), but I do think they're sweet looking.

The problem is, they in no way resemble real sheep.

Real sheep are (dare I say it?) not as cosmetically appealing. Some of them have strange, piercing eyes, positioned so close together as to make them look cross-eyed. None of them are anywhere near as white as the kind in the store. They've got stuff hanging all over them, from food to worse, and consequently they don't smell very nice either (and that's on a cool breezy day; in the heat of summer, look out!).

Now, that's not to say that sheep aren't lovable. By no means. They have so many needs and are so dependent on their shepherd that you can't help but want to take care of them. And they need a *lot* of care, because—please don't think I'm being cruel when I say this—sheep are *stupid*.

They will eat grass until they get to the roots, then eat the roots so the grass will never grow back, then bleat about, wondering where their grass went, when all the while delicious green grass is ten feet away.

They are not smart animals. They also can be "cast down," which means they get in a comfy little spot and stretch just so and suddenly they are on their backs with all four of their little feet up in the air, and they are *stuck*. Can't you just hear them: "Help, I've fallen, and I can't get up!" Bleat. Bleat.

Enter the kind shepherd who hears this bleating, finds the sheep, and helps it back on its feet, because if left that way, the sheep is doomed, and it's at least smart enough to know that much.

So you see, when Jesus said that we are like sheep, this was not a compliment. He clearly stated that we aren't as intelligent as we think we are, nor do we know what is best for us, nor can we keep ourselves out of danger. You can't even think of the word *sheep* in Scripture without also thinking of the words *gone astray*. They are also creatures of habit and stubborn to boot. Is that us, or what?

Here's the happy ending: We have a Shepherd who loves us, knows us, cares deeply for us, watches over us, looks out for us, keeps His staff on hand to lift us out of danger. He feeds us from His rich pastures, He leads us to still waters, He restores our souls . . . what a Shepherd!

For you were like sheep going astray, but have now returned to the Shepherd and Overseer of your souls.
I Peter 2:25

The next time you see a sheep—even on television—give thanks for having a loving God who is your Shepherd.

Precious Moments With God

Avis McGriff Rasmussen

Begin and end the day with him who is the Alpha and Omega, and if you really experience what it is to love God, you will redeem all the time you can for his more immediate service.

Susanna Wesley

How do we capture those precious moments with God and worship Him throughout each day? For those of us who have busy schedules, we often ponder this important question. The answer lies in having a quiet time with God, but we can also weave times of worship into our daily activities.

Before rising out of bed each morning, we can begin the day by thanking the Lord for at least five blessings in our lives. Once out of bed, we can continue in worship by finding a quiet place to pray and read. I usually retreat to the living room.

Since our minds are less cluttered at the beginning of the day, we are, essentially, giving God the first fruits of our thoughts. It's often these first thoughts which will influence our attitude of worship during the remainder of a day. Ask God to help you to focus your thoughts on Him.

While preparing for the day, we can silently rehearse scripture we've memorized or learn new verses. We can also listen to the Bible on tape. Listening to Scripture allows us to reflect on God while engaging in other tasks. This is also a great way to have the Word seep into the ears of the whole family.

We can also worship God through a family prayer time. My husband gathers our family for a time of morning prayer before we head into the day. I continue praying, and praising God along with my son, while driving him to daycare. Then I pray for my employer and co-workers on the way to work. I also pray for the members of my church as I drive past our church office.

To worship God while working, we can listen to the Bible on tape, rather than talk radio. This can help to reduce much of the stress during the day. When I do listen to radio ministry programs, I join in the prayers at the end of the messages. I also silently recite scripture during the day, or pray for the needs of others, such as ministry leaders. Often, I have an extended time of Bible Study rather than eating lunch.

Another great way to worship is by singing praise songs to the Lord. In the evenings, my family sometimes sings along with praise music to encourage a time of worship. You may also want to keep what I call "daily worship reminders" handy around the house. I keep a small flip calendar, which contains sayings and scriptures, as well as a bowl filled with Scripture cards on the dining table. As my family has its meals, we can choose a Scripture to read. And at the end of the day, we have a family devotional.

By worshiping God, we make a conscious effort to align ourselves to His will. I find those precious moments with God in each day by keeping Him at the center of my thoughts. I am enriched each time I seek the Lord. Let's begin and end our days with God on our minds.

I will praise You, O LORD, with all my heart . . . I will be glad and rejoice in You; I will sing praise to Your name, O Most High.

Psalm 9:1–2

Create your own daily worship reminders, like Scripture cards. Place them in visible areas around your home to encourage your family to pray through the day.

How Deep Is Your Debt?

Lois Hudson

Pay every debt, as if God wrote the bill.

Ralph Waldo Emerson

What debts do you owe? Plastic money has made it easy to have what we want when we want it. It doesn't feel like we're spending money when we whip out the charge card. But the Bible warns us: *Let no debt remain outstanding, except the continuing debt to love one another, for he who loves his fellow man has fulfilled the law* (Romans 13:8).

Certainly the first debt is the debt of love for Jesus Christ, because of the cost of salvation which He freely purchased for us. But that debt cannot be repaid except in obedience to His command to love. Jesus said both the law and all the things the prophets spoke of were summed up in the command to love the Lord and to love our neighbors (Matthew 22:37).

Are you working on your debt of love? It's one that will never be "paid in full" but increases in value even as we work to pay it off. We owe it to Christ to love one another. You've heard of IOU's for gifts of love: a home-cooked meal, an afternoon of baby-sitting, a car wash, shopping for a shut-in, a movie with a grandchild, lunch with a friend, running errands, a trip to the beauty parlor. How many ways can you expand this list to bolster up a sister in Christ, a family member, or a neighbor? Perhaps even someone who is seeking Christ?

Years ago I purchased a set of small cards imprinted "*I love you because . . .* " They were fun to share with family and friends and gave me the opportunity to show appreciation for them. For the occasion of our thirty-fifth wedding anniversary, I got the bright idea of filling out thirty-five cards telling my husband "*I love you because . . .* " in thirty-five different ways. When he opened my gift, I couldn't gauge his reaction beyond his initial apparent appreciation. There were other people present, other gifts to open, and it wasn't the time for him to stop and read each of the thirty-five cards. But seven years later, I was cleaning out his desk at his office after he had died. I found the little box of cards in the top drawer of his desk closest to the front. The well-worn box and much fingered cards showed me how much my heartfelt gift had meant to him.

Tell your family and friends you love them. Tell your Christian family you love them. Tell your Lord and Savior you love Him. You never know when you might not have another chance.

The commandments . . . are summed up in this one rule:
"Love your neighbor as yourself."
Romans 13:9

Create your own "I love you because . . ." cards
with colorful card stock from the stationery store.
Enclose them in letters, gifts, lunch boxes,
Christmas stockings, wherever!

Small Gesture; Abundant Joy
CINDY BAILEY

The joys of parents are secret, so are their grieves and fears.
Francis Bacon

As I sat on the piano bench waiting for the pastor to announce the next hymn, I watched a young father struggling to keep his two little girls under control. His wife had died only a few weeks before following a long battle with cancer. Our church had encircled the family with compassion throughout the long ordeal, but now life had returned to normal. It was time to move on.

Patiently, this grief-worn dad leaned across the pew time and again, whispered quiet instruction to his daughters as he simultaneously tried to participate in praise and worship. My heart went out to him. I was reminded of the years I had watched my own husband fuss with our two little girls Sunday after Sunday while I fulfilled my duties as church pianist. And then I remembered how we learned to pack a special "activity bag" for each child, filled with stickers, crayons, and non-messy snacks. Now was the time to make a couple of these "Goin' to Church" bags for someone else.

At home, I found some farm scene fabric scraps, which I cut into strips about 14 by 36 inches long. Next, I folded the fabric in half, lengthwise, right sides together, and stitched. Then I turned under the raw edges of what would be the top of the bag and stitched it down.

To form a casing for the drawstring, I folded about one inch of the top down to the inside of the bag and stitched across the length. Next, I sewed the other long side up to the casing. For the drawstring, I used a 30-inch section of clothesline. I threaded it through the casing with a large safety pin, and finally tied the string in a knot. Of course, you may purchase a canvas bag instead of making one.

I filled the bags with age-appropriate items, including art materials, Bible flash cards, tiny boxes of cereal, and one hardback book to be used as a "desk." Some items were new; others gently used. The next Sunday, I watched my own daughters present the bags to these little ones and their father. For an instant, the burdens lifted from his face as his daughters squealed with delight. My own girls beamed. Such abundant joy—even for a few moments—from such a small gesture.

As I played the introduction for a praise chorus, I felt as if someone was trying to get my attention. I looked up and the young father winked at me before he closed his eyes and lifted his hands to the Lord in praise.

Is there someone within your influence who could benefit from this idea?

Let us hold unswervingly to the hope we profess, for he who promised is faithful. And let us consider how we may spur one another on toward love and good deeds.
Hebrews 10:23–24

Our Inheritance

TONY EVANS

Faith is the Christian's foundation, hope is his anchor, death is his harbor, Christ is his pilot, and heaven is his country.

Jeremy Taylor

I love to go to the Texas State Fair here in Dallas because I love roller-coasters. And there's more food than you could ever eat. Now I usually get into the fair free because one of my church members gives me tickets. My admission to the fair is a gift paid for by someone else. So let's call the fair heaven.

Once I'm on the fairgrounds, there is so much to do: the rides, the circus, the games, an incredible array of exhibits. I could just go from one thing to another all day long. All of that is available to me simply because my entrance to the fairgrounds gives me access to it. I got in free because someone paid for my ticket. I wasn't denied entrance to the fair, and no one will ask me to leave. I can walk around all day and enjoy the exciting sights, sounds, and smells of the state fair.

But to enjoy everything the fair has to offer to its fullest, I need more than an admission ticket, because at the State Fair, the rides and the food are not free. You have to buy coupons for them. So to fully enjoy the fair, what I need to do is "inherit" the fair. That is, I need someone to say to me, "Tony, this is all yours. Here are all the coupons you will ever need. Enjoy everything you see at no additional cost. You've been a faithful servant, and this is your reward."

All true Christians will enter the kingdom. They will be at the fair, if you will. And it's far better to be at the fair than to miss it completely. There's no comparison. But it's a terrible thing to be at the fair and not be able to ride. It's terrible to have access, but not be a full participant.

Look at it another way. Our oldest son, Tony, Jr., is prominently mentioned in the will Lois and I have drawn up, as you would expect. He's our son, and nothing can change that.

He can, however, be disinherited, even though he cannot be "de-soned." In fact, our will says if any of our children adopt a godless lifestyle from which they do not repent, then the blessings of our inheritance are to be passed on to the other children.

Tony, Jr., is my son by birth. But he is my *heir* by merit. Only by living a consistent Christian lifestyle can he inherit my "kingdom." The inheritance his father has waiting for him ought to motivate him to live right. You know what ought to motivate you and me to live right? The inheritance our Father has waiting for us!

Praise be to the God and Father of our Lord Jesus Christ! In his great mercy he has given us new birth into a living hope through the resurrection of Jesus Christ from the dead, and into an inheritance that can never perish, spoil or fade—kept in heaven for you.

I Peter 1:3–4

Bring out of storage some treasured piece and enjoy it.

Turtle On A Fence Post

MILLIE BARGER

*If you were driving down the road and saw a turtle on a fence post,
wouldn't you wonder how it got there?*

Chuck Swindoll

A turtle doesn't have the ability to climb a post, so someone had to put it there. The turtle can stretch its neck and look around, or draw back into its shell and sit there doing nothing. Who would want to be a turtle like that?

Before I became a speaker for Christian Women's Clubs, I mentioned to a friend that I would feel intimidated by a sophisticated group of women. She replied, "Well, just remember, you're the one on the platform and they're in the audience. That should tell you something."

Whenever I accept an invitation to speak, I remember her words and also those about the turtle. I tell God, "I'm merely Your turtle on a fence post." He is the Someone responsible for putting me on the fence post.

After I spoke at one club, a woman remarked, "We like you. You speak to us on our level." I took that as a compliment. I also remembered that a fence post is not very high. As a turtle, I try not to draw back into my shell, but to stick my neck out and share my testimony of what God has done in my life. Over a period of six months, I spoke at twenty ladies' meetings—either Christian Women's Club or church groups—and was amazed at the number of women who responded and prayed to receive Christ as Savior.

Who wouldn't want to be a turtle on God's fence post?

*You are the light of the world. . . . Neither do people light a lamp and put it
under a bowl. . . . let your light so shine before men that they may . . . praise
your Father in heaven.*

Matthew 5:14–16

> If you're feeling overwhelmed by too many projects, group similar ones together and do all those at the same time.

All Aboard The "Barna-Bus"!

BONNIE COMPTON HANSON

We are made kind by being kind.
Eric Hoffer

Young Mike wiggled in his seat during morning worship service as our pastor discussed the Book of Acts. "Barnabas," the pastor said, "was a real encourager in the Early Church. Barnabas especially encouraged Paul." Suddenly Mike sat up. "Wow, Mom!" he cried. "Can we take a ride on 'Barney's Bus,' too?"

No, Barnabas was not a purple dinosaur puppet. Indeed, he was once just plain Joseph, a Levite of Cyprus. But the early church found him such a rich and constant resource of kind, helpful words and deeds that he's been known as "Barnabas"—a nickname meaning "Son of Encouragement"—ever since.

Can you think of someone like that in your own life? Someone who could see potential in you that no one else could and pushed you to realize it? Someone willing to go the extra mile for you, to trust you, to help you, to encourage you when the bottom seemed to fall out of your life? Someone willing to talk, to smile, to sympathize, to be a real friend?

You can be someone's "Barnabas," also! Think of those around you in your home, neighborhood, school, work, or church. Perhaps it will be a shy, insecure young man no one else talks to or a young girl sensitive about her appearance. Or maybe it will be an immigrant trying hard to understand a new land or an "at-home Mom" swamped with responsibilities. Do you know an elderly shut-in or a shy visitor at church? Also consider a new Christian looking for the next step in his Christian walk.

People needing smiles, warmth, handshakes, words of encouragement, listening ears, home-baked muffins, rides, coffee, and a chance to talk about their joys or sorrows. Well, that's where you come in! You can even be a "Barnabas" to your own pastor and church leaders!

What can you say to someone to encourage them? Obviously not criticism. Neither does God want you to use shallow flattery, "feel-good" sound bites, or anything not grounded in the Scripture. Instead, look for the best in others and you'll be delightfully surprised to find it.

So, all aboard the "Barna-bus Express"! There's plenty of room on board. The "fare" repays you richly. And the "ride" can last you a whole lifetime of joy!

> *. . . whatever is true, whatever is noble, whatever is right, whatever is pure, whatever is lovely, whatever is admirable—if anything is excellent or praiseworthy—think about such things.*
>
> Philippians 4:8

Send flowers anonymously to a relative or friend and see if you hear of their delight through the grapevine. Regardless, you'll receive much pleasure from it.

Working Wives
And Gourmet Gastronomics
June Hetzel

*We'd better go easy on "stick to the ribs" food,
because that's not where it usually sticks.*

Unknown

Given a choice, wouldn't we all love to eat out every night? Like most American women, I'm a wife who works inside and outside the home. After a hard eight- to ten-hour day at the office, the last thing I want to do is add two hours of meal preparation and clean-up. As a result, I'm nearly always in favor of eating out. However, over time, I've learned that too much of a good thing is a bad thing. Check my thighs or pocketbook and you'll see proof. Recognizing that cooking a meal at home is ten times healthier and ten times more economical, I'm desperate for simple recipes that can be prepared "in a snap." Here's my number one favorite and personal variation on Ten Bean Soup:

Step One: When You Grocery Shop. Purchase six to ten bags of a variety of beans and legumes; one large onion; one can of Italian stewed tomatoes; and cooked, lean ham.

Step Two: When You Get Home. Open all the bags of beans and empty them into one large airtight container. These beans will easily provide fifteen to twenty economical, healthy meals.

Step Three: Before You Go to Bed. Place about two cups of dried beans in a crock pot. Fill the crock with water. Swirl and rinse two times. Then, fill the crock pot with water again and allow the beans to soak overnight.

Step Four: When You Wake Up. Pour the water off the beans. Add one to two cups of chopped ham, a chopped onion, one can of stewed Italian tomatoes, salt and pepper, and dried hot chilies if your family likes spicy soups.

Fill the crock pot three-quarters full with water. Place the lid on the crock, plug in, and turn on high.

Step Five: Time to Eat! When you wearily return home after a hard day's work, the aroma of freshly cooked ham and beans will greet you at the door, immediately lifting your spirits. Dinner is ready! Serve the beans hot from the crock pot with a side salad (coleslaw or tossed green) and bread (cornbread or biscuits). Serve several consecutive nights with a variety of side dishes.

Remember, a chef is a person with a big enough vocabulary to give soup a different name every day, so when you serve this dish to your family, be creative. Here are some ideas: Best Bean Soup, Ham Hock Southern Soup, and Gourmet Gastronomic Delight! Or freeze or refrigerate the soup, intermingling with other favorites. Even Daniel, Shadrach, Meshach, and Abed-nego (Daniel 1) knew the value of simple foods as they tested vegetables and water against the king's wine and delicacies.

Simple wins every time, so try this quick, hearty, healthy recipe and simplify your culinary life, reduce fat calories, increase proteins and natural legumes, and save dollars and time!

> *Then God said, "I give you every seed-bearing plant on the face of the*
> *whole earth and every tree that has fruit with seed in it.*
> *They will be yours for food . . ."*
> Genesis 1:29

Health Rule: Eat like a king for breakfast, a prince for lunch, and a pauper for dinner.

Getting Quiet In A Noisy World

Pamela Enderby

A public man, though he is necessarily available at many times, must learn to hide. If he is always available, he is not worth enough when he is available.

Elton Trueblood

For months, I thrived on a "spiritual high" after receiving Christ as my personal Savior. God coddled me with an acute sense of His presence and changes toward godliness seemed to come quickly. However, my spiritual honeymoon gradually faded. Mothering three small children, four years old and under, living on a shoestring budget while church planting and craving close friendships threw me into a tailspin.

Finally, I collapsed under all the pressure and began to understand my need to be alone and quiet before Christ. At first, my mind raced with tasks on my "to do" list, but I didn't give up. Eventually, while sitting quietly before the throne of grace, I learned to hear God's still small voice and glean truth from Scripture as my outer world kept spinning.

You, too, can shut the door to your world of noise and restlessness. These ideas will help.

Adopt a plan. In your daytimer, record a daily "appointment with God" that tells when and where you will meet with Him. Consider buying a Bible Study book and praise music to enhance your time.

Adjust priorities. Skip a soap opera or movie, shorten telephone conversations, or turn off the radio. Instead, meet with God.

Admit and surrender. Call out to God for wisdom, strength, and guidance. Nurture inner peace by giving your concerns, your time, your agenda, and yourself to God.

Avoid distractions. After the phone, TV and radio are turned off, kids' needs carry on. However, with a consistent reminder, "play quietly while

Mommy has her quiet time," children's interruptions will fade. Reward obedience with an extra bedtime story or a special treat. With older children, serve their breakfast picnic style while they watch their favorite video. Hang your "do not disturb" sign as a reminder and set a timer to avoid running late for work. Or consider including the children for a few minutes before sending them off to play.

Arrange childcare. While raising four children six years old and younger, I'd escape to my bedroom after dinner while my husband took charge. If your spouse is unavailable, make plans with a trustworthy neighbor to care for your children a few mornings a week for one hour. Later, return the favor.

When I make time to receive God's love, accept His strength, and claim His promises, I can face life with renewed courage and experience inner joy and peace in a noisy world.

> *Great peace have they who love Your law,*
> *and nothing can make them stumble.*
> Psalm 119:165

If your drinking glasses are stuck hopelessly together, separate them fast by filling the top one with cold water and dipping the bottom in hot water.

One Lone Daffodil

Barbara J. Anson

. . . all at once I saw a crowd, A host, of golden daffodils. . .
William Wordsworth

With a gasp of wonder and a sigh of relief, I spotted the first brilliant sign of spring on a gray and windy morning late in February. I had been gazing out the window during my quiet time. "Oh, God, will this long, cold, wet winter ever come to an end?" As my eyes swept over the dull monotone landscape so typical of this season, my mood was as colorless and gloomy as the leaden sky.

Suddenly my attention was riveted by the first bright yellow daffodil of the season. It was like a golden ray of sunshine. As that one exquisite blossom waved bravely in the breeze, it seemed to expand in my mind until I pictured Wordsworth's host of golden daffodils. Then I began to envision my whole yard being full of spring flowers with their beautiful colors and exquisite shapes. The song of birds seemed to fill the air, too.

With my thoughts refocused on the beauty and promise of spring, my spirits lifted and the sky no longer seemed as gray as it had moments earlier. "Thank you, God, for capturing my attention this morning with one perfect golden daffodil. Thank you for lifting my spirits and expanding my vision. As you showed me this first sign of spring, I am reminded that your compassion is new every morning (Lamentations 3:22,23). You are faithful. Spring will always follow winter, whether in my soul or in nature. Open my eyes to see the beauty in every situation and every season."

When the long winter months seem unending or your mood is as gloomy as a gray February morning, let God gently remind you of the first spring daffodil's promise. Imagine the warmth of spring with its abundant flowers and sweet birdsong being just around the corner. Know that as He did for me, God is always willing to lift your spirits when you focus on all He has provided. Aah, what an abundance of warmth and beauty is contained in the simplicity and promise of one lone daffodil.

Flowers appear on the earth; the season of singing has come,
the cooing of doves is heard in our land.

Song of Songs 2:12

Plant some spring bulbs in your yard or place a silk daffodil on your desk to remind you of God's compassion and faithfulness.

The River

SHARON NORRIS

Nothing endures but change.

Heraclitus

While flying home to Los Angeles from Portland, Oregon, after a writer's conference, we flew over a river. From above, I watched as the river twisted and turned through the landscape. I noticed how, at every point where the river had to change direction, the water rippled much more turbulently than when it flowed through the straightaways. Yet, from above, the entire river was beautiful. It was easy to see how the water could not get from one end of the river to the other, without following its age-old, preset course.

That river made me think of myself and my Christian walk. Like the entire course of the river, God sees where I started and where I have to go. But like the water, I'm just flowing along, with no way of knowing when the next change in direction is coming. I notice that when I get to a curve, a turn in the course, I ripple much more turbulently than when I was flowing through the straightaways.

I must learn a lesson from the river. I know that, with Him as Creator and Designer, my life from beginning to end will flow as one beautiful river. He alone knows where the changes in that course need to be; He alone is best equipped to coordinate both the direction and the sharpness of the turns. However, I alone have the choice as to how I take the turns. I can flow smoothly, taking the curves like a track star on the inside lane, or I can meander turbulently around the corners, complaining every step of the way. It's my call.

But the one thing I must remember is this, I *will* take the curve. God will see to it that I round that bend because He knows it takes that curve to reach His desired end for me. To skip that curve is to go the wrong way and violate His will for me.

What bend in the river are you facing? Choose today not to meander turbulently around the curve, but to flow smoothly in the center of the course. And know this, there's a straightaway just around the bend.

All the days ordained for me were written in your book
before one of them came to be.
Psalm 139:16b

While waiting for food to cook, complete one small task,
like rearranging one drawer in the kitchen.

Letters Of Encouragement

JOANNE YOONA PARK

A faithful friend is finer still than all other treasures upon this earth.

Flavia Weeden

"Did you know that the Bible is a love letter written just for you?" asked my Sunday School teacher. Spellbound, I sat in the classroom unable to answer the question. Then I knew. Penetrating and fascinating my heart, the answer enlightened my inquisitive twelve-year-old mind.

As a pre-teen, letter writing was an all too familiar means of communication. I grew up writing letters to a family overseas and scribbling notes to girlfriends during English class. Every day, the anticipation of getting a reply excited my youthful heart. That day I learned that God had a special message for me. Ever since, the Bible has been the source of encouragement in my spiritual walk and I too wanted to share letters of good news with whom I love.

Growing up, I received many cards from my parents, friends, and spiritual mentors. Unexpected get-well cards healed my stomach flus while friendship cards tickled my heart. Thank-you cards inspired me and other times brought tears. And every year, the birthday cards reassured me of the love and joy of friendship. Having experienced the delight of God's Word and the words of loved ones, God taught me to exalt and pray for others through writing. I promised God that every time I thought of a friend during the week, I would write a letter of encouragement and lift the friend up in prayer. Because of this, I prepared a big colorful box full of cards, letter sets, markers, stickers, and stamps ready to send whenever I thought of a friend.

These days, letter writing is considered an ancient form of communication to most people. E-mails, fax, and telephones have taken over. I use them too when I do business. However, when it comes to personal relationships, I still love sending letters through the U.S. Postal Service. I decorate them to make them fun, personal, and meaningful.

Some friends laugh when they hear that I still send letters through the mail. They joke around that it's a waste of time. But again and again, the friends who laugh are the ones who call and thank me when they receive a letter of encouragement.

For example, my friend Christy recently moved and came across an old box filled with dozens of letters I had written over the seven years we've been friends. Christy told me she read them one by one, giggling, laughing, and crying. While Christy confesses that she hates letter writing, she faithfully keeps in touch by calling. But once in a while, she does surprise me with a funny card. These out-of-the blue surprises have brightened both of our days, causing us to reflect upon our friendship. And over the years, Christy and I have kept in touch and grown in our friendship.

Just as I learned from my Sunday school teacher, the Bible is a letter written to us by God. It encourages, sharpens, and penetrates our soul and brings us good news. Likewise, we should share good news with our loved ones by sending letters of encouragement. Not only will they be surprised by the unexpected gift, they'll be tickled with joy and might even call you. Just wait and see.

Your statutes are my heritage forever; they are the joy of my heart. My heart is set on keeping your decrees to the very end.
Psalm 119:111–112

When you're reminded of a friend during the week, write a letter of encouragement and lift the friend up in prayer.

Making The Most Of God's Gifts

Frances Gregory Pasch

All wealth is the product of labor.
Locke

Are rising food prices putting a strain on your budget? Would you like to save money and have fun at the same time? I saved thousands of dollars over the years while raising our five sons. It took patience and perseverance but it truly paid off. How? By buying wisely and using coupons.

Start by checking weekly food ads in your local newspaper. Compare prices of at least three markets near your home. Circle items you regularly buy and check the meat specials. Plan your meals around the sale items. Then select the two stores with the best prices and make a shopping list for each. You'll save more money by going to at least two supermarkets, but if you only have time for one, then pick the store with the best overall prices.

Clipping coupons will add to your savings. They're available in most Sunday newspapers. You'll also find coupons in magazines, on the product packaging, or inside it. You can maximize your savings even more by looking for stores that offer double coupons. This means that the store will double the face value of each coupon. But be sure to check each store for restrictions before you start.

Supermarkets also offer their own weekly coupon specials. Many markets now have clipless coupons. The market gives you a plastic card which the checker scans before ringing your order. The scanner automatically picks up the coupon savings. You can also use a manufacturer's coupon from your collection on the same item for additional savings.

Smart shoppers carry their coupons with them at all times. If you only have a few, put them in an envelope. As your collection grows, put them in a 4 x 6 file box. Separate them with dividers in alphabetical order according to categories, such as cake mixes, juices, toiletries, etc. You can increase your coupon collection by buying extra copies of your paper weekly. It pays to stock up even without a coupon. When there's an exceptionally good sale on a product you need, buy at least two or three of that item. Eliminate another item from your list that you can really do without. The following week stock up on another sale item. Eventually you will have your own stock-pile for emergencies.

Here are a few more tips to help you become an even smarter shopper:

1. Eat before you shop—it helps avoid impulse buying.
2. Shop alone, when possible—others influence your buying.
3. Shop in the early morning or early afternoon when lines are shorter—your time is worth money, too.
4. Bring the store ad with you, in case prices are marked incorrectly.
5. Get a raincheck when a sale item is out of stock.
6. Learn to spot a legitimate sale by becoming familiar with regular everyday prices. Just because something is on a display rack doesn't mean it's a bargain.
7. Look for unadvertised in-store specials.
8. Look for specially marked packages.
9. Keep a record of your savings as an incentive to keep "shopping smart."

As you follow these guidelines, you'll save money abundantly!

The man who had received the five talents brought the other five. "Master," he said, "you entrusted me with five talents. See, I have gained five more."
Matthew 25:20

> Put your savings in a separate account, if possible, and treat yourself to something special that you would not have been able to afford.

Gone But Not Forgotten

KENDRA PRINCE

A dog is the only thing on earth that loves you more than he loves himself.

Josh Billings

My family is blessed to own a Pembroke Welsh Corgi named "Becca." Truth be told, Becca owns us. In her five years with the Prince household, she has managed to wrap each of us around her paw. Corgis have a way of doing that!

Recently, my mother and I attended the AKC dog show in town. Of course, we were most interested in the corgis. The corgi competition included obedience trials. In one part of the obedience trial, the corgis are lined up and given a command by the handler to lie down and stay. The handlers then leave the ring for several minutes. The corgis are graded on how well they maintain position while their handler is out of sight.

Our hearts went out to one little corgi who had trouble staying still. The longer her handler was gone, the more restless she became. She sat up and even barked once, as if to say, "Where are you?" Then she laid back down. It looked as if she tried to fool the handler into thinking she had been obedient by lying down again. However, she sat back up in time to see her handler making her way back to the ring. Her relief at seeing the handler was mixed with her sorrow at failing to obey.

How often have we failed to obey God's commands just because He is "out of sight"? How often have we become restless while waiting for a sense of His immediate presence? Just as the corgi's obedience, or lack of, reflects on the handler, our obedience or lack of, reflects on God. His Word gives us His commands and His Spirit within us should give us a sense of His presence.

We ran into Becca's breeder at the dog show. She told me that obedience training isn't hard but it takes spending a lot time with the dog. If the handler hasn't spent sufficient time training the dog, it shows in the ring. We will be more successful at obeying God's commands by spending time with Him.

So be careful to do what the LORD your God has commanded you; do not turn aside to the right or to the left. Walk in all the way that the LORD your God has commanded you, so that you may live and prosper and prolong your days in the land you will possess.

Deuteronomy 5:33

This week, commit anew to studying God's commands and following them. Ask God for a fresh sense of His presence so that you will be even more motivated to obey.

Just Simple Hospitality

SHARON RAIVO REMMEN

The road to a friend's house is never long.

Danish proverb

Not long ago, friends of mine stopped by unexpectedly for a late morning visit. We had a nice talk along with a cup of coffee. While chatting, I debated with myself about asking them to stay for lunch. But since all I could offer that day was a simple sandwich or soup, I decided against it.

Later, after they left, my decision troubled me. Was the simpleness of what we would eat so important? Or was the hospitality I wanted to offer them even more important?

A few days later, I happened to recall a visit to a relative's home many years before. My cousin and his wife had invited us to stay for a light supper. We had grilled cheese sandwiches and home-made cherry sauce for dessert.

Although this happened nineteen years previously, I still hadn't forgotten that meal! Not only because it tasted good, but because the added ingredients of genuine hospitality and warm friendship had made that homey supper a memorable one.

I realized what my lesson was. It's not the food itself that counts, but the meaning and love behind it. Next time I will offer friends that simple meal. What will you do?

Practice hospitality.
Romans 12:13b

Keep a small pad and pencil on your bedside table. If you awaken in the night with a thought you want to remember, you can quickly and easily jot it down.

The Power Of A Few Kind Words

Joy Anna Rosendale

The greatest thing a man can do for his heavenly Father is to be kind to some of His other children.

Henry Drummond

I trudged up the sidewalk toward my car after a hard day at work, fretting about my boss and office politics. Christians aren't supposed to worry—but I couldn't calm my hammering thoughts. With the late afternoon sun shining full in my face, I didn't realize at first that someone was coming toward me.

His thick eyeglasses glinted in the golden light and the young man hung his head as soon as he realized I'd spotted him. As we got closer, he glanced up at me and his face got red. He turned his face and stared hard at the grass, his arms hanging rigid like two sticks, as the distance between us narrowed.

We were just about to pass each other on the sidewalk when he sucked in a big breath, hunched up his shoulders and squinted at me, connecting with my eyes just for a second. "God bless you," he said.

"What did you say!" The last thing I expected was for him to speak to me.

He winced, took another big breath and said louder, "G-God bless you!"

I stopped, turned around, and stared after him as he shuffled on up the sidewalk. With his shoulders still hunched and his head down, he walked so stiffly that he almost limped, as if he were thinking, "She must think I'm a real jerk!"

I didn't. I thought he was practically an angel with a message from heaven. God was trying to speak to me, and He chose a terribly shy young man of whom it would cost a lot to tell me that He cared about my stress at the office. I mattered to Him. And He wanted to bless me.

A few weeks later I was laid off from my job and found a much better position. God did bless me. But I've never forgotten the kind words spoken by that shy young man. In tough times or in happy, they hover like a benediction over me and lodge in my heart. A simple effort on the young man's part has blossomed into lasting benefit for me. He will never know until he gets to heaven the power of his few kind words.

Probably, you too have said kind things to people. Maybe you've said "God bless you" to a store clerk or given a coworker a compliment. You may have said "I love you" to a child or written a note of encouragement to a friend who was hurting. You carry in your heart and in your mouth the power to permanently bless another's life. And you too will never know until you get to heaven the power of a few kind words.

The mouth of the righteous is a fountain of life . . .
Proverbs 10:11a

Make a list of the kind things you've said and done each day
for a week, and plan opportunities to increase your efforts.

Shredded Tissue

Suzy Ryan

Failure is only the opportunity to begin again, more intelligently.
Henry Ford

Earlier in the week, my seven-year-old son cut his lip during his baseball game. I patched it up, then put some extra tissue in his back pocket.

Unfortunately, when I did the load of dark clothes, I forgot to remove it from his uniform. I didn't know whether to laugh or cry when white spotted laundry peeked out from the washer. Never claiming victory over the bottomless basket of laundry is daunting enough, without having to "scotch tape" the Kleenex from a load full of clothes.

While starting to tackle this monster mess, God impressed on me that the shredded tissue is similar to sin. If it sits unconfessed in our heart, silently like the hidden tissue in my son's back pocket, it creates havoc with our lives. It stains the fabric of our soul and bleeds into every area of our existence.

When we finally confess our transgressions, God's detergent of grace cleans the initial wound of sin and the consequences of not confessing it. Then we are blemish free and ready for the abundant life that He promises us.

If we confess our sins, He is faithful and just and will forgive us our sins and purify us from all unrighteousness.

I John 1:9

Pray for God to convict you of the small and large sin in your life. As soon as He reveals your transgressions, immediately confess them to your forgiving Father.

Approaching the Throne

DEBBI TAYLOR

If you mean to know God intimately, you must begin by taking the time to listen to His voice.

Unknown

One peaceful summer morning, I arose early while the house was still, eager to spend some quiet time alone with my Father. With my favorite Bible, personal journal, and a cup of steaming cocoa beside me, I read Hebrews 4:16, meditating on the concept of approaching the throne room of my Heavenly King. Vivid pictures of royal, resplendent surroundings filled my imagination. And on an elevated dais, the Almighty One, robed in glorious garments awaited my entrance. As much as I tried to imagine coming boldly into the presence of the King of the Universe, the more I gazed upon His splendor and majesty, I could only imagine approaching His throne room with overwhelming humility and reverence.

As I reflected quietly in my heart, vacillating between trembling awe and a longing to march boldly into His presence, God illuminated Hebrews 4:16 with a tender scene that forever changed my perspective. Midst the grandeur of this exalted throne room of the King of Kings, I envisioned a little girl running toward the King, her face alight with excitement and joy. Though it was evident He was absorbed in important matters, He paused from His sovereign duties, a radiant smile lighting His face. His eyes shone as His open arms warmly welcomed this child who leapt into His embrace.

Immediately, I heard His still, small voice whisper to my heart, "It is right for you to worship Me as your King, enthroned in majesty. But remember that you are the daughter of the King, the one I welcome into My presence without hesitation. See the smile that lights up My face and the twinkle in My eyes when I see you come into My throne room? Nothing brings greater joy to a parent than the spontaneous expression of love from their beloved child. And this is the joy you bring to My heart when you choose to run to My presence; when you choose to spend time with Me over all your other options."

Joy and gratitude welled up in my heart with the profound realization that when I come to the throne as a child, presenting my concerns to my Heavenly Daddy, my simple expression of love delights His heart.

Let us then approach the throne of grace with confidence, so that we may receive mercy and find grace to help us in our time of need.
Hebrews 4:16

> Make a note of how you spend your money for a week and then decide how you could have been wiser financially.

Send A Card
Margaret Primrose

O Master, let me walk with Thee
In lowly paths of service free.
Washington Gladden

I love to send cards, so I send a lot of them. There is always someone who would welcome a "Happy Birthday" or simply needs to know "You've been a blessing to me."

Doesn't it cost a lot? Well, it could if I did not know that the personal touch is more important to my friends and family than the size and market value of the card. Packages of cards, sales, and discount stores help to keep the cost manageable. Usually the best bargains are at thrift stores and garage sales. Sometimes I have paid as little as three cents each for cards and note paper of top quality.

Often the lowest-priced cards are blank, but that leaves space for creativity. On one a dog had his mouth close to another's ear. Inside the card I wrote, "It's time to whisper something in your ear. You're special."

I like postcards, especially when I don't have much time to write a note and want to save postage. A package of 4" x 6" file cards is a good choice. Available in several colors besides white, their size provides a bit more space than cards sold at the post office. Often I draw a line through the middle of the back of a card. The address goes on one half, the note on the other.

Stickers help to dress up cards. Once a cardinal on a corner of the front helped me say, "A little bird told me . . ." A bough of apples on peach background seemed right for Thanksgiving. A border of happy faces spurred me into writing:

> These happy-face stickers
> Are here to say,
> "I'm thinking of you.
> Please have a nice day."

Cartoons, old photos to which I can add a caption and even a cookie cutter have given me ideas. The duck I cut out after drawing around the cookie cutter was the impetus for "Just paddling by to tell you 'Hi!'" A few swishes with a blue magic marker gave the duck a pond in which to swim.

Occasionally I can turn a used greeting card into a picture postcard by trimming off the back with a paper cutter.

Perhaps some day you and I may want to experiment with dried or tatted flowers and even calligraphy. But right now we all know someone who needs encouragement. Why not send her a simple card? It may be just what she needs.

. . . let us encourage one another . . .
Hebrews 10:25b

Even if you can't send a card, find a way to encourage
someone today.

Spring All Year
DURLYNN ANEMA GARTEN

Come, gentle spring! ethereal Mildness! come.
James Thomson

Our winter was unusually cold in 1998–99, so cold that three-quarters of our plants froze. Whenever I looked outside during December, January, and February, I viewed brown, ugly shrubs and perennials. As the cold continued I despaired of seeing green again—and vowed in the future only to cultivate those plants which remained green during the onslaught of cold.

However, by the end of February, the sun once again exuded warmth—as only can happen in central California. One day of sunshine was my incentive to survey my outside disaster. With clippers in hand, I invaded the yard, ready to attack all those ugly brown and brittle branches.

But imagine my surprise! Hidden beneath the dead milieu were small green stubs and leaves, eagerly awaiting the sun to begin the growing process once more. Even the branches of the Europa daisy bent at my touch, not dead at all, only waiting for spring, as my lantana always does.

As I gazed at this harbinger of warmer days, I thought about our lives. Do we sometimes allow the ugly brown to overwhelm us until we forget the beauty beneath the surface of our lives? Do we become so overburdened with life's chores we forget to gaze underneath to what God has given us?

God gave us spring to remind us of renewal, reseeding, and new growth. Green buds are ready to spring forth, just as life springs forth for all of us when we trust God. As spring arrives this year, why not vow to place new growth in your life every day, instead of waiting for the next spring?

There is a time for everything, and a season for every activity under heaven.
Ecclesiastes. 3:1

Check your fire extinguisher to make sure it is still useable.

The Bright Spot In The Fog

DONNA J. ADEE

As endless as God's blessings are,
So should my praises be
For all His daily goodnesses
That flow unceasingly!

Adams

Alone for the day, I looked out at the dreary fog. Such a heavy fog all day is unusual for Kansas. The cold damp day brought on a melancholy sadness, following the joyous excitement of the holidays with our children and grand-children.

As I worked on letters and cards neglected during the busy days of family activities, I kept looking out the window for some sign of the fog dissipating. No sign of the sun; just dreary, heavy fog continuing for the day.

Suddenly as I sat there looking out the window, something bright caught my eye. In a small tree some forty feet from the house, I saw a bright flicker of color. It couldn't be! Nothing would be out in this miserable fog. I ran for the binoculars, hoping they would improve my vision through the fog

Focusing quickly, I trained the binoculars on that tree. There he was, the most brilliant crimson cardinal, twisting and turning as if to show me his best side. He wasn't melancholy or sad in the fog. He was going on with the life that the Creator had made for him.

By concentrating on the foggy, dreary weather, I forgot to focus on God and His lessons in the melancholy times. Rather than focusing on what I could do to encourage others, I was focusing on "poor me" who was all alone on a melancholy day.

What are you focusing on today? If it's something sad, it's most likely coloring your perspective in a dreary fog. Why not focus on God's goodness instead? His goodness is constant regardless of your circumstances. A new outlook may help you see His goodness when it wasn't apparent before.

But my eyes are fixed on you, O Sovereign Lord; in you I take refuge—
don't give me over to death.

Psalm 141:8

Make a list of your "inheritances in Christ" as mentioned in the first chapter of Ephesians.

Mommy, Pleeeze Can I Buy It?

BONNIE WATKINS

*An object in possession seldom retains the same charm
that it had in pursuit.*

Pliny the Younger

Needing to have so many "things" is a current American obsession. Particularly in children, the "gimmee" expectation can be frightening. How many weary mothers have you seen give in to their children's loud demands of a new toy with every trip to the store? Teaching children to live a simple life doesn't mean that life has to be stripped to the bare essentials or be boring; it just means that you are more creative in making the essentials more fun and entertaining.

With pre-schoolers, everything can be a game, and this makes simple living more fun. We use special names for things: blackeyed peas and brown rice go by the old Cajun name of Hoppin' John. My five-year-old gets the biggest kick out of this. We always repeat the old rhyme, "I love you once; I love you twice. I love you better than beans and rice," while eating this humble fare. We all get into the kitchen and prepare food together on Mexican Night and eat inexpensive bean chalupas or turkey tacos.

A trendy restaurant in town serves baked potatoes with different toppings for the main course and we do our own at home, using the restaurant's name and a homemade menu. Making a menu or using candles can make any ordinary fare exciting for children. Do be careful with candles, however. Once I walked away and left the boys unattended. My five-year-old sauntered in to relay that his two-year-old brother had "set the table on fire" with his napkin!

These children can also decimate a ream of paper in an afternoon. I hate to plead economics when they want to write the numbers from one to one hundred, one number per page. So, I have found ways to save on everyday items. Companies are usually happy to part with excess computer paper. Butcher paper or brown grocery bags split open to make perfect art paper.

These paper-eating children also love connect-the-dot pictures, but they can go through an entire book in one afternoon. I use simple coloring books and make my own dot pictures by using a blank piece of paper over the picture to trace and randomly supply dots.

We make our own finger paints and play dough. Recipes for these items are found in many cookbooks with children's recipes, or in craft books for children available at the public library. And the library is another source of inexpensive entertainment of borrowed books or activities centered on reading.

Put your mind to providing simple alternatives for your children. You'll be glad when they think that homemade toys are more fun than store toys.

For we brought nothing into the world, and we can take nothing out of it.
I Timothy 6:7

Invite neighborhood children over to share simple living activities. You'll be teaching them simplicity and ministering at the same time.

Abundant Grace
KATHLEEN DALE WRIGHT

Happy are the simple followers of Jesus Christ who have been overcome by His grace, and are able to sing the praises of the all-sufficient grace of God in Jesus Christ with humbleness of heart.
Dietrich Bonhoeffer

We received a letter from a sixty-five-year-old friend, which told about her recent mission trip to Mexico. She wrote about God's unusual provision of their material needs on this trip, and of ways in which God had used them to bring others to know Jesus Christ. However, her remarks about the provision of God's grace touched me the most. At the beginning of her letter, she'd told about preparing for her trip to Mexico. This included loading materials for repairing a church building into the back of her pickup truck.

"I was trying to move a heavy board and leaning over the rails pulling," she wrote. "I knew I probably couldn't move it, but, for some reason, I kept on pulling until my ribs cracked. I began to pray because I couldn't get my breath. I said, 'Lord, how can I go and do work on the church with broken ribs?' When I kept pressing the Lord, he said, 'Ask for rib-grace.' I'd never heard that before but I said, 'Okay, Lord, I'll claim rib grace.'"

Somehow this simple story gave me a fresh insight into appropriating God's grace for any need. We would all like to be healed of every sickness or delivered from every trying situation immediately. But we know that this just isn't the way life works. We often have to endure sickness and pain and loss. But we have the opportunity each day to tap into God's exceedingly abundant grace for each need.

We often get a preconceived idea about the meaning of a word like "grace." And it sometimes takes couching the word in new terms, such as "rib grace," to open the floodgates of understanding. In the New Testament, only one Greek word is used for grace: charis. The Amplified Bible gives charis two general meanings: 1) unmerited favor and 2) spiritual strength. One dictionary calls grace "an excellence of power granted by God."

What kind of grace do you need today? Do you need housecleaning grace, job coping grace, child training grace, spending grace, care giving grace, tithing grace, or saving grace? The list could go on and on. So, let us come boldly today to God's throne of grace, to receive His unmerited gift, excellence of power, and spiritual strength, so that we can appropriate all we need to serve Him joyfully and live an abundant life.

And God is able to make all grace abound to you, so that in all things at all times, having all that you need, you will abound in every good work.
II Corinthians 9:8

If you're having trouble keeping track of where your cash is going, try this. Put your week's recreation money, lunch money, grocery money, etc., into marked envelopes for a while and write each "withdrawal" on the outside of that envelope.

Seizing The Day
VEDA BOYD JONES

Consider that this day ne'er dawns again.
Dante Alighieri

It was a rare day in February. The temperature, which should have been around forty, soared past the seventy mark on the back porch thermometer. And there was wind.

I paced outside in the Ozark sunshine, restless, pensive. With sudden resolve, I marched inside the house to the phone.

"This day was made for sailing," I told my husband, once his secretary connected us. "Can you get away?" We were half-owners of a seventeen-year-old sailboat, which was sitting in the sun at the lake. There was nothing fancy about the boat, but it was watertight and danced along the surface of the water when the wind filled her sails.

"What about the boys?" he asked.

"School's out at three. They have piano lessons, but I know they'd be glad to skip them this once."

He looked over his schedule and decided he could go in early the next day to make up the work. I called the piano teacher, who was thrilled with the gift of a free hour.

I put the chicken that was thawing for supper in the refrigerator, packed sandwiches and drinks, and within an hour the four of us were at the lake. The boys laughed with glee at playing hooky from piano. My husband's eyes twinkled as we piled our gear on the boat and set sail.

We had no destination. We sailed where the wind took us. We laughed and gazed at God's wonders. The trees on shore were still bare, a sight we hadn't seen from this angle because we'd never sailed in February. Birds soared overhead. A warm breeze filled our sails, and water lapped against the boat.

As the sun neared the horizon, the temperature took a nosedive. We huddled in our jackets and turned the boat toward the dock.

We had taken the day God had given us and made the very most of it. We'd spent quality family time together. The cheerful faces around me reflected the effect of being spontaneous and seizing the day.

The boys promised to practice their piano a little extra the next day. I vowed to make tomorrow's supper a feast, and my husband was headed in early to work the next morning. We would not slight our regular responsibilities, but we enjoyed the special February day God had given us.

When was the last time you did something spontaneous? Try something small even today. It'll make your day abundant.

This is the day the LORD has made; let us rejoice and be glad in it.
Psalm 118:24

Don't plan every minute of your day. Give yourself free time so that you can rearrange responsibilities and enjoy a spontaneous event.

Protected by a Mother's Wings
KATHY COLLARD MILLER

The same love of God that melted the icy fingers of death now warms my heart.
David Carpenter

I recently heard about the experience of a forest ranger walking through an area of Yellowstone National Park after a fire swept through the area. He came across the sickening sight of a bird seemingly petrified in ashes, perched statuesquely at the base of a tree. Although deeply saddened at the sight, the ranger knocked the bird's body over with a stick. Suddenly, three tiny chicks scurried from under their dead mother's wings.

What had given that mother bird the courage to face that fire, willing to sacrifice her own life to keep her babies safe? Only the love of a parent could have empowered her to resist her urge to fly away. She could have left her progeny behind and saved her own life, but she stood her ground and hoped her offspring would be protected sufficiently from the flames.

Those baby birds may have resisted being confined under their mother's wings, but she knew what was best. Through their obedience, they survived the fire. In her sacrifice, she demonstrated her incredible love.

God has done the same for you and me. He sent His Son, Jesus, to sacrifice His own life, in order to keep us safe from sin's destruction. Will we take shelter under His loving wings? Will we huddle beneath His protection or go our own way into the fire's heat? He knows what's best and offers the greatest love anyone could give us—the sacrificial love of a Heavenly Father.

He will cover you with his feathers, and under his wings you will find refuge; his faithfulness will be your shield and rampart.

Psalm 91:4

The next time you hear the song of a bird, remind yourself of your Heavenly Father's love and whisper "thank you, Lord."

Treasured Times

EVA MARIE EVERSON

Row, row, row the boat,
Gently down the stream.
Merrily, merrily, merrily, merrily,
Life is but a dream!
Traditional Children's Song

Nearly twenty years ago, when I was expecting my daughter, the popularity of breast feeding was once again on the upswing. Organizations like La Leche League met in homes, churches, schools, and hospitals. One of my first decisions as a new mother was to breast feed my baby, so I sought the nearest chapter of La Leche League for instruction.

Reactions to my decision varied. "Why are you being taught to do what other mammals do naturally?" my grandmother asked with a chuckle.

"What do you mean 'instead of the bottle'?" my mother-in-law gasped.

Even my mother expressed concern. "Are you sure you want to nurse for so long?"

"Six months," I said. "Six months and then I'll wean her to a bottle."

Wishful thinking. Six months stretched like the marks across my body to sixteen months. It was no longer a matter of my decision, my knowledge, or my choice. It was my daughter's choice. She vehemently refused to take the bottle, pushing it away whenever I tried to entice her with it. No, no! The breast was in; the bottle was out!

Naturally by the sixteenth month, feedings were infrequent at ten in the morning and at ten at night: naptime and bedtime. I had recently introduced Jessica to a Tommy Tippee cup, the yellow, round-bottomed, two-handled cup with a mouth piece. Juice, watered-down cola, and water went into the cup. The milk was still in me.

One night, as ten o'clock neared, I sat in my rocker and called to my little one. "Jessica? Are you ready to nurse and go to sleep?"

She stood before me, dressed in her footed pajamas, her fuzzy blond hair whisping around her cherub face. "No," she said gently shaking her head. "I want a cup."

"No, sweetie. The cup doesn't have milk. Mommy has milk."

"I want a cup," she repeated, then turned. I watched her little padded bottom sway left to right as she proceeded toward the kitchen. Dutifully, I followed her.

My baby never nursed again. Countless times over the years I have said, "I wish I had known the last time was *the last time*. I would have enjoyed it more." As she approaches adulthood, I can name other "last times" I wish I had known about. The last time I carried her on my hip, the last time she called me Mommy, the last time we sang "Row, Row, Row The Boat" together, and the last time I had to drive her anywhere.

Every moment that we spend with our children, even the argumentative times, are silver treasures. We should never allow them to tarnish, but instead, identify them as the valuable gifts they are. Every "time" could be the last time. Never take them for granted, but recognize their fragility and hold them close to your heart.

But Mary treasured up all these things and pondered them in her heart.
Luke 2:19

> Never walk through the house empty-handed.
> Take a stray object closer to its rightful place.

Children's Day

SUZY RYAN

You know you are a mother when, you stop criticizing the way your mother raised you.
Unknown

"When is Children's Day?" I whined to my mother after my second grade class created a flower wall hanging for Mother's Day.

You know her answer. "Every day is Children's Day."

Now, as a mother of three young children, I know the question will travel full circle. While pondering an answer for my own babes, I smile at how I bristled at the drudgery of being a child.

As an exhausted mother reminiscing about my youth, I fantasize about . . .

- being sent to my room for a time-out. I promise I will not come out until called.
- someone coaxing me to eat my veggies and fruit while keeping me away

from the chocolates that call my name. I promise to appreciate the time it takes to make that crunchy salad and succulent fruit plate.

- planning three recesses a day for me to run and play. I promise to run hard, swing high, and slide fast.
- being put to bed early. I promise not to complain. Really, seven is not too early for me.
- having a hot bubble bath poured for me. I promise to scrub the dirt and not splash the water.
- someone demanding I read one book a day. I promise to write a book report and keep track of the minutes spent reading.
- someone compelling me to write thank-you notes. I promise to use good penmanship if they are addressed and mailed for me.
- being forced to drink ice-cold water. I promise not to snivel for a sugar-laden soda or a syrupy juice concoction.

But alas, as a mom that isn't going to happen.

My eight-year-old son, just came in from playing catch with his friend and asked, "Mom, why isn't there a children's day?" (His class must be working on Mother's Day gift.)

I still did not have an adequate answer. I hesitated when the echo that cascaded from my mouth sounded (yikes!) just like my mother.

"Every day is Children's Day," I replied. Confused, he shot back outside. I chuckled to myself. He will understand one day. In time, he will understand.

Even though no one will do those things for you, why not do one of them for yourself and make every day a Mother's Day?

Sons are a heritage from the Lord, children a reward from him.
Psalm 127:3

Keep a journal of the precious things your child says.
Write in it once a month and when the child turns eighteen,
present the journal as a birthday gift.

The Gift

KAREN POLAND

*Thou who hast given so much to me,
give one thing more—a grateful heart!*

George Herbert

This year was special for me. The Lord gave me a gift. I don't recall asking for it. I don't think I even realized that I needed it; however, when it arrived, everything changed for me.

I have always been amazed at what can result from a small seed of discontentment. A broken marriage can be sparked by a small irritation or disappointment, which grew into despair and abandonment. Or it may be an unfulfilled dream or failure that journeyed down the road to depression and hopelessness. In the most secret places of our hearts, I would guess that all of us have struggled with the "if onlys."

As a mom consumed by the unending needs of my family, I have sometimes allowed my heart to wander into discontentment. As a wife experiencing episodes of distance and alienation from my husband, I have traveled in my mind to dissatisfaction. Although this was not always a burning problem, it was still there. Moments of questioning, "Why is it that I cannot give my whole heart to this task—or to this person?" At times it was as if something was missing inside of me.

But the Father met me this year. At a moment that I cannot define, He gave me a gift. I do not recall reaching out for the hem of His garment, yet I feel as though I have touched it. The gift was contentment. Suddenly I have come to see it all more clearly. I have realized the value in all that I have . . . my husband . . . my children . . . our ministry. I have just taken notice that my husband makes the effort to kiss me each time he leaves the house. Now, rather than simply receiving his kiss, I give one as well. I am amazed that he never stopped after all those times that I never reciprocated. I watch him with an overflowing heart, as he plays and wrestles with the children. Where does he get such energy after a long day of work? My "mother heart" is renewed to look beyond the hassles and find the fun. Laughter is back.

Why not reach out for the hem of His contentment?

But godliness with contentment is great gain.
I Timothy 6:6

Set up separate work areas for doing different kinds of projects and keep your needed materials in that area.

Do You Fake It?
MILLIE BARGER

Resolved, never to reprove another except I experience at the same time a peculiar contrition of heart.
Henry Martyn

My friend, Wilma tired of fastening her seat belt, draped the strap over her shoulder but did not buckle it. When her little grandson climbed into the back seat of her car, his mother reminded him, "Fasten your seat belt."

He asked, "Shall I fake it like Grandma?"

Grandma Wilma realized her grandson had received the wrong message from her carelessness. When she told me about it, I thought of how that applies to our spiritual actions. The way we behave and the opinions we express influence others more than we realize, even when we don't think they're watching.

We should ask ourselves whether our actions are consistent with the beliefs we espouse. Or, do others see things which make them think we're faking our faith? We can say we trust God, but when we worry or fret, what are we communicating?

The next time you put on your seat belt, ask yourself, "Am I faking anything in my walk with God?"

> *So that you might be able to discern what is best and may be pure*
> *and blameless until the day of Christ.*
>
> Philippians 1:10

> Do a chore like cleaning out the medicine cabinet
> or a kitchen drawer (brought into the bathroom)
> while supervising a child in the bathtub.

Right before My Eyes

PATTY STUMP

Faith is believing beyond the optic nerve.
Unknown

Before scooting our kids to school, my husband noticed that our son, T. J., needed a bit of assistance with his 'hairstyle.' With a brush in one hand and styling gel in the other, my husband launched a surprise attack on the wayward strands, catching our unsuspecting son off guard.

"Leave my hair alone! I want it the way God made it!" T. J. exclaimed.

While a few minor adjustments could have improved his appearance, we realized that his outlook on the situation was worth respecting.

Later, as I caught a glimpse of my reflection in the mirror, I found myself critical of the face that greeted me. If only my skin, my hair, and my figure looked a little different. Within a matter of moments, I found myself lacking in numerous areas, leaving me discouraged and disappointed with my "lot in life." What a way to start the day!

Then I recalled my five-year-old's words: "Leave it alone; I want it the way God made it." Taking another glance in the mirror, I realized it wasn't my appearance that needed to be adjusted, but my attitude. I had become focused on what I perceived to be shortcomings. Consequently, I overlooked God's creativity in my fashion and form. Psalm 139:14 states that we are fearfully and wonderfully made—created by God himself. Furthermore, it encourages us to give thanks to God, accepting our form and features as His design.

It's easy to become discouraged and discontent when our eyes become fixed on ourselves. Yet, when we shift our focus from our flaws to our Father, we can discover an endless assortment of things to be thankful for. Things right before our eyes! For example, we have vision to behold what God has created, the ability to smell the fragrance of flowers or a favorite meal, arms to hug with and fingers that can simplify daily tasks, the ability to laugh, and even the capacity to cry. Yet our list doesn't end there. Beyond ourselves, the world around us surrounds us with sights, sounds, smells, and experiences that can give us a glimpse of God's abundant handiwork and creativity. Yet in order to see His wonders, we mustn't look for perfection, but rather look with a perspective that is grounded in an attitude of gratitude.

Each day seek to see the wonders of His work. Adjust your focus; shifting your perspective from how you think things should be to how God has created them. In doing so, you'll quickly discover an abundance of God's handiwork—sometimes simplistic yet simultaneously majestic, often unnoticed yet incredibly noteworthy.

Give thanks in all circumstances, for this is God's will for you in Christ Jesus.
I Thessalonians 5:18

Take time today to thank God specifically
for three attributes
He created in you!

Credits

For Our Own Good from *When God Doesn't Make Sense*, by James Dobson, Tyndale, IL., 1993. Used by permission. [12]

On Display from *Sincerely . . . Gigi*, by Gigi Graham Tchividjian, Zondervan, MI, 1984. [90]

A Rabbit on the Swim Team from *Growing Strong in the Seasons of Life*, by Charles R. Swindoll, Multnomah, 1983. [94]

Avoiding Stress Fractures from *Promises and Priorities*, by H. Norman Wright, Servant Publications, MI, 1997. Used by permission. [225]

The Value of Rebounding from *Returning to Your First Love*, by Tony Evans, Moody, IL, 1995. Used by permission. [165]

Simplicity of Time from *Freedom from Tyranny of the Urgent*, by Charles E. Hummel, InterVarsity Press, IL, 1997. Eagle Publishing owns the rights for Europe and British Commonwealth. Used by permission. [99]

Bogged Down Thinking from *Taming Tension*, by W. Phillip Keller, Baker Book House, MI, 1979. Used by permission. [231]

Priorities adapted from *The Man in the Mirror*, by Patrick M. Morley, Wolgemuth & Hyatt, TN. [239]

Eternity in Our Hearts from *Eternity*, by Joseph M. Stowell, Moody, IL, 1995. Used by permission. [175]

God's Silence from *My Utmost for His Highest*, by Oswald Chambers, Discover House Publishers, MI, 1963. Used by permission. [36]

Who Pushes Your Swing? from *On the Anvil*, by Max Lucado, Tyndale House, IL, 1985. Used by permission. [108]

Have You Any Wool? from *Mirror, Mirror on the Wall, Have I Got News for You!*, by Liz Curtis Higgs, Thomas Nelson, TN, 1997. Used by permission. [245]

A $100 Gift from *On Becoming A Real Man*, by Edwin Louis Cole, Thomas Nelson, TN, 1992. Used by permission. [185]

A Glimpse from *Men and Women*, by Dr. Larry Crabb, Zondervan, MI, 1991. Used by permission. [43]

Our Heavenly Father from *Seven Secrets of Effective Fathers*, by Ken R. Canfield, Tyndale House, IL, 1992. Used by permission. [115]

Our Inheritance from *Returning to Your First Love*, by Tony Evans Moody, IL, 1995. Used by permission. [252]

A Planning Getaway from *Love to Love You*, by Bill and Pam Farrel, Harvest House, OR, 1997. Used by permission. [31]

The Welcome of Background Music adapted from *It's About Home*, by Patsy Clairmont, Vine (Servant), IL, 1998. Used by permission. [33]

A Good Friend Speaks the Truth from *A Good Friend*, by Les and Leslie Parrott, Vine, IL, 1998. Used by permission. [147]

Every Problem Holds Positive Possibilities from *Tough Times Never Last, But Tough People Do*, by Robert H. Schuller, Thomas Nelson, TN, 1983. [5]

Communicate In Love from *Marriage Moments*, by David and Claudia Arp, Vine, IL, 1998. Used by permission. [77]

Life Is Short—Celebrate Now! from *Mama, Get The Hammer! There's A Fly On Papa's Head!*, by Barbara Johnson, Word, 1994. Used by permission. [222]

Don't Blow Out the Candles from *Because of Love*, by William and Patricia Coleman, Vine, IL, 1998. Used by permission. [159]

Slow Down That Conversation from *The Hidden Value of a Man*, by Gary Smalley and John Trent, Ph.D., Focus on the Family, 1992. [8]

Tips From A Bunny from *Shop, Save and Share*, by Ellie Kay, Bethany House Publishers, MN, 1998. Used by permission. [124]

Of Servants and Kings from *From the Heart of a Child*, by Dawn Richerson, New Hope Publishers, Birmingham, AL, 1999, www.newhopepubl.com, 1-800-968-7301. Used by permission. [25]

Contributors

Nora Lacie Abell lives on and writes from the Colville Confederated Tribes' Reservation in eastern Washington State. Her experiences as health care professional, wife, mother, and tree farmer give her a unique perspective on rural America. Contact: Long Rifle Ranch, Inchelium, WA 99138. [139]

Donna J. Adee, a homemaker from Minneapolis, Kansas, has with her husband, Ellis, written the true story of their son, *God's Special Child—Lessons from Nathan and Other Special Needs Children*. Donna wrote *Miriam's Dilemma* and *The Courtship of Miriam* and the one in process: *Miriam and Timothy Face Life*. [219, 223]

Audrey Allen is a wife, mom, and grandma who enjoys her family, home, and garden. She is a published freelance writer/poet and is a Master Writer for Warner Press. Contact: (661) 588-8167. [70]

Beverly J. Anderson, Colfax, California, is a freelance writer. An elder and active in cell group ministry at Auburn Presbyterian Church, she also serves as Facilitator for Placer County Caring Connection, a network of churches. Contact: bja@foothill.net. [226]

Durlynn Anema-Garten, Ph.D., Ed.D., Christian counselor, is author of 12 books and numerous inspirational articles, and adjunct faculty member of Western Seminary. She presents at women's workshops/retreats and for Christian school faculties. Contact: 401 Oak Ridge Court, Valley Springs, CA 95252. (209) 772-2521. durverga@caltel.com. [276]

Barbara J. Anson, wife, mother, grandmother, and former dental hygienist, speaks and writes with a passion for the practical application of biblical truths as she encourages women in their Christian walk. Contact: 1415 Tom Fowler Dr., Tracy, CA 95376. oanson@pacbell.net. [148, 261]

Cindy Bailey writes abundant features and columns for the Pittsburgh/ Greensburg *Tribune-Review* and Waynesburg (PA) College. Her devotionals, songs, and photos have appeared in various publications, including *Why Fret That God Stuff?* Contact: R.D.#1, Box 191-B, Waynesburg, PA 15370. (724) 852-2563; cinswind@greeenepa.net. [250]

Esther M. Bailey and her husband Ray keep abundance in their marriage with fun dates on Thursday and Saturday of each week. Contact: 4631 E. Solano Dr., Phoenix, AZ 85018. (602) 840-3143. baileywick@juno.com. [103, 243]

Vivian Lee Baniak is a freelance writer and speaker with strong Bible emphasis for Christian women's events. Contact: 7914 Teak Way, Rancho Cucamonga, CA 91730. mmviviandy@integrityonline7.com. [201]

Millie Barger, wife, mother, and grandmother, is the author of several books, including the novel, *Like Abigail*. She speaks in churches and at Christian Women's Clubs in Arizona. Contact: (602) 863-2231. lbarger@juno.com. [254, 290]

Margarita Garza de Beck is a freelance writer and also pastors Cristo la Roca, an Hispanic outreach of the church where she and her husband are members. Contact: 58 Denwood Dr., Jackson, TN 38305. argaritabeck@msn.com. [154]

Kelly Bell is a pastor's wife, director of Women's Ministry, and mother of two! She enjoys teaching and speaking to women's groups, along with writing Bible Studies and devotionals for women. Contact: P.O. Box 95, Murrieta, CA 92562. (909) 677-5667. kbell@ccmurrieta.com. [178, 202]

LeAnne E. Benfield regularly contributes to *Journey* and *Southern Lifestyles*. Her work has also appeared in *Discipleship Journal*, *Devo'Zine*, *Stand Firm*, *Georgia on My Mind*, *Threads of Gold*, and more. Contact: (770) 271-9123 or Lbenfield@mindspring.com. [206]

Ellen Bergh leads the High Desert Christian Writers Guild, where writers realize their God-given dreams. Contact: 3600 Brabham Avenue, Rosamond, CA 93560-689. mastermedia@hughes.net. [69]

Joan Rawlins Biggar, a former teacher, is the author of two series of adventure-mystery books for young people set in the Pacific Northwest. She enjoys nature, kids, and indulging her curiosity through writing. Contact: 4425 Meridian Ave. N, #3 Marysville, WA 98271. [208]

Delores Elaine Bius has sold over 1,900 articles and stories in 27 years of writing. She is a widow and speaks at writer's conferences and women's meetings. Contact: 6400 S. Narragansett Ave., Chicago, IL 60638. (773) 586-4384. [83]

Cheryl Brasuell serves on staff at Fellowship Church as the Director of Women's Ministry. Her passion for God runs deep and can be felt in her writings. Contact: P.O. Box 1780, Frisco, TX 75035. sbrasuell@aol.com. [228]

Ina Mae Brooks is retired after working as a church secretary and as a program manager for an Independent Living Center. Volunteer work, freelance writing, bird watching, and enjoying her grandchildren occupy most of her time. Contact: imbrooks@talleytech.com. [209]

Barbara Bryden works as a freelance writer and part-time ESL teacher. She lives with her husband and black calico cat in a house surrounded by an ever expanding perennial garden. Contact: 1439 37th Avenue SE, Olympia, WA 98501. dvff75b@prodigy.com. [81]

Libby C. Carpenter is a freelance writer and former educator. Previously published in *God's Abundance*, *God's Unexpected Blessings*, and *Why Fret That God Stuff?*, she desires to minister through her writing. Contact: 426 Aderholdt Road, Lincolnton, NC 28092. (704) 435-2932. [229]

Sandra Palmer Carr is a wife, mother, and grandmother, and a member of the Christian Writer's Fellowship of Orange County. She brings the hope of Jesus through poetry, stories, drama, and devotionals. Contact: 9421 Hyannis Port Drive, Huntington Beach, CA 92646-3515. (714) 962-0906. [173]

Sandy Cathcart, freelance writer, speaker, musician/singer, shares a message of encouragement for believers to put feet to their faith. Contact: 341 Flounce Rock Rd., Prospect, OR 97536. (541) 560-367. 5222.3643@compuserve.com. [28, 116]

Jeri Chrysong, a poet and humorist, resides in Huntington Beach, California, with teenaged sons, Luc and Sam. Her work has been featured in newspapers, devotionals, and the *God's Vitamin "C" for the Spirit* series. Jeri enjoys watching her kids participate in sports, and her Pug puppy, "Puddy." [179]

Cathy S. Clark, together with her husband Duane Clark, ministers in music around the world. She is a freelance writer, songwriter, and homeschool teacher to her two children. Contact: P.O. Box 461, Lancaster, CA 93584. duaneclark@qnet.com. [21]

Glenna M. Clark and her husband have been missionaries with Wycliffe Bible Translators for 40 years. Their fields of service include Jamaica, the Philippines, and Central America. They have three grown children. Contact: 5200 E. Irvine Blvd. #380, Irvine, CA 92620. (714) 832-5434. Burton_Glenna@Juno.com. [75]

Joan Clayton's sixth book has just been released. She's the religion columnist for her local newspaper. Joan and her husband, Emmitt, reside in Portales, New Mexico. Contact: joan@yucca.net. [46]

Doris C. Crandall, an inspirational writer, lives in Amarillo, Texas. She is the co-founder of the Amarillo Chapter of Inspirational Writers Alive!, a group dedicated to Christian writing. Doris devotes much of her time to helping beginning writers hone their skills. [29]

Linda Cutrell is inspired to write on her day set apart with the Lord, where she fasts from the world. Linda has sold articles to *Decision, Joyful Woman, Celebrating Life, Purpose,* and *Expressions.* Contact: 5370 East Forster Ave., Columbus, IN 47201. [215]

Christine R. Davis is mother to three sons, writer, full-time secretary, and teaches garden/craft classes at Powell Botanical Gardens in Kansas City. She enjoys crafts and tending her flower, herb, and gourd gardens. Contact: crdavis113@aol.com. [163]

Gloria H. Dvorak is a wife and mother of three grown children and grandmom of six. She has been a religious freelance writer for ten years and resides in Illinois. [39]

Pamela Enderby, mother of five, teaches Bible Studies, mentors women, and leads an evangelistic prayer group. She has been published in books by Kathy Collard Miller (*Why Fret That God Stuff?*) and Lynn Morrissey (*Seasons of a Woman's Heart*). Contact: enderbyhome@compuserve.com. [259]

Marjorie K. Evans, former school teacher, is a freelance writer of many published articles. She enjoys grandparenting, reading, church work, her Welsh corgi, and orchids. She and Edgar have two sons and five grandchildren. Contact: 4162 Fireside Cir., Irvine, CA 92604-2216. (949) 551-5296. [68, 105]

Eva Marie Everson is a wife and mother living in Orlando, Florida, where she writes for several ministries and publications. She is the co-author of *Pinches of Salt, Prisms of Light*, and is an active speaker and teacher. Contact: (407) 695-9366. PenNhnd@aol.com. [212, 285]

Rusty Fischer is an editor for an educational publisher in Greensboro, North Carolina. He and his wife Martha enjoy traveling, walking in the park, and seeing movies together. Contact: MFis245583@aol.com. [56]

Mary Bahr Fritts, author of *The Memory Box, If Nathan Were Here*, and 150+ articles, won her twelfth award—The Anna Cross Giblin Research Grant from SCBWI. She lives in Colorado Springs with husband, sons, and too many cats. Contact: (719) 630-8244. mmfwriter@aol.com. [149]

Donna Garrett began another career after raising four children and baking three thousand cakes/pies/brownies. A variety of magazines have published her articles on leisure, religion, children, seniors, and the handicapped. Contact: 3009 Merino Dr., Roanoke, VA 24018. [204]

Linda Gilden is a wife, mother, and freelance writer and editor. She is the author of over 200 articles and has contributed to several books. Her favorite pastime is reading while floating in the lake, surrounded by splashing children. [171]

Kathryn Higginbottom Gorin is a freelance writer from Surrey, British Columbia, Canada. She has been married for three years, has a young son, and is expecting her second child in July, 1999. Contact: (604) 594-5884. [110]

Alice King Greenwood is a Bible teacher, poet, songwriter, and pianist. She and her husband Morris, retired school teachers, are parents of five children and grandparents of twelve. Contact: 4022 Candy Lane, Odessa, TX 79762. (915) 366-9281. greenwoodsr@earthlink.net. [132, 241]

Kathleen Hagberg is married, the mother of three children, a newspaper columnist, author of a book of children's verses, and a director of Children's Ministries. Contact: 41 Bittersweet Trail, Wilton, CT 06897. (203) 762-0541. Khagberg@hope.com. [101, 106, 188, 190]

Bonnie Compton Hanson has published several books, plus poems, stories, and articles (including in the Chicken Soup books). Contact: 3330 S. Lowell St., Santa Ana, CA 92707. (714) 751-7824. bonnieh1@worldnet.att.net. [255]

Marilyn J. Hathaway is a retired R.N., community volunteer, and freelance writer of devotionals conveying the message, "Look what God is doing; see what He can do in your life." Contact: 2101 Mariyana Ave., Gallup, MN 87301. (505) 722-9795. [198]

David Hauk is a licensed optometrist in addition to being a writer. His writing interests include poetry, devotionals, essays, and non-fiction. David lives in Reading, Pennyslvania, with his wife, Debra, and children, Matthew, Daniel, and Abigail. Contact: PraisePen@aol.com. [111]

Sarah Healton, Ed.D. is retired. She co-authored *Anytime Craft Series*, with her daughter, and has articles in *God's Abundance*, *God's Vitamin "C" for the Spirit of Women*. She loves writing, sewing, and gardening. Contact: 6669 Belinda Dr., Riverside, CA 92504. [60]

Linda Herr and husband James Wheeler, along with their children, Alice, Mary Ona, and Joseph, are re-entering North American culture. Their latest term in the Middle East involved English teaching and community development work in the Gaza Strip, serving with Mennonite Central Committee. [113]

June Hetzel is Associate Professor of Education at Biola University and a freelance writer/editor. Contact: 241 W. Patwood, La Habra, CA 90631. DJuneH@aol.com. [257]

Lois Hudson writes for and edits a daily devotional published monthly by her church, writes curriculum and fiction, leads Bible Study classes and workshops, oversees small group ministries, and composes music. Contact: 17921 Romelle Ave., Santa Ana, CA 92705. (714) 532-4626. [249]

Pauline Rael Jaramillo is a journalist and freelance writer. Her published works include research, political issues, profiles, and personal experience articles; short stories, one-act plays, and poetry. She is bicultural and bilingual (Spanish/English). Contact: P.O. Box 225, Rimforest, CA 92378. mija100@earthlink.net. [118]

Marilyn Jaskulke is a freelance writer with publications of children's stories and devotionals. Contact: 254 Avenida Madrid, San Clemente, CA 92672. (949) 361-8428. mar68jask@aol.com. [119]

Lorraine Jennings is an herbal columnist and feature writer for *The Ageless Times*, freelance writer, entertainment musician, and retired public relations executive. Devoted Christian, wife, mother, grandmother, and great-grandmother, she loves life! Contact: 8000 Village Oak #A-1 San Antonio, TX 78233. lyloace@swbell.net. [120]

Jane Tod Jimenez lives with husband, Victor, and two teenagers in Tempe, Arizona. Appreciating life's variety, she has had careers in real estate, accounting, and teaching. When not working, she's either quilting, cooking, or gardening. Contact: jvjimenez@yahoo.com. [79]

Nelda Jones is a grandmother and writer with poetry, devotionals, and articles in several publications, including Starburst books. She is also desktop publisher and editor of a church newsletter. Contact: Rt.1, Box 81, Edgewood, TX 75117. (903) 896-4885. nfjones@vzinet.com. [122]

Veda Boyd Jones is the author of twenty-one books including eight inspirational romances. She and her husband, Jimmie, have three sons and live in the Ozarks of Missouri. [193, 282]

Ellie Kay, author of *Shop, Save and Share*, is an international speaker, radio and television veteran, humorist, mother of five, and wife of an Air Force fighter pilot. Contact: Shop, Save & Share Seminars, P.O. Box 229, Ft. Drum, NY 13603. halfwit5@juno.com. [124]

Jodi Karnick is a freelance writer, speaker, child advocate, and foster parent. She works with troubled children in southern Wisconsin and spends her spare time sailing, rapelling, and rollerblading. Contact: wedgie@chorus.net. [49]

Lettie J. Kirkpatrick currently mothers four sons. She also writes and speaks about family, parenting, holidays, and Christian living. Contact: 373 Charles Circle, Cleveland, TN 37323. Phone and fax: (423) 479-2063. [167, 233]

Erma Landis is a wife of 48 years, mother of six, grandmother of 17, and becoming a first-time great-grandmother in the Fall. Her interests include bird-watching, travelling, photography, and reading. Contact: 690 E. Oregon Rd., Lititz, PA 17543. [151]

Faye Landrum is a retired nurse and freelance writer. She has published three books and over a hundred articles in children and adult publications. Contact: 7871 Beecher Road SW, Pataskala, OH 43062-8587. (740) 927-2790; fax: 740-927-2795. FAYELAND@aol.com. [85]

Marilyn Neuber Larson taught fourth grade for thirty years. She is also a conference speaker and author of more than 100 stories and articles for both children and adults. Contact: HCR 69, Box 886, Moriarty, NM 87035. (505) 298-1003. [183, 213]

Janie Lazo is a busy working mom who also homeschools, writes, and assists with her church's music ministry. Contact: 21241 S. Santa Fe Ave., Apt. #3, Long Beach, CA 90810. [156]

Georgia Curtis Ling is a mom, wife, author, and speaker. She lives with her husband, Phil, their son Philip, and his cat, Alice. Contact: 3610 Shore Avenue, Everett, WA 98203. [136]

Helen Luecke is an inspirational writer of short stories, articles, and devotionals. She helped organize Inspirational Writers Alive!/Amarillo Chapter. Contact: 2921 S. Dallas, Amarillo, TX 79103. (806) 376-9671. [181]

Katherine Lundgren is a graphic designer, artist, and writer living with her husband of twenty-three years. They have one grown son. Her favorite reading is the Scriptures and biographies. Contact: 5960 Havilland Lane, Riverside, CA 92504. jklund1@juno.com. [78, 145, 220]

Marty Magee is a medical transcriptionist who has written for a take-home paper to fill in her empty nest. She and her husband, David, live miles from their two daughters. Contact: 3051 East Sierra Avenue, Fresno, CA 93710. (559) 325-0456. redwr10104@aol.com. [128]

Joann Matthews is a public speaker and entrepreneur. She started her own training and consulting business in response to her passion for teaching and training. Contact: (254) 547-3672 or jmattsalt@aol.com. [11]

Jane E. Maxwell, R.N., is a mother of four children and grandmother of two. Writer of inspirational and health articles, devotionals, and essays, she is also involved in ministries to single mothers, victims of domestic violence, and children. Contact: 1704 Pearl St., Vestal, NY 13850. [100]

Ruth E. McDaniel is a Christian writer (published nearly 1,000 items in eight years), full-time caregiver, mother (three), grandmother (eight), and co-leader of St. Louis Christian Writer's Group. Contact: 15233 Country Ridge Dr., Chesterfield, MO 63017. [38]

Susan McElmurry lives in Portland, Oregon, with her husband, Douglas, and son, Griffin. Some of their favorite activities include camping, cross-country skiing, hiking, and reading. They attend Spring Mountain Bible Church. She teaches part-time at an area high school. Contact: macruadh@iccom.com. [14]

Lucy Whitsett McGuire is the editor of *Reflections Evangelical Presbyterian Church* magazine, editor of *Connection* women's newsletter, author *of Help for the Introvert*, and chairman of EPC Committee on Pastor's Wives Ministry. Contact: 48028 Andover Dr., Novi, MI 48374. lucyw@mich.com. [16, 26]

Jan McNaught is a minister's wife, grandma, and friend. Jan likes home decorating, bargain hunting, crafting, and calligraphy. She enjoys writing and speaking about God's Word, and especially discipling new believers. Contact: P.O. Box 330, Cheney, WA 99004. (509) 235-5572. ejmcnaught@juno.com. [130]

Jennifer Anne F. Messing is the author of numerous articles and poems published in fourteen magazines. She teaches writing, is a licensed hairstylist, and a worship vocalist. The Messings have two daughters and reside in Oregon. Contact: 70721.550@compuserve.com. [131]

Kathy Collard Miller is a mother, wife, speaker, and author of forty books including *Through His Eyes*. She speaks nationally and internationally on viewing life through God's perspective. Contact: PO Box 1058, Placentia, CA 92871. (714) 993-2654. Kathyspeak@aol.com. [6, 284]

Rosalie J.G. Mills is a freelance writer and speaker, published in *God's Abundance*, *Seasons of a Woman's Heart*, and Plastow Publications. She is currently co-authoring a book chronicling God's healing and restoration in her life. Contact: (818) 548-8981. rmills7777@aol.com. [17]

Lynn D. Morrissey is the author of *Seasons of a Woman's Heart*, *Treasures of a Woman's Heart*, and a contributing author to numerous bestsellers; CLASSpeaker (specializing in prayer-journaling; women's topics); and vocalist. Contact: PO Box 50101, St. Louis, MO 63105. http://members.primary.net/~lynnswords/. [196]

Sherrie Ward Murphree is a Bible teacher, church musician, and freelance writer of inspirational articles and devotionals. Her bachelor's degree is in English and speech. She loves to encourage others. Contact: 1302 E. 52nd, Odessa, TX 79762. [166]

Amberly Neese is passionate about Christ. Her humor and enthusiasm have encouraged thousands at various retreats and camps. She ministers in Southern California with her husband of seven years, Scott. Amberly recently received her master's degree from Biola University. Contact: (714) 847-3573. [22]

Deborah Sillas Nell is a writer, artist, and counselor. She lives with her husband Craig and six-year-old daughter Sophia. Contact: 735 McAllister St., Hanover, PA 17331. craignell@hotmail.com. [47]

Stephanie E. Nickel is a wife and homeschooling mother of three. She runs a freelance writing business from her home. She also runs a creative writing consulting business for home educators. Contact: 39-405 Wellington St., St. Thomas, ON N5R 5T7. [51]

Sharon Norris is a published author and popular speaker who touches the lives of her audiences at conferences, women's retreats, seminars, church, and school programs. P.O. Box 1519, Inglewood, CA 90308 or SajWriter@aol.com. [95, 224, 262]

D. J. Note is a wife, mother of two teenagers, a member of Oregon Christian Writers, Mom's-In-Touch Int'l., and a regular contributor to *Cascade Horseman* magazine. Her love of God, family, and country life inspire her writing. Contact: djnote@juno.com. [20]

Karen O'Connor is an award-winning author and Christian speaker, known for her ability to inspire audiences with gentle humor and straightforward truth. She is the author of 35 books, including *Basket of Blessings* and *Squeeze the Moment*. Contact: (619) 483-3184. wordykaren@aol.com. [34]

Joanne Yoona Park is an editor at Glencoe/McGraw-Hill. She enjoys reading and writing children's literature. Joanne loves traveling to exotic places with her fiancé, Nathan. The two are getting married this summer. Contact: 5015 Onyx Street, Torrance, CA 90503. jpark116@aol.com. [264]

Golden Keyes Parsons, Matters of the Heart Ministries, is a CLASSpeaker/writer/musician, specializing in Bible teaching, women's, mother/daughter conferences. She teams with her pastor/husband to lead couples' conferences. Contact: PO 764, Red River, NM 87558. (505) 754-1742. bgpar@taosnet.com. [157]

Frances Gregory Pasch is married, and has five sons and six grandchildren. Her writing has appeared in numerous publications. She leads a Christian women's writers' group and enjoys encouraging beginners. Contact: 165 Norwood Ave., North Plainfield, NJ 07060. (908) 755-2075. paschf@mail.eclipse.net. [266]

Allison Pittman lives in a whirlwind. Besides being a high school English teacher, she is the harried wife of a very understanding man, and the mother of three active little boys. Contact: (The Disaster Area) 158 Meadowland, Universal City, TX 78148. [86]

Betty Chapman Plude is a freelance writer and speaker. She is the author of *A Romance With North San Diego County Restaurants*, numerous magazine and newspaper articles, and two newsletters. Contact: 834 Cessna St., Independence, OR 97351. (503) 838-4039. Fax: (503) 838-3239. pludeea@open.org. [50]

Karen Poland is a homemaker and minister's wife living in Corpus Christi, TX. She and her husband Hugh have three daughters, Kayse, Jayme, and Ally. She enjoys reading, writing, and encouraging others. Contact: Kpoland@aol.com. [54, 289]

Janet E. Pratt is a full-time mother, home school educator, and freelance writer. She lives with her husband Ramie, and two children, Jacob and Rianne. Contact: 11625 Chesapeake Drive, Reno, NV 89506. (775) 677-2061. JanetPratt@aol.com. [44]

Kendra Prince has been writing Christian drama for ten years. She is very thankful for a Heavenly Father who is the first and foremost author of creativity. Contact: KPrince697@aol.com. [268]

Sheila Rabe is a popular writer of romance novels as well as inspirational books. Her latest books are *I Hate Whining Except When I'm Doing It* and *It's a Wonderful Midlife.* [169]

Avis McGriff Rasmussen is a speaker and accomplished poet, including "Beneath My Skin I Have A Soul." She has also authored numerous inspirational stories. Contact: P.O. Box 5954, Orange, CA 92863. (714) 771-3093. dennisr@simongreanleaf.org. [187, 247]

Sharon Raivo Remmen is an author and a speaker for Stonecroft Ministries. A former social worker, she also enjoys gardening, music, reading, and animals. Contact: 324 Casitas Bulevar, Los Gatos, CA 95032. [269]

Kayleen J. Reusser has published a variety of articles in *Decision, Today's Christian Woman, The Christian Reader, Grit,* and *Business People.* She is married to John and has three children. Contact: 1524 N. Sutton Cir. Bluffton IN 46714. (219) 824-8573. kyreusser@juno.com. [57, 160]

Dawn Richerson is an Atlanta-based writer and author of *From the Heart of a Child: Meditations for Everyday Living,* a collection of devotions based on conversations with her son, Luke, available from New Hope Publishers, (www.newhopepubl.com.) Contact (770) 381-7058. dbixrich@aol.com. [25]

Laura Sabin Riley is a wife, mother, author, and passionate speaker. She is the author of *All Mothers Are Working Mothers*, a devotional book for stay-at-home moms (Horizon Books), and numerous short stories. Contact: P.O. Box 1150, Yuma, AZ 85366. RileysRanch@juno.com. [58]

Joy Anna Rosendale is an executive secretary, the leader of the Single Ladies' Fellowship at her church, and a student at Biola University, where she is earning a degree in Organizational Leadership. Contact: joyfullyjoy@earthlink.net. [270]

Tiziana Ruff was born in 1953, in Genova, Italy. She is the mother of two beautiful children, Sharon, 26 and Anthony, 11, and married to her wonderful best friend, Robert. She enjoys being the Lord's servant who is completing her day by day. [88]

Suzy Ryan lives in Southern California with her husband and three small children. Her articles have appeared in *Today's Christian Woman*, *Woman's World*, *The American Enterprise*, *Bounce Back Too*, *Seasons of a Woman's Heart*, and various newspapers. Contact: KenSuzyR@aol.com. [272, 287]

Terry Fitzgerald Sieck is an author and professional speaker with 25 years of experience. She and her husband Larry live in San Diego. Contact: LSieck@Pacbell.net. [41]

J. A. Stackhaus is originally from Louisiana and now resides in the Kansas City area with her husband and two children. She is a legal assistant, freelance writer, and volunteer with Prison Fellowship Ministries. [91]

Carolyn Standerfer is an inspirational writer, homeschool teacher, and leader of personal and relational recovery groups. She resides in California's high desert with her husband and three children. Contact: 4847 West Avenue N, Quartz Hill, CA 93536-2465. carolyns@hughes.net. [93]

Patty Stump is a wife, mother of two, popular speaker for retreats and special events, writer, Bible Study teacher, and Christian counselor. She communicates Biblical truth with humor, insights, and practical application. Contact: P.O. Box 5003, Glendale, AZ 85312. (602) 979-3544. [53, 152, 291]

Lea L. Tartanian, a medical secretary, writer, and a member of Toastmasters, has written for 24 publications. Her goals are to publish inspirational books, conduct journaling workshops, and be an inspirational speaker. Contact: 3012 Phyllis Street, Endwell, NY 13760. (607) 754-3671. [235]

Debbi Taylor finds joy in encouraging students in her roles as school administrator, teacher, and writer. Contact: 7754 McGroarty Ave. Tujunga, CA 91042. (818) 352-4808. Debbi777@aol.com. [273]

Karen Taylor is a freelance writer whose inspirational short stories, poems, and articles appear in nationally and internationally circulated publications. Contact: 5530 NW Osprey Place, Portland, OR 97229. (503) 645-4906. KTfrelnc@aol.com. [236]

June L. Varnum is the author of various articles, devotions, and book reviews, and is a speaker and amateur photographer. She teaches Sunday School and has led Bible Studies, prayer groups, and workshops. Contact: P.O. Box 236, Loyalton, CA 96118-0236. (530) 993-0223. jvarnum@psln.com. [97, 182]

Susan Waterman Voss lives with her husband and three sons in Atkins, Iowa. Her writings have appeared in *The Lutheran Witness, My Devotions, Children's Ministry,* and several other Christian publications. [66, 134]

Lori Wall is a single parent of three children, poet, and in-house playwright for Pasadena's Exodus Theatre Troupe. She is self-publishing a poetry book to minister to AIDS victims. Contact: PO Box 41-701, Los Angeles, CA 90041. (626) 585-1305. [237]

Bonnie Watkins began learning simple living as a dairy farm daughter outside of Houston, Texas. Living with her husband and two sons in Austin, she teaches literature and writing at Hyde Park Baptist High School. She is a member of Austin Christian Writers' Guild. [279]

C. Ellen Watts writes for Christian markets. Author of four books, with two more in progress, this mom to 5 and grandmother to 16 also serves through workshops and as an encourager to fledgling writers. Contact: 702 Alderwood Ln, Nampa, ID 83651-2477. (208) 466-0813. [137]

Leslie Whitworth lives on a ranch in the Texas Hill Country. She is a bilingual kindergarten teacher and enjoys kayaking, gardening, and being with her children, Sophie and Ned. Contact: HC16, Box 14, Castell, TX 76831. lesw64@ctesc.net. [62]

Naomi Wiederkehr has had one book published and over 160 articles, devotionals, and book reviews. Her special interest is teaching little children. She worked in libraries for 30 years. Contact: 705 Stucky, Apt. 212, Berne, IN 46711. (210) 589-2445. [162]

Cassandra Woods is a management engineer, writer, and speaker. Her writing has been published in various publications, and she enjoys challenging others to reach their full potential. Contact: P.O. Box 13311, Birmingham, AL 35202. CWjoy@aol.com. [240]

Kathleen Dale Wright is a wife, mother of three, grandmother of eight, and great-grandmother of one. She sold her first article 20 years ago and is a CTM in Toastmasters International. Contact: 19122 N. Highway 71, Mountainburg, AR 72946. (501) 369-4286. bkwright@earthlink.net. [281]

Susan Kimmel Wright shares her space with a husband, three teenagers, and assorted animals. She's published many articles and a children's mystery series (Herald Press), as well as previous *God's Abundance* contributions. Contact: 221 Fawcett Church Rd, Bridgeville PA 15017. wereallwright@icubed.com. [64]

Leeann S. Yamakawa, devotional writer, poet, vocalist, and avid reader, is involved in discipling hurting women. She lives with her husband Glenn and two daughters, Jeannie and Annie. Contact: 3439 Cambridge Ave., Jackson, MI 49203. (517) 782-6270. [199]

Martha B. Yoder, forced from nursing by post-polio problems, writes for Christian Light Publications, Starburst Publishers, and has nine children's story tapes for Gospel Sunrise, Inc. Contact: 1501 Virginia Avenue, Apt. 159, Harrisonburg, VA 22802. (540) 564-6560. [177]

Jeanne Zornes writes and speaks with wit and Biblical faithfulness. She's written six books, including *When I Felt Like Ragweed, God Saw A Rose.* Contact: Apple of His Eye Ministries, 1025 Meeks St., Wenatchee, WA 98801-1640. [23, 191]

Other Books by Starburst Publishers®
(partial listing – full list available upon request)

God's Abundance for Women—*Compiled by Kathy Collard Miller*

Subtitled: *Devotions for a More Meaningful Life.* Following the success of *God's Abundance*, this book will touch women of all ages as they seek a more meaningful life. Essays from our most beloved Christian authors exemplify how to gain the abundant life that Jesus promised through trusting Him to fulfill our every need. Each story is enhanced with Scripture, quotes, and practical tips providing brief, yet deeply spiritual reading.
(cloth)   ISBN 1892016141   **$19.95**

More God's Abundance—*Compiled by Kathy Collard Miller*

Subtitled: *Joyful Devotions for Every Season.* Editor Kathy Collard Miller responds to the tremendous success of *God's Abundance* with a fresh collection of stories based on God's Word for a simpler life. Includes stories from our most beloved Christian writers, such as Liz Curtis Higgs and Patsy Clairmont, that are combined ideas, tips, quotes, and scripture.
(cloth)   ISBN 1892016133   **$19.95**

God's Abundance—*Edited by Kathy Collard Miller*

Over 100,000 sold! This day-by-day inspirational is a collection of thoughts by leading Christian writers such as Patsy Clairmont, Jill Briscoe, Liz Curtis Higgs, and Naomi Rhode. *God's Abundance* is based on God's Word for a simpler, yet more abundant life. Learn to make all aspects of your life—personal, business, financial, relationships, even housework a "spiritual abundance of simplicity."
(cloth)   ISBN 0914984977   **$19.95**

Promises of God's Abundance—*Edited by Kathy Collard Miller*

Subtitled: *For a More Meaningful Life.* The Bible is filled with God's promises for an abundant life. *Promises of God's Abundance* is written in the same way as the best-selling *God's Abundance*. It will help you discover these promises and show you how simple obedience is the key to an abundant life. Scripture, questions for growth, and a simple thought for the day will guide you to a more meaningful life.
(trade paper) ISBN 0914984-098 **$9.95**

Stories of God's Abundance—*Compiled by Kathy Collard Miller*

Subtitled: *for a More Joyful Life.* Following the success of *God's Abundance* (100,000 sold), this book is filled with beautiful, inspirational, real-life stories of God, Scriptures, and insights that any reader can apply to their daily lives. Renew your faith in life's small miracles and challenge yourself to allow God to lead the way as you find the source of abundant living for all your relationships.
(trade paper)   ISBN 1892016060   **$12.95**

God's Unexpected Blessings—*Edited by Kathy Collard Miller*

Over 50,000 sold! Learn to see the unexpected blessings in life. These individual essays describe experiences that seem negative on the surface but are something God has used for good in our lives or to benefit others. Witness God at work in our lives. Learn to trust God in action. Realize that we always have a choice to learn and benefit from these experiences by letting God prove His promise of turning all things for our good.
(cloth)   ISBN 0914984071   **$18.95**

Why Fret That God Stuff?—*Edited by Kathy Collard Miller*

Subtitled: *Stories of Encouragement to Help You Let Go and Let God Take Control of All Things in Your Life*. Occasionally, we all become overwhelmed by the everyday challenges of our lives: hectic schedules, our loved ones' needs, unexpected expenses, a sagging devotional life. *Why Fret That God Stuff* is the perfect beginning to finding joy and peace for the real world!
(trade paper)   ISBN 0914984-500   **$12.95**

Seasons of a Woman's Heart—*Compiled by Lynn D. Morrissey*

Subtitled: *A Daybook of Stories and Inspiration*. A woman's heart is complex. This daybook of stories, quotes, scriptures, and daily reflections will inspire and refresh. Christian women share their heartfelt thoughts on Seasons of Faith, Growth, Guidance, Nurturing, and Victory. Including Christian women's writers such as Kay Arthur, Emilie Barnes, Luci Swindoll, Jill Briscoe, Florence Littauer, and Gigi Graham Tchividjian.
(cloth)   ISBN 1892016036   **$18.95**

The **God's Word for the Biblically-Inept™** series is already a best-seller with over 100,000 books sold! Designed to make reading the Bible easy, educational and fun! This series of verse-by-verse Bible studies, Topical Studies and Overviews mixes scholarly information from experts with helpful icons, illustrations, sidebars and time lines. It's the Bible made easy!

The Bible—God's Word for the Biblically-Inept™

An excellent book to start learning the entire Bible. Get the basics or the in-depth information you are seeking with this user-friendly overview. From Creation to Christ to the Millenium, learning the Bible has never been easier.
(trade paper) ISBN 0914984551 **$16.95**

Revelation—God's Word for the Biblically-Inept™—*Daymond R. Duck*

End-time Bible Prophecy, expert Daymond Duck leads us verse-by-verse through one of the Bible's most confusing books. Follow the experts as they forge their way through the captivating prophecies of Revelation!
(trade paper)   ISBN 0914984985   **$16.95**

Daniel—God's Word for the Biblically-Inept™—*Daymond R. Duck*

Daniel is a book of prophecy and the key to understanding the mysteries of the Tribulation and End-Time events. This verse-by-verse commentary combines humor and scholasticism to get at the essentials of scripture. Perfect for those who want to know the truth about the Antichrist.
(trade paper)   ISBN 0914984489   **$16.95**

Health and Nutrition—God's Word for the Biblically-Inept™—*Kathleen O'Bannon Baldinger*

The Bible is full of God's rules for good health! Kathleen Baldinger reveals scientific evidence that proves the diet and health principles outlined in the Bible are the best for total health. Learn about the Bible Diet, the food pyramid and fruits and vegetable from the Bible! Experts include Pamela Smith, Julian Whitaker, Kenneth Cooper, and T.D. Jakes.
(trade paper)   ISBN 0914984055   **$16.95**

Men of the Bible—God's Word for the Biblically-Inept™—*D. Larry Miller*

Benefit from the life experiences of the powerful men of the Bible! Learn how the inspirational struggles of men such as Moses, Daniel, Paul, and David parallel the struggles of today's man. It will inspire and build Christian character for any reader.
(trade paper)   ISBN 1892016079   **$16.95**

Women of the Bible—God's Word for the Biblically-Inept™—*Kathy Collard Miller*

Finally, a Bible perspective just for women! Gain valuable insight from the successes and struggles of such women as Eve, Esther, Mary, Sarah, and Rebekah. Interesting icons like Get Close to God, Build Your Spirit, and Grow your Marriage will make incorporating God's Word into your daily life easy.
(trade paper)   ISBN 0914984063   **$16.95**

What's in the Bible for™ Women—*Georgia Curtis Ling*

What does the Bible have to say to women? Find out in the second release from the **What's in the Bible for . . .**™ series. Women of all ages will find Biblical insight on the topics that are meaningful to them in six simple sections including Faith, Family, Friends, Fellowship, Freedom, and Femininity. From the editors of the *God's Word for the Biblically-Inept*™ series, this book also uses illustrations, bullet points, chapter summaries, and icons to make understanding God's Word easier than ever!
(trade paper)   ISBN 1-892016-11-7   **$16.95**

The Weekly Feeder—*Cori Kirkpatrick*

Subtitled: *A Revolutionary Shopping, Cooking and Meal Planning System*. The Weekly Feeder is a revolutionary meal planning system that will make preparing home-cooked dinners more convenient than ever. At the beginning of each week, simply choose one of the eight pre-planned weekly menus, tear out the corresponding grocery list, do your shopping, and whip up a great meal in less than 45 minutes! The author's household management tips, equipment checklists, and nutrition information make this system a must have for any busy family. Also included with every recipe is a personal anecdote from the author emphasizing the importance of good food, a healthy family, and a well-balanced life.
(trade paper)   ISBN 1892016095   **$16.95**

God Stories—*Donna I. Douglas*

Subtitled: *They're So Amazing, Only God Could Make Them Happen*. Famous individuals share their personal, true-life experiences with God in this beautiful new book! Find out how God has touched the life of top recording artists, professional athletes, and other newsmakers such as Jessi Colter, Deana Carter, Ben Vereen, Stephanie Zimbalist, Cindy Morgan, Sheila E., Joe Jacoby, Cheryl Landon, Brett Butler, Clifton Taulbert, Babbie Mason, Michael Medved, Sandi Patty, Charlie Daniels, and more! Their stories are intimate, poignant, and sure to inspire and motivate you as you listen for God's message in your own life!
(cloth)   ISBN 1892016117   **$18.95**

Since Life Isn't A Game, These Are God's Rules—*Kathy Collard Miller*

Subtitled: *Finding Joy & Happiness in God's Ten Commandments.* We often hear life being referred to as a *game*, but we know this is not really true. In life there is only one set of rules and those are God's. God gave us the Ten Commandments for our good—to protect and guide us. In this book, Kathy Collard Miller explains the meaning of each of the Ten Commandments and illustrates how they are relevant in today's life. Each chapter includes Scripture and quotes from some of our most beloved Christian authors including Billy Graham, Patsy Clairmont, Liz Curtis Higgs, and more! Sure to renew your understanding of God's rules.
(cloth)   ISBN 189201615X $16.95

More of Him, Less of Me—*Jan Christiansen*

Subtitled: *A Daybook of My Personal Insights, Inspirations & Meditations on the Weigh Down™ Diet.* The insight shared in this year-long daybook of inspiration will encourage you on your weight-loss journey, bring you to a deeper relationship with God, and help you improve any facet of your life. Each page includes an essay, Scripture, and a tip-of-the-day that will encourage and uplift you as you trust God to help you achieve your proper weight. Perfect for companion guide for anyone on the Weigh Down™ diet!
(cloth)   ISBN 1892016001   **$17.95**

Desert Morsels—*Jan Christiansen*

Subtitled: *A Journal with Encouraging Tidbits from My Journey on the Weigh Down™ Diet.* When Jan Christiansen set out to lose weight on the Weigh Down™ Diet she got more than she bargained for! In addition to *losing* over 35 pounds and *gaining* a closer relationship with God, Jan discovered a gift—her ability to entertain and comfort fellow dieters! Jan's inspiring website led to the release of her best-selling first book, *More of Him, Less of Me*. Now, Jan serves another helping of *her* wit and *His* wisdom in this lovely companion journal. Includes inspiring Scripture, insightful comments, stories from readers, room for the reader's personal reflection and _Plenty_ of **Attitude** (p-attitude).
(cloth)   ISBN 1892016214   **$16.95**

Purchasing Information:
www.starburstpublishers.com

Books are available from your favorite bookstore, either from current stock or special order. To assist bookstore in locating your selection be sure to give title, author, and ISBN #. If unable to purchase from the bookstore you may order direct from STARBURST PUBLISHERS. When ordering enclose full payment plus shipping and handling as follows: Post Office (4th Class)—$3.00 (Up to $20.00), $4.00 ($20.01-$50.00), 8% ($50.01 and Up); UPS—$4.50 (Up to $20.00), $6.00 ($20.01-$50.00), 12% ($50.01 and Up); Canada—$5.00 (Up to $35.00), 15% ($35.01 and Up); Overseas (Surface)—$5.00 (Up to $25.00), 20% ($25.01 and Up). Payment in U.S. Funds only. Please allow two to three weeks minimum (longer overseas) for delivery. Make checks payable to and mail to: STARBURST PUBLISHERS, P.O. Box 4123, LANCASTER, PA 17604. Credit card orders may also be placed by calling 1-800-441-1456 (credit card orders only), Mon-Fri, 8:30 a.m. to 5:30 p.m. Eastern Standard Time. Prices subject to change without notice. Catalog available for a 9 x 12 self-addressed envelope with 4 first-class stamps.